THE 12 VOLT DOCTOR'S
PRACTICAL HANDBOOK

for the boat's electric system

by

C. PLATH
NORTH AMERICAN DIVISION
ANNAPOLIS, MARYLAND

Publisher: C. Plath North American Division
222 Severn Avenue
Annapolis, MD 21403

ISBN number: 1-878797-00-X

Introduction

You may think that making a wiring diagram for your boat would be a monstrous headache, and the results as useful as a street map of Brooklyn viewed from ten feet away. But read how simple it is when you take small steps, one area and one sketch at a time, whenever you happen to look at a particular detail. Eventually, you will have a collection of sketches which is your wiring diagram.

With the diagram, trouble shooting will be much easier, and so will planning. Repairs will be much faster, too. Sooner or later, you will decide that as designed, the boat's electrical equipment is less than perfect. You may want lights in new places, switches in different locations, add instruments and equipment, run electricity from better charged batteries. The step from knowing your boat's electrics to making changes will come quite naturally. Start with a relatively easy subject and later you will be surprised by the degree of confidence you have gained. Your boat will then fit your personal expectations in a way no one else can match with any amount of hired repair service.

Annapolis, September 1983
Ed Beyn

Contents

Very Basic Electricity: the Plumbing Equivalent.

It is easy to see how electrical units are related to each other if you compare them with experiments with water.

Let us compare a battery with a supply of water under pressure. In **Sketch 1**, a weighted piston presses on water. The pressure is measured by the pressure gauge which may indicate in pounds per square inch (PSI). The gauge is our equivalent to a voltmeter.

Connect a garden hose nozzle to the water supply, and have the nozzle shoot a

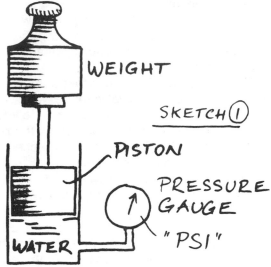

jet of water into the air. With greater weight on the piston, **Sketch 2**, there will be a higher water jet. The height of the jet could serve as a measurement of pressure.

Compare electrical current or Ampere to water current or flow rate: we could measure water flow rate with a bucket, by catching the falling water

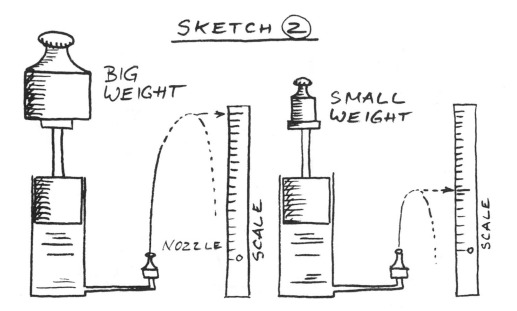

1

jet and counting, in gallons per minute. Other flow rate meters could be propellers or paddle wheels in the water line, much like your boat's speed-ometer impeller.

Instead of the weight on the piston, we could use more water to generate the weight and pressure, by making the water container tall enough until we reach the desired pressure (voltage), and wide enough for the needed capacity, our battery size.

Now let us experiment and take some measurements, to show how things are related. Connect a valve to the water supply, **Sketch 5**. While the valve is turned off, flow rate is zero. What do you think the pressure gauges will show? The one on the left will show the pressure of the water supply, the one on the right will show zero. The closed valve resists water flow perfectly, it has infinitely high resistance.

Next, open the valve in **Sketch 5** enough to let some water flow. Let us assume that the left pressure gauge reads 12 Volts and the one on the right zero, and that the water flow rate into the bucket is 5 Ampere. How much water will flow if we double the supply pressure from 12 to 24 Volts? The flow rate will double, to 10 Ampere. And the resistance of the valve in that setting, by Ohm's law, is Pressure or Voltage divided by flow rate or Ampere, namely

$$\text{Resistance} = \frac{\text{Pressure}}{\text{Flow Rate}} = \frac{\text{Volt}}{\text{Amp}} = \frac{12}{5} = \frac{24}{10} = 2.4$$

SKETCH ④

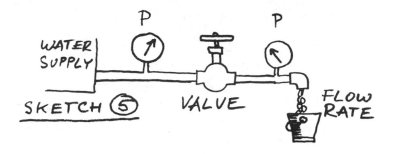

SKETCH ⑤

Where would we install a paddle wheel flow rate meter, our ammeter equivalent, in this experiment? We could install it anywhere in the line, left or right of the valve, since the flow rate is the same everywhere.

Sketch 6 shows an electrical circuit: ammeters at any of the locations marked "A" would give the same reading, all locations are suitable to measure current.

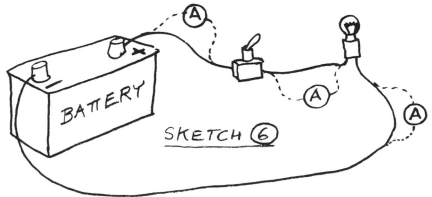

SKETCH ⑥

Would any size of flow rate meter work? No. Look at **Sketch 7**: The paddle wheel meter is so small that a large drop in pressure occurs at the meter: pressure upstream is the pressure in the water supply, and pressure downstream is essentially zero. The resistance of this small ammeter equivalent is too high for this application. The flow rate meter in **Sketch 8**, on the other hand, does not resist flow at all. But it is so large that the small

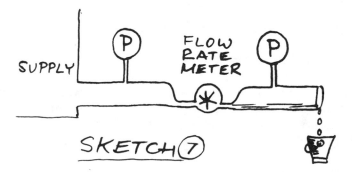

SKETCH ⑦

3

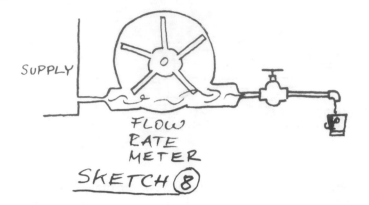

SUPPLY

FLOW
RATE
METER

SKETCH (8)

flow in the pipes (note sizes) will not move the paddle wheel. In an electrical example, this would be a 60 A ammeter not responding to a current of only one Ampere.

About meters in general: note in all of the sketches that the pressure gauges are connected by a "T" to the main water lines. Very little flow rate is involved with pressure gauges or voltmeters, the lines may be small or the wires thin but they must withstand pressure: wires must have insulation to withstand the involved voltage. Flow resistance of voltmeters is very high: there is no flow through pressure gauges which makes their resistance infinitely high. All voltmeters use a small amount of current, you could compare their function best with the method of measuring the height of the water jet in **Sketch 3**. The best voltmeters do their measurements with the smallest current or the thinnest water jet. The best voltmeters will have the greatest resistance.

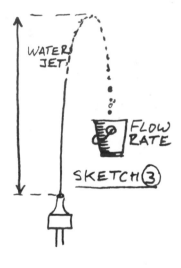

WATER
JET

FLOW
RATE

SKETCH (3)

Ammeters, on the other hand, are installed in the main line of flow and must have low resistance because all current must pass through them, to be measured (shunt type ammeters are the only exception, detailed later in the book). Ammeters for very high currents will have extremely low resistance, while meters for only low ranges of current will have somewhat higher resistance. We will see in a moment why that is no problem. First, a sketch which shows an electrical circuit with both voltmeter and ammeter. In **Sketch 9**, ammeter "A" is connected in the supply wire to the lamp, the

4

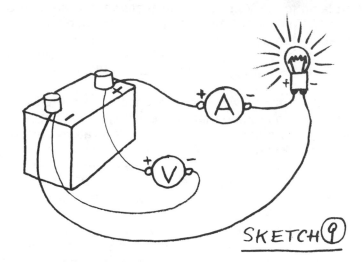

SKETCH ⑨

flow of lamp current is measured by the ammeter. Voltmeter "V" measures the tension or pressure of the supply. Lamp current does not flow through the wires of the voltmeter.

Let us talk about power. We measure it in horsepower, or in Watt (kW, kilowat = 1000 Watt). The paddle wheel machine in **Sketch 10** shows how we can generate mechanical power from our water supply: we direct a water jet at the paddles so that they turn. To generate the same power at the paddle wheel, we can use water of lower pressure and choose a big jet, or use water at higher pressure which allows us to use

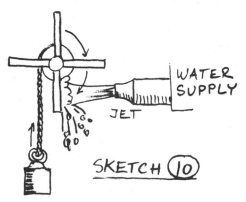

WATER SUPPLY

JET

SKETCH ⑩

less volume, because the water jet is faster due to the higher pressure. Power is determined by both flow rate and pressure, by both Ampere and Volt. One Watt is generated when a current of one Amp flows, from the tension of one Volt.

Think of a 40 Watt lamp ("light bulb") at home: connected to 110 Volt, only 0.36 Ampere need flow to generate 40 Watt. On the boat, a 40 Watt lamp draws 3.3 Ampere when on 12 Volt. But in both cases, Volt times Amps give us the 40 Watt. How are the lamps different? The one for 110 volt is designed to have a much higher resistance, namely about 300 Ohm (calculated from 110 Volt and 0.36 Ampere as discussed with **Sketch 5**). If you connected this bulb to 12 V, the pressure would be only about one tenth of 110 V, and only about one tenth of the current would flow, approximately 0.036 Ampere. On 12 Volt, that would only be 0.036 times 12 = 0.4 Watt which shows why the 40 Watt household lamp would not work onboard.

5

The 40 Watt lamp for 12 Volt has a resistance of only about 4 Ohm, as calculated from 12 Volt and 3.6 Ampere. If you connected this lamp to 110 Volt at home, about ten times the pressure or voltage would force about ten times 3.6 Amps of current through this lamp: a very short surge of power of 36 Amps times 110 Volt = 3960 Watts would destroy the lamp and blow a fuse.

With household electricity, we always talk about Watt when we discuss power. On the boat, we assume that all electricity is used at 12 Volt and mostly talk in terms of Ampere instead. We talk flow rate but mean power: each Ampere equals 12 Watt, and a battery with 100 Ampere hours supplies 1200 Watt hours or 1.2 kilo Watt hours: the units of our household electric meters. Ampere multiplied by Volt give Watt, and 1000 Watt or W are one kilo Watt or kW. We have seen earlier that resistance affects flow rate or current. Look at **Sketch 5** again: as you close the valve, you increase resistance and reduce flow rate. What happens if there are two resistances (bottle necks!) in the same water pipe? In **Sketch 11** we have two resistors "in series." These bottle necks in the pipe are called R_1 and R_2. If we knew their values in Ohm, we could calculate the flow rate into the bucket. In series, their values are simply added together. If their total were one Ohm, one Volt would cause a current of one Ampere. If the total resistance were 10 Ohm instead of 1 Ohm, only one tenths of current would flow, all just as you would expect.

Now to the pressure gauge or voltage readings: two of them are obvious. The voltage at left will be the supply voltage, 12 volt, and at right, with no other restriction coming, it is zero. The voltage between the resistors though is not easy to guess but very significant as we will see in the following example. The voltage between the resistors will be half the supply voltage if the resistors are alike. With other sizes, the size ratio determines how the voltage is divided. If the resistors were 10 and 2 Ohm, the voltage drop at the resistors would also be at a ratio of 10:2. **Sketch 12** shows the electrical diagram and how the voltages are measured. On the boat, many problems are related to resistors in series, and this subject is so important that we should look at some examples.

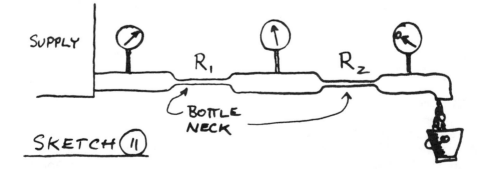

SUPPLY

R_1

R_2

BOTTLE NECK

SKETCH (11)

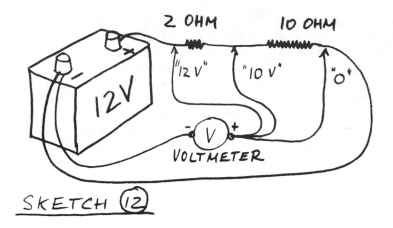

2 OHM   10 OHM

"12 V"   "10 V"   "0"

12V

VOLTMETER

SKETCH ⑫

First example: There is a switch for the compass light. The lamp in the compass is rated 1W. The switch is slightly corroded and has developed contact resistance of 5 Ohm. How will that affect the compass light?

Answer: the compass light draws: 1 Watt divided by 12 Volt = 0.083 Ampere, it has a resistance of: 12 Volt divided by 0.083 Ampere = 144 Ohm. Adding another resistor of 5 Ohm, the switch, in series to the lamp will increase total resistance to 149 Ohm, the effect will hardly be noticeable.

Second example: The same type of switch is used to switch a 40 Watt cabin light. This switch also has corroded and developed 5 Ohms resistance at its contacts. Will that affect the cabin light?

Answer: On 12 Volt, the cabin light draws:
40 Watt divided by 12 Volt = 3.3 Ampere, it has:
12 Volt divided by 3.3 Ampere = 3.6 Ohms of resistance.
Adding the switch resistance in series with this lamp will more than double the total resistance, so that the current will be reduced to:
12 volt divided by 8.6 total Ohm = 1.4 Ampere which flow through switch and lamp. This lamp will therefore hardly glow at all.

    And another problem, at the switch we now have a voltage drop of 7 Volt (12 Volt split by the ratio of resistances, or 12 divided by 8.6, multiplied by 5), so that 7 Volt times 1.4 Ampere = almost 10 Watt of heat are generated at the switch contact.

Third example: the starter motor on your engine is rated 3000 Watt. A battery cable terminal has developed very slight contact resistance at a battery post, the resistance is only 1/100 of an Ohm and now is in series with the starter motor. Can you start your engine? Can you find the battery connection by hand touch? Answer: The starter motor uses:
3000 Watt divided by 12 Volt = 250 Ampere, its resistance is:
12 Volt divided by 250 Ampere = 0.048 Ohm. The added resistance of 0.01 Ohm is series brings the total resistance to 0.058 which allows only:

7

12 Volt divided by 0.058 Ohm = 207 Ampere, so that power is reduced to: 207 Amps times 12 Volt = 2484 Watts instead of 3000 Watt. And of these 2484 Watts, not all are applied at the starter motor. Of the full 12 Volt, about 2 Volts are dropped at the added resistance at the battery post which corresponds to:

2 Volt times 207 Ampere = 408 Watt, so that only 2484 minus 408 = 2076 Watt are trying to turn the engine, about two thirds of normal, perhaps barely enough. The 408 Watt at the battery post are enough to make that post and terminal *HOT* in seconds. You would easily find it by just feeling the cable connections until you find the hot one. Much less resistance of almost perfect connections, makes itself noticeable by the generated heat during starting.

The Plumbing Equivalent: Table of Units and Relationships

Electrical	Equivalent
Potential, Tension	Pressure
Volt	Pounds per Square Inch, PSI
Current	Flow Rate
Ampere	Gallons per Minute
Power	Power
Watt	Watt or Horsepower
Work	Work
Watt hours	Watt hours, Kilowatt hours, Horsepower hours, Man hours, Joules, BTU
An increase in voltage causes an increase in current	An increase in pressure causes an increase in flow rate.
An increase in resistance causes a decrease in current	An increase in resistance causes a decrease in flow rate
To do more work in the same time, more Watt are needed.	To do more work in the same time, more power is needed.
Volt times Amp = Watt. Greater Watt may be from higher Amps or Volts, or both.	More power may come from greater water pressure, or from higher flow rate, or both.
The same Wattage may come from high voltage but low current, or low voltage but high current.	The same work may be done with high water volume under low pressure, or low volume at high pressure (water jet on turbine for example)

8

Volt, Ohm, Ampere, Watt Calculated

Here are some examples with numbers. In **Sketch 1,** the resistor R could be a piece of electrical equipment. Ammeter A and voltmeter V show how they must be connected.

$$4 \text{ Ohm} = \frac{12 \text{ Volt}}{3 \text{ Amp}}$$

$$12 \text{ Volt} = 3 \text{ Amp} \times 4 \text{ Ohm}$$

$$3 \text{ Amp} = \frac{12 \text{ Volt}}{4 \text{ Ohm}}$$

$$12 \text{ Volt} \times 3 \text{ Amp} = 36 \text{ WATT}$$

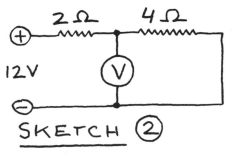

SKETCH ①

In **Sketch 2,** two resistors are in series. The total resistance is 2 Ohm plus 4 Ohm = 6 Ohm. Then,

$$\frac{12 \text{ Volt}}{6 \text{ Ohm}} = 2 \text{ Amp are flowing}$$

SKETCH ②

If you measure the voltage between the two, meter V would show 8 Volt. The voltage drops 4 V at the first resistor, 8 V at the second. Power at the first resistor is

$$2 \text{ Amp} \times 4 \text{ Volt} = 8 \text{ Watt}$$

power at the second resistor is

$$2 \text{ Amp} \times 8 \text{ Volt} = 16 \text{ Watt}$$

which adds up to a total of

$$24 \text{ Watt} (= 2 \text{ Amp} \times 12 \text{ Volt})$$

With two resistors or loads in parallel, **Sketch 3,** calculate the current for each one:

$$\frac{12 \text{ Volt}}{8 \text{ Ohm}} = 1.5 \text{ Amp, and } \frac{12 \text{ Volt}}{4 \text{ Ohm}} = 3 \text{ Amp}$$

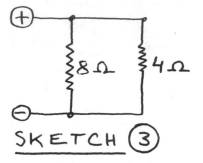

SKETCH ③

The total current is

$$1.5 \text{ Amp} + 3 \text{ Amp} = 4.5 \text{ Amp}$$

so that the two resistors act as a single resistor of

$$\frac{12 \text{ Volt}}{4.5 \text{ Amp}} = 2.66 \text{ Ohm}$$

Power on the left is 12 Volt × 1.5 Amp = 18 Watt, and on the right 12 Volt × 3 Amp = 36 Watt, or a total of 18 + 36 = 54 Watt (same as 12 Volt × 4.5 total Amps.)

How To Make and Use a Test Light

A test light is a most versatile trouble shooting tool which you can make yourself. It consists of a 12 V lamp and two test leads, as in **Sketch 1**. Easiest to use are the lamps ("light bulbs") with single contact bayonet base, see the lamp list in this book. The test wires are directly soldered to the lamp: one to the tip at the base, and one to the side of the brass base. Use a lamp number 67, 97, 631, 1155, or 1247, two pieces of stranded number 18 or 16 wire, as flexible as possible, and each about two to three feet long, with a plug or alligator clip soldered to the ends.

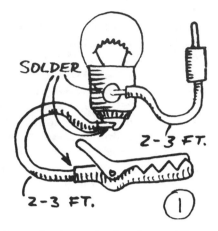

With only a few exceptions, all wires and terminals on the boat are either at plus 12 Volt, or at zero Volt or ground level, and so by design or because of a problem. Also, all wiring on the boat is so relatively heavy that the extra load of the test light will never matter. In the contrary, the load of the test light of about ½ A can find poor connections which a Volt Ohm Meter (VOM) could not.

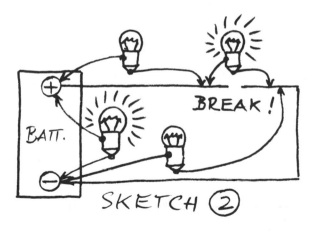

Sketch 2 shows a battery and a circuit which we are going to test. Note that the circuit has a break. This break in the wire can be our "load." It matters little to the test light (TL) whether the break is a completely open gap in the wire or is a light or some other equipment which lets some current flow. Now see why two of the test lights are on, and two are off. One is lit because its wires are touched to the battery terminals so that there is a difference in voltage, potential, pressure, between the two points touched. The TL across the break also lights because the two points at each side of the break are connected by wires to the plus and minus battery terminals. The TL at top, left, remains dark because both its test wires touch points which are at plus twelve Volt, so there is no force to make a current flow through the light. The same is true for the TL at lower right: it touches two points which are both at the battery minus level, again, there is no difference and no current flows, so the light remains

11

dark. In a real trouble shooting case, **Sketch 3**, you are trying to find why the lamp does not work. A break or poor contact in the positive wire would keep the TL dark if it were touched as at "A." A break or poor connection in the minus wire would keep the TL dark if touched to the points at "B."

The following example is typical for most circuits on the boat which consist of a positive wire with one or more switches, a load such as a light, motor, or instrument, and a minus wire without any switches, connected to ground. **Sketch 4** shows a battery, connected to a main switch, panel circuit breaker (for example "Cabin Lights"), toggle switch (for

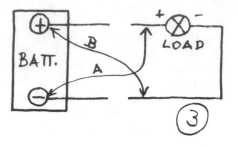

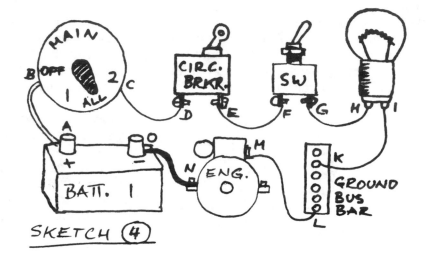

SKETCH ④

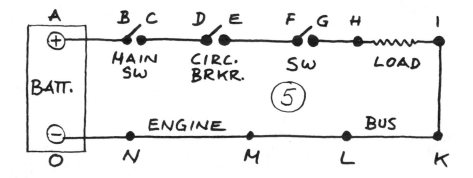

example the switch of a cabin light), a ground bus bar (which could also be a terminal strip to which many ground wires are connected), a ground wire to the engine block, and the heavy ground wire between battery minus terminal and engine block. The same is shown in **Sketch 5** as a wiring diagram, all terminals are labelled with a letter so that trouble shooting can be systematic. To test the switch SW with the test light at terminals F and G hold one test wire to F and the other to G as in **Sketch 6**.

Trouble Shooting the Circuit in **Sketches 4** and **5** with the test light:

First step: Turn all three switches on. If the cabin light does not work, touch test light to H and I: TL lights up, replace lamp or improve contacts at lamp base. If the TL remains dark, the problem is elsewhere.

Second step: to test all switches and positive wires between A and H, leave all switches turned on. Connect one test light wire to ground or minus, for example at O, N, or M, and leave connected. Test this ground by touching the other TL wire to A (TL lights), then to B, C, D, E, F, G, and H, in that order. TL normally lights up. However:

TL dark at A: completely dead battery, very unlikely.
TL dark at B: poor battery cable connections, unlikely to affect small load.
TL dark at C: poor main switch contact. Exercise the switch.
TL dark at D: faulty wire or connections at C or D.
TL dark at E: poor contact in circuit breaker, exercise it.
TL dark at F: faulty wire or connections E or F.
TL dark at G: poor contact in the switch, try to exercise switch.
TL dark at H: faulty wire or connections G or H.

Third step: clip one test wire to A, B, C, D, E, F, G, or H if they were found to be all right, or to another source of plus 12 Volt, and leave connected. Verify by touching the other TL wire to O (TL lights),then to N, M, L, K, and I in that order. The TL will normally light up. However, you have found a poor ground where the test light remains dark. For example, the TL lights at M and L, but not at K: poor connection at the ground bus bar terminals.

All of the faulty connections and poor switch contacts including accidentally open switches can be verified if the load (cabin light in this example) draws at least one Ampere when it is working. If you connect the test light wires across a switch with poor or open contacts as in **Sketch 6**, the TL will light up, brighter with greater Watt or Amp ratings of the load. See **Sketch 2** for the explanation.

Another trouble shooting example will follow later and describe how to trouble shoot battery, main switch, and engine starting circuit.

A test light extension wire may often be necessary. Make by soldering alligator clips to a length of stranded No. 16 or 18 wire. To test wiring in the mast, this extension wire must be long enough to let you reach the mast top.

The Volt Ohm Meter, VOM

This instrument is most useful if it has a direct current or DC range from 0 to 15 Volt, and a low Ohm range, for example one with 100 Ohm or less at the center of the scale. Unfortunately, most VOMs have 0 - 10 V DC and 0 - 50 V DC ranges, one too small, the other too large for good resolution of readings near 12 Volt. The most rugged meters have taut band meter movements, almost indestructible even if dropped. Since none except the most expensive are waterproof, you should start with a ten dollar variety and replace it when necessary. There is one such VOM available with convenient 0 - 15 V DC range.

Before taking a reading, the meter needle must be adjusted to zero which is done with a small screw on the meter. Resistance (Ohm) measurements require a battery which you can leave out if you do not need that function. Since the battery slowly ages, prior to Ohm measurements another adjustment is necessary. Turn "Ohm Adjust" control so that the needle points to 0 Ohm, with test wires touched to each other.

Many Volt Ohm meters are very sensitive, a normally desirable feature not needed for our applications and which can sometimes cause confusion. For example, in **Sketch 1**, switch A may be closed but have very poor contact. Switch B is open. A sensitive VOM would indicate full 12 V when connected as shown, and imply that switch A is all right. A test light connected to the same points as the VOM would remain dark.

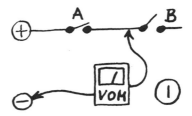

WARNING: since most meters have alternating current (AC) ranges as well, be warned of the shock hazard of 110 VAC.

For your notes:

Wiring Diagrams

Why your boat probably does not have one

There may be a wiring diagram for your engine, usually in the engine manual, or supplied by the builder. This diagram usually includes wiring of the starter, alternator, engine instruments, and controls such as key switch and start button switch. It usually shows one battery and sometimes mentions optional main switches and second batteries. Such diagram is a good starting point for a complete wiring diagram of the boat but it will be incomplete and may show details which were not fitted on your boat.

Why a wiring diagram is helpful

The wiring diagram shows what electrical equipment is there, and how it is connected. It shows exactly how electricity reaches a light through circuit breakers, switches, junctions, and wires: details which you cannot possibly remember nor trace, since many of them are hidden from view. But the details in the wiring diagram often allow you to pinpoint the most likely cause of trouble, it lets you search for problems systematically, it shows how best to connect new equipment or to make changes in the wiring. Finally, making up a wiring diagram is a superb opportunity to inspect those details which are visible, and to reason how the wires are connected which are hidden inside of liners, bulkheads, wiring ducts, mast, or uniformly covered with red engine paint.

How to make your boat's wiring diagram one step at a time

First of all, it is not necessary to have one all-encompassing master wiring diagram for the boat. Such diagrams do exist for some boats, they have serious disadvantages though. First of all, such sheet of paper is too big to handle on board. The detail which you may be looking for is hard to locate and difficult to keep in focus as you compare it to actual components on the boat. Finally, you will make changes over the years, but correcting and changing such master wiring diagram is almost impossible.

Instead, our "wiring diagram" will be a number of smaller diagrams which you can make up, one at a time as mood and opportunity arise, collect in a ring book or file, with enough room on each page to add notes, changes, comments, and easy enough to re-draw when necessary. Later on, we will decide how to subdivide the master diagram. Possible sections, each one one page, could be:

1. Batteries with main selector switch, starter and solenoid, battery monitoring instruments, battery charging equipment.
2. Ships main circuit breaker panel.
3. Mast wiring.
4. Cabin lights.
5. Instruments and radios.
6. Engine wiring.
7. Boat's 110V AC wiring.

Electrical Components

First step toward wiring diagrams is to identify electrical components, then decide on a uniform method of showing them with a symbol, and describing their wiring with uniform symbols in the diagram.

Batteries

Batteries have two terminals, meaning two connections, isolated from each other, called plus and minus. One or more wires may be connected to the plus and the minus terminals, but no wire connects directly from the plus terminal to the minus terminal of the same battery. Let us draw the boat's 12 Volt batteries as a rectangular box as in **Sketch 1**, with a small circle and plus or minus sign as the terminals. Replaceable batteries such as flashlight batteries, batteries in calculators, portable radios, other electronic equipment are often shown as in **Sketch 2**. If no plus or minus signs are used, the short bar is the plus or positive terminal. Batteries are often made up from a number of cells which are "stacked" or connected in

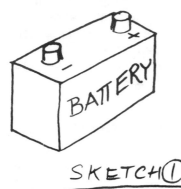

SKETCH ①

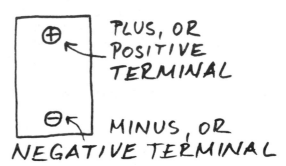

SYMBOL:

PLUS, OR POSITIVE TERMINAL

MINUS, OR NEGATIVE TERMINAL

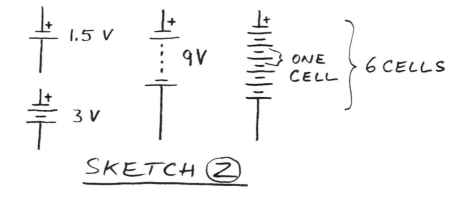

1.5 V

3 V

9V

ONE CELL } 6 CELLS

SKETCH ②

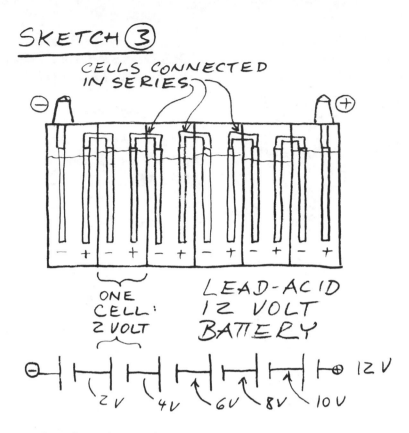

SKETCH ③

CELLS CONNECTED IN SERIES

ONE CELL: 2 VOLT

LEAD-ACID 12 VOLT BATTERY

⊖ — 2V — 4V — 6V — 8V — 10V — ⊕ 12V

series, so that the voltage of each cell contributes to the voltage of the battery as in the examples of **Sketch 3**. In the diagrams, the capacity or size of batteries is normally not shown, but the voltage or number of cells is sometimes indicated.

Switches

The simplest switch has two terminals which are either connected to each other so that current can flow, or disconnected and insulated from each other. Confusingly, the switch is called "closed" when the terminals are connected and allow current flow, and "open" when disconnected. This switch with two terminals is called a single pole, single throw switch.

A switch with three terminals is used as a selector switch, it can connect one "common" terminal to either of two other terminals and is called a single pole, double throw switch (abbreviated SPDT). Our normal battery selector switch is a SPDT switch with a special feature: the contact "makes" before breaking, meaning that throwing the switch from contact "1" to contact "2," it makes contact with terminal 2 before breaking contact with terminal 1, in the "ALL" or "BOTH" position. A similar but smaller SPDT switch is used to select automatic or manual bilge pump operation, or to use a voltmeter to measure battery 1 or battery 2. Single pole switches with

19

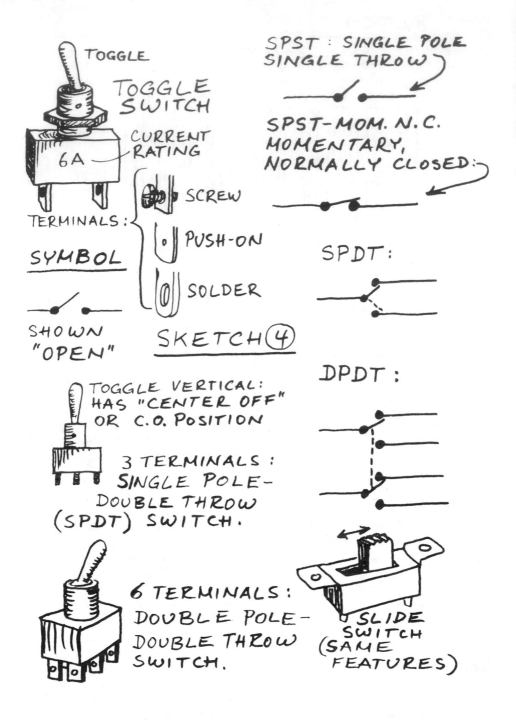

TOGGLE

TOGGLE SWITCH

CURRENT RATING

6A

TERMINALS:

SYMBOL

SHOWN "OPEN"

SCREW

PUSH-ON

SOLDER

SKETCH ④

TOGGLE VERTICAL: HAS "CENTER OFF" OR C.O. POSITION

3 TERMINALS: SINGLE POLE- DOUBLE THROW (SPDT) SWITCH.

6 TERMINALS: DOUBLE POLE- DOUBLE THROW SWITCH.

SPST : SINGLE POLE SINGLE THROW

SPST - MOM. N.C. MOMENTARY, NORMALLY CLOSED:

SPDT :

DPDT :

SLIDE SWITCH (SAME FEATURES)

three or more contacts are in use, as are switches which combine two single pole switches and are called double pole, as in "double pole single throw switch."

Sketch 4 shows some of the more common switches and their symbols for the wiring diagram. Note that some switches are shown "open" and some "closed," and that switch contacts may be designed to remain in contact only while held in a position against spring tension. Such switches are called "momentary," and require the additional description "normally open" or "normally closed," depending on contact position "during rest." An example of a single pole, single throw, normally open, momentary switch is the starter button switch. An example for a normally closed momentary switch is the "kill" switch on many outboard motors which interrupts the ignition.

Wires

For the wiring diagram, you will have to distinguish between four sizes of wires as you inspect the boat's electrics. The heaviest, biggest type has a diameter of ½ inch or more and connects the battery terminals to the battery main selector switch, to the starter solenoid, and engine block. Such wires are often called "battery cables" although they only have a single copper conductor made from many thin strands of wire. This heavy wire is also used to connect electric windlasses and any other equipment which draws large currents.

The next smaller wire size you will find as the supply wire to the electric switch panel, and on some of the engine controls. It is about the size of a pencil, noticeably bigger than the mass of wires which are used to connect individual lights or components to circuit breakers or fuses. You may find one such pencil sized wire connected to the "C" terminal of the battery main switch, together with another heavy wire. One supplies plus 12 Volt to the electric panel, the other, starting current to the engine.

Recognizing the differences in wire sizes, and using the colors of wires, will help you trace wires. In most cases, you will only be able to see a wire at the ends. In between, the wire may become an unidentifiable part of a wiring bundle, or may run in a wiring duct. Notice the size of wires most abundant behind the electric panel or at the circuit breakers or fuses. These will be about ⅛ inch in diameter, and hopefully several different colors will have been used. We will discuss in a moment how, with reason and pencil and paper, we fit these wires correctly into the wiring diagram.

Very thin individual wires, and several in a cable, are used to connect electronic instruments, wind instruments, log, speedometer, and so on. Because of their size and profuse color coding, these instrument wires are usually easy to follow. Since such instruments use very little current, their electric supply wires are also usually thin: you may spot them at the main electric panel where some will be connected to plus 12 Volt and to minus or ground.

If your boat is wired for shore electricity, 110 VAC, you will likely have such wiring connections blended right into your 12 Volt wiring. Often, similar terminal blocks and wire sizes and colors are used, and sometimes investigating the wiring behind the main panel is hazardous indeed:

CAUTION: Disconnect the shore power cable and remove it, or place a tape over the cable socket on the boat while you inspect any of the wiring. Identify all of the 110 VAC circuit breakers which often have uninsulated terminals. Look out for 110 V pilot lights, reverse polarity lights, AC voltmeters and ammeters which may be located on the same panel as the 12 V units and may at the back of the panel all look alike. All 110 V meter, light, and breaker terminals are a shock hazard, as are the wire terminal blocks or barrier strips which are often used. Make certain that you recognize all wires and cables used for the shore power lights, outlets, and appliances, and label them.

Wires in the wiring diagram are usually represented by thin solid lines regardless of the actual wire size. Only sometimes, for emphasis, are heavy wires shown by heavier black lines. One of the important features of the wiring diagram is simplicity, it must show at a glance how things are connected. Therefore, the components in the diagram are oriented and arranged to make the interconnecting wires, lines here, simple. Switches, meters, and components, will be shown exactly as wired, but may be turned so that up and down, left and right, may not match their real position if that helped to make the wiring diagram easier to comprehend.

Another wiring diagram simplification is based on the fact that we switch all equipment off at the positive wire. The wiring between positive battery terminal and lights and appliances contains the switches, fuses, circuit breakers, while the negative side remains permanently connected to ground or minus. Wiring diagrams are often simplified by omitting all connections of the minus wires and, only, showing a minus symbol at terminals. Many of the wiring details are shown in **Sketch 5**. Details of wire sizes and current carrying ability will follow in another chapter.

Lights

Cabin light wiring and wiring within the mast will almost always be inaccessible. Still, you will be able to make a complete and accurate wiring diagram with the method described later, as long as you know about all lights and their functions. The procedure is made slightly more complicated by lights which do not work. Almost all cabin lights will have their own on-off switch, either a single pole, single throw toggle or slide switch, or a rotary switch, sometimes at the back of a lamp socket fitting. More rarely is a whole group of cabin lights switched by a single switch. Mast lights, on the other hand, have their switches on the electric panel or nav. station

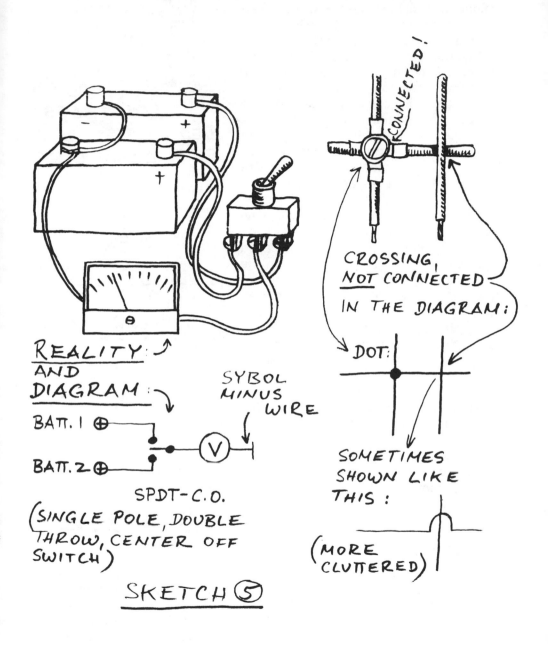

CONNECTED!

REALITY: ↗
AND
DIAGRAM:

BATT. 1 ⊕

BATT. 2 ⊕

SYBOL
MINUS
WIRE

SPDT–C.O.
(SINGLE POLE, DOUBLE
THROW, CENTER OFF
SWITCH)

SKETCH ⑤

CROSSING,
NOT CONNECTED

IN THE DIAGRAM:

DOT:

SOMETIMES
SHOWN LIKE
THIS:

(MORE
CLUTTERED)

panel, a long distance away from the lights and normally with wiring junctions or terminal blocks or boxes (see below) between switch and light. If in doubt, see the details on mast wiring in a later chapter.

Light output of a light is related to the current which, in turn, may give you a clue to the wire size: compass light and instrument lights will draw only a fraction of an Ampere (A) and may use very light wire, individual running lights and smaller cabin lights will use about one Ampere each and will use that most common wire size discussed in the paragraph on wires. Spreader lights or deck lights will almost always use greater currents and use heavier than average wires which you may spot. The light bulbs in light fixtures are called "lamps," a lamp list follows later in the book. In the wiring diagram, lamp sizes are usually ignored and all lamps shown with the same symbol. If there are two lamps in a light fixture, two lamps should be shown in the diagram. Especially with lamps and lights, the minus wire is usually not shown in the wiring diagram since it is obvious that there must be one. However, we will discuss ground wires in the sections about trouble shooting, to see how easily they are overlooked. Several symbols are in use for "filament" or "incandescent" lamps, pick one, then use it consistently. See **Sketch 6**.

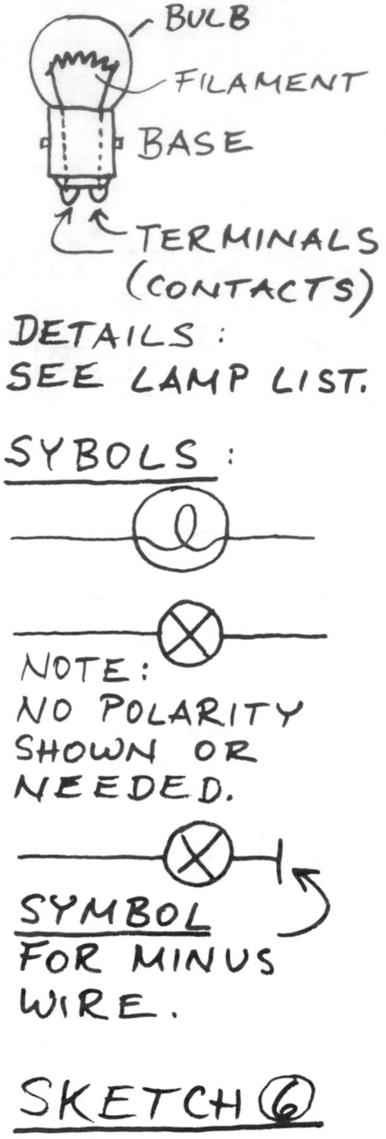

BULB
FILAMENT
BASE
TERMINALS
(CONTACTS)
DETAILS :
SEE LAMP LIST.

SYBOLS :

NOTE :
NO POLARITY
SHOWN OR
NEEDED.

SYMBOL
FOR MINUS
WIRE.

SKETCH 6

Circuit Breakers and Fuses

For the purpose of the wiring diagram, treat circuit breakers as single pole switches, sketch them the same way but identify them with their Ampere rating if known, and "C.BRKR." or similar abbreviation, see **Sketch 7**. Fuses protect from excess current but cannot be switched. Usually fuse holders are installed with single pole switches in series, see **Sketch 8**. In the wiring diagrams, you should try to maintain the order in which circuit breakers or fuses are arranged on the electric panel since you will from time to time be looking at the back of such panel, wiring diagram in hand but circuit breaker labels out of sight.

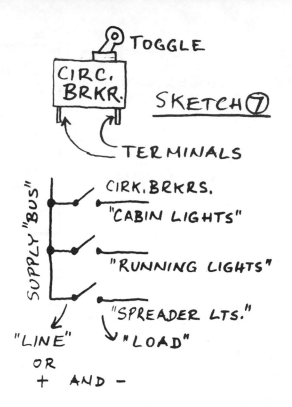

TOGGLE

CIRC. BRKR.

SKETCH ⑦

TERMINALS

SUPPLY "BUS"

CIRK. BRKRS.

"CABIN LIGHTS"

"RUNNING LIGHTS"

"SPREADER LTS."

"LINE"
OR
+ AND −

"LOAD"

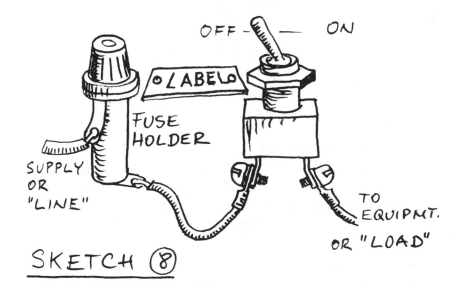

OFF ―― ON

LABEL

FUSE HOLDER

SUPPLY
OR
"LINE"

TO EQUIPMT.
OR "LOAD"

SKETCH ⑧

WIRING DIAGRAM:

FUSE
5 A

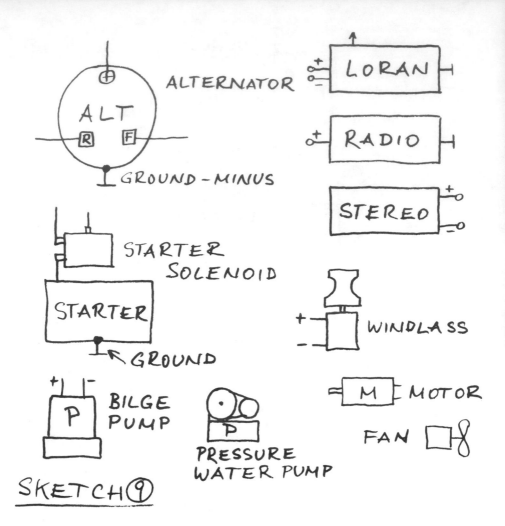

ALTERNATOR

ALT
R F

GROUND - MINUS

STARTER
SOLENOID

STARTER

GROUND

BILGE
PUMP

PRESSURE
WATER PUMP

SKETCH 9

LORAN

RADIO

STEREO

WINDLASS

M MOTOR

FAN

Other Pieces of Equipment

For the wiring diagram, we will lump all other equipment into one group which will contain the alternator, engine starter motor and solenoid, electric bilge and pressure water pumps, other equipment with electric motors, radios, navigation receivers, other electronics. All of these will be connected to 12 Volt, all will have at least a plus and minus terminal, and almost all are complicated enough so that we do not want their internal wiring as a part of the boat's wiring diagram. Many of these we will treat later in the book. Their internal diagrams are often essential to have but should be filed on a separate page. For our wiring diagram we proceed as follows: if the component is round, like the alternator, we represent it with a circle. If it is longish like a starter motor, with solenoid on its back, let us use silhouettes which will look similar but without the clutter of details. Show

26

pumps as boxes with a letter P, for example, or show your type of bilge pump in profile, show electronic equipment as boxes with labels and, if possible, a note which helps you find their wiring diagram and manual. Is a sketch necessary? Here it is, **Sketch 9**, with circles and boxes.

Example: How to make a wiring diagram:
Batteries, Main Switch, Starter, Solenoid

This part of the master wiring diagram will start with the battery "cables" because they are easy to see and trace, and the battery main or selector switch and engine starter motor are all wired with similarly heavy wire, or "cable."

To make your wiring sketch, start with a large piece of paper. Or use a pad of tracing paper and start on its last page: you can then make changes by folding a new page on top and trace any part of old drawing. Draw a rectangle, battery symbol, for each battery on board. Mark plus and minus terminals. Draw a main switch, or two if your boat is so fitted. Then draw starter and solenoid, for example as in **Sketch 10**. Do not enter any wires yet, and leave ample space between the components.

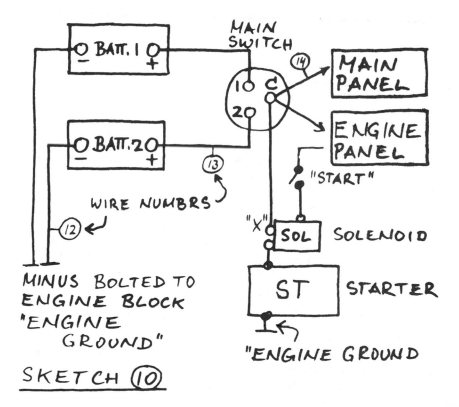

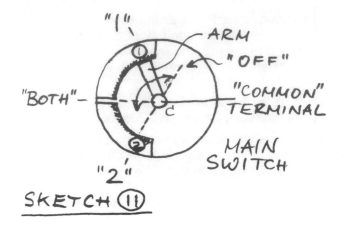

"1" ARM "OFF"
"BOTH"- "COMMON" TERMINAL
"2" MAIN SWITCH

SKETCH ⑪

On the back of the battery main switch, terminals are labelled "1," "2," and "ALL" or "BOTH." If you can see the number one terminal, begin with the heavy wire connected to it, and trace it to a battery plus terminal. That battery will be No. 1. Enter the wire in the diagram. Trace the heavy wire from terminal "2" to plus post of battery No. 2. The remaining heavy wire should then run from the third main switch terminal into the area of the starter, on one side of the engine.

If you cannot see the numbers on the back of the main switch, you can identify the batteries by taking off one heavy wire from one battery plus terminal (do not touch to ground), then turn the switch to "1" and "2" while trying cabin lights. The main switch position will tell you which battery you have disconnected. Mark your batteries if they do not carry numbers now. Enter the wires in the diagram. Then locate the minus terminals of each battery and trace the minus wires to a bolt on the engine: your boat has "negative ground." The ground connections are rarely as in **Sketch 10** but more often have the battery minus posts interconnected, and only one wire to ground at the engine. In the rare case that your boat should have "positive ground," label the battery terminals in the diagram as they are actually wired.

You will likely find some smaller wires also connected to the battery main switch. While you have the terminals identified, look for a medium sized wire (number 10 or 12 American Wire Gauge, see section in this book) which supplies the boat's electric panel, and another similar wire to the engine panel or ignition key switch and starter switch. Note the "X" in **Sketch 10**. The engine panel wire is often connected to this solenoid terminal instead of terminal "C" of the main switch. This solenoid terminal is large; do not confuse with the much smaller terminal from the "Start" button. Enter the wires in the diagram as you locate them.

If your boat has more than two batteries, they may either be connected in parallel, as a bank, as batteries 1A and 1B in **Sketch 12**, or switched separately with an additional main switch as in **Sketch 13**.

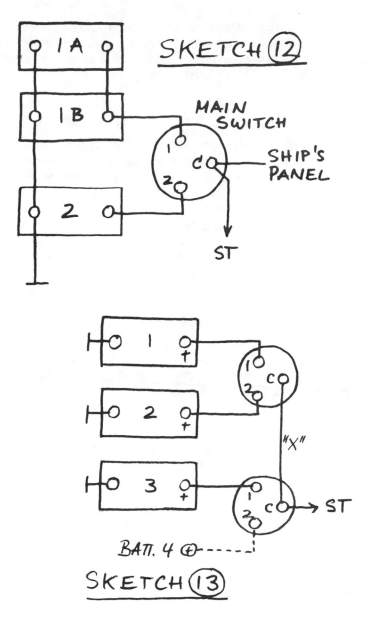

SKETCH 12

MAIN SWITCH

SHIP'S PANEL

ST

SKETCH 13

BATT. 4 ⊕------

"X"

Any number of batteries may be connected as 1A and 1B, and then are used as one large battery. All positive terminals would be interconnected, and all negative terminals connected to ground. If three or more batteries are switched (selected) separately, more than one battery main switch is needed. Inspect your system and sketch it as you see its wiring.

On some boats, a separate "engine" battery is used for engine starting only, with one or two "house" batteries supplying all other electricity. Such system would not have the connection marked "X" in **Sketch 13**. The starter would be connected to the lower main switch at "ST" while the electric panel, with all of the boat's circuits, would be connected to the "C" terminal of the upper main switch. We will discuss the relative merits of such systems in the section on batteries. At this point, try to make a drawing as complete as possible, of what is there.

Wire Numbering

Since you will see wires connected to the main switch or to the battery which have not become a part of this section of your wiring diagram, note their existence. For example, with the "main panel" wire in **Sketch 10**, note the color and size of such wire and consider numbering. Wire numbers are discussed in the section on electrical materials. Numbers are best placed near the ends, terminals, of each wire, and marked in the wiring sketches. Put numbers on yet unidentified wires which you find connected to a component. You will later come across the other end of such wire and will then be able to tell what that wire does.

Engine Panel and Controls

This section of the master wiring diagram may already be on hand in your engine manual. However, compare it to the actual components and wiring which is easy enough: check whether your engine panel actually has key switch, warning lights, meters, alarms et cetera as listed.

Sketch 14 shows two types of key switches. The one at top has two terminals and two positions, ON and OFF. The other has three or more terminals and three or more positions: an OFF and ON position, and one momentary ON position for starting. Both switches will have one supply terminal with the wire coming from main switch or terminal "X" in **Sketch 10**. Try to trace and compare color, and number the wire at this end. The switch with three or more positions may have more than one SPST switch, connecting to one or more terminals as the switch is turned. Test by the switch functions. There will be only one momentary switch position, its terminal connected to the small terminal on the starter solenoid, shown in sketches.

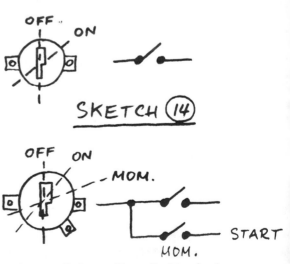

KEY SWITCHES :

SKETCH (14)

If there is no key switch, you will either have a switch or circuit breaker labelled "Engine" on the main electric panel, or there may be a fuel or oil pressure switch on the engine which is normally open, closing with pressure, and switching electricity to the engine instruments, alternator charge light, engine alarms, and alternator regulator. Some of these details are in the Alternator Section.

In **Sketch 15** you see an accumulation of possible components and functions which may all be switched ON from the key switch. There will

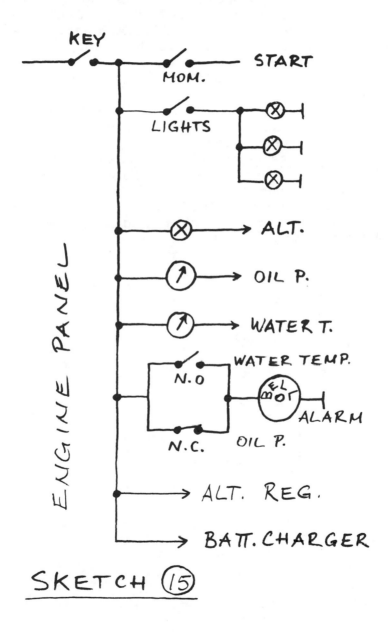

SKETCH ⑮

always be a momentary starting switch, separately as shown, or as part of the key switch itself. Instrument lights will have their own ON-OFF switch in most cases. The "ALT" light is the "idiot light" as used on automobiles, the other wire from the light will be connected to a terminal on the alternator (details in the section on alternators). Oil pressure gauge and water temperature gauge may be the mechanical or electrical variety. If the latter, the gauge meters have one terminal connected to plus twelve volt, and another wire connected to a sensor or sender at the engine (details in the section on engine alarms). One kind of engine alarm is shown here, consisting of a bell or horn connected to two switches, both mounted on the engine: the normally open water temperature switch closes with high temperature, the normally closed oil pressure switch opens when pressure reaches normal levels. Such alarm will sound when the key is turned on and will stop once the engine runs. However, see **Sketch 16** for other engine alarms. The ALT. REG. wire will lead to the alternator regulator. However, some alternators do not require this wire connection. Finally, a wire is sometimes used to switch off shore power operated battery chargers while the engine is running. If you find a thin wire from this engine panel terminal leading to the "converter" or battery charger, mark it as such. Label and number any of these wires at the panel and in your drawing, note any additional wires for later identification.

Another alarm system is shown in **Sketch 16**; remember that wire connections are marked by dots. This alarm, used on Yanmar engines, has three warning lights connected to three places on the engine, plus one buzzer alarm common to all three. The ALT wire is connected to a terminal of the alternator which has 12 Volt only when the alternator is working, the W.T. water temperature sensor is an open switch which closes if water

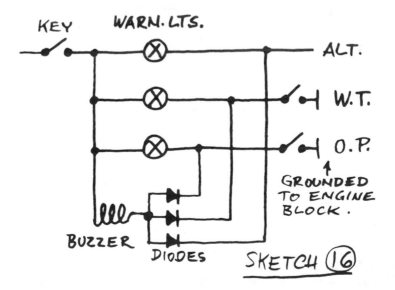

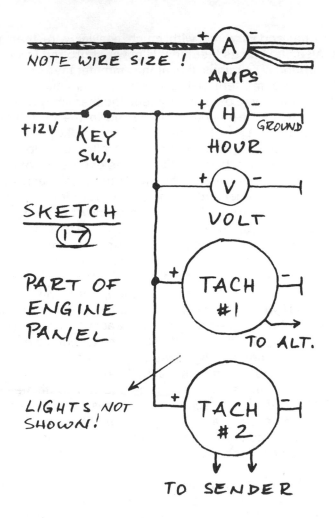

NOTE WIRE SIZE !

+12V KEY SW.

SKETCH (17)

PART OF ENGINE PANEL

LIGHTS NOT SHOWN!

AMPS

HOUR GROUND

VOLT

TACH #1 TO ALT.

TACH #2

TO SENDER

temperature rises beyond a limit, and the oil pressure sensor is a normally closed switch which opens with normal oil pressure. Only three single wires lead to the engine, the senders make contact to their housing which is in electrical contact with engine block and ground. If any one wire is connected to ground, the buzzer alarm sounds but only the corresponding warning light lights up. There are isolating diodes in the buzzer unit, shown in the sketch. The diodes conduct only in one direction and keep the three warning lights isolated to their own warning circuit. With key switch on, the alternator and oil pressure lights will go on and will sound the alarm before the engine is started.

Several other instruments may be present in your engine panel, see **Sketch 17**. From the key switch, which is the same as shown in the previous sketches, wires carry plus 12 Volt to an engine hour meter, a voltmeter, and two kinds of tachometers. Please note that the "A" ammeter is wired differently from all other panel instruments. The ammeter measures current, flow rate, and is wired with much heavier wire than the other instruments. Also, its "minus" terminal is never at ground level and is not connected to ground. The minus sign at the ammeter merely indicates that this is the "downstream" terminal. Sometimes, this ammeter terminal is used to supply electricity to other equipment and there may be two or more wires connected to that terminal, as indicated in the sketch. The other instruments in **Sketch 17** will come alive when the key switch is turned on, or when electricity is supplied to them by an alternative to a key switch, for example by a panel switch or circuit breaker, or by a fuel or oil pressure switch on the engine which closes when the engine has been started.

The wires to the hour meter and voltmeter may be quite light or thin since very little current is required. The hour meter may be incorporated in a tachometer and then will not have visible wiring. Note that the minus wiring is not shown but has been replaced by a ground symbol in the sketches. Also, note that the connections to the key switch are simplified by using lines and dots in the sketch, but in reality will have one wire from the key switch to each of the instruments. In addition, there will be instrument lights, each with its own plus and minus wire and possibly a "lights" switch, so that such a panel will appear a confusing tangle of wires when you first inspect its back. But if you use the wiring diagram technique of first sketching the components, then adding wires as you identify them, the sketch will eventually show you how things are working.

Two kinds of tachometers are shown in **Sketch 17**, both are connected to plus 12 Volt and ground. Tachometer #1 has another wire which is connected to a terminal of the alternator. This terminal supplies alternating current, directly from the stator windings of the alternator. The frequency of this alternating current is proportional to the speed of the engine.

Tachometer #2 uses a transducer or sender which sends pulses of electricity. The sender may be mounted so that it senses the teeth of the flywheel (the same teeth into which the starter motor engages), or teeth of another gear of the engine, or the blades of the fan of the alternator, directly behind the pulley of the alternator. Or the sender may be a unit with its own shaft, driven by the engine.

On gas engines, the tachometer will be the #1 type and the sensing wire connected to the ignition: the tachometer uses pulses generated by the points. In all cases, tachometers are calibrated to show actual engine RPM for proportional pulses or alternating currents which depend on pulley size ratio for alternators, number of teeth on flywheels, or number of cylinders of gas engines. Most tachometers have a calibration screw at the back of the housing, usually under a seal or cap.

As mentioned elsewhere, erratic readings of the tachometer are often caused by a slipping alternator belt. The symptom can be amplified by increasing the electrical load on the alternator: switch all pumps and lights on, to see if the tachometer display decreases in spite of constant engine speed.

To make the wiring diagram of the engine panel, start by making a sketch with only the components and instruments which you actually have. Use the engine manual to help you with details and possibly with color codes of the wiring. Unfortunately, color coded wires are often uniformly coated with engine paint. The use of wire numbering is strongly recommended. Attach a number marker at one end of a wire, for example at a terminal of an instrument or switch, then trace the wire and label the other end with the same number. Enter the wire with its number in your sketch. Mistakes will usually become obvious in the sketch: it shows the terminals of all components. If any terminal remains without its wire or wires, it shows you that the sketch is not yet complete. If the sketch shows a wire which connects two terminals of the same component, or a wire which connects plus 12 V to ground, you have probably made a mistake. You may leave any difficult details for later. Often, you discover wiring details which may belong to the engine while, for example, looking at cabin light wiring.

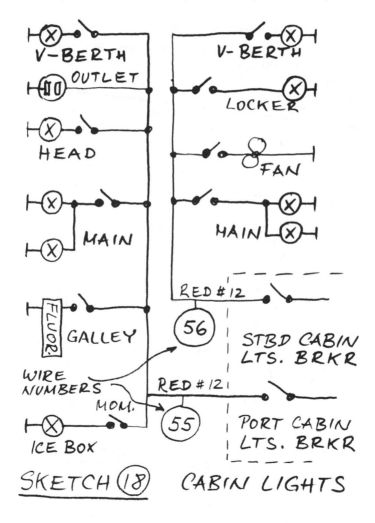

SKETCH (18)   CABIN LIGHTS

Cabin Lights

This section of the master wiring diagram will almost always be quite easy to make, even though much of the actual wire may be out of sight, in wiring ducts or conduits, in bulkheads, or behind liners. Include in this diagram any 12 V outlets, cabin fans, etc. Enter in your sketch the lights, approximately as they are located throughout the boat, light switches, chart lights, bunk and reading lights, outlets, fans, and the one, two, or more main panel circuit breakers for cabin lights. Try which lights are connected to each breaker. Then complete the diagram which will be similar to **Sketch 18**. How the wires actually reach each cabin light may remain a secret unless there are problems which make trouble shooting necessary. If the lights are bright, and one light does not dim when another is switched on (see trouble shooting techniques), no wire tracing or numbering is necessary except in the area at the main panel.

Mast

Since the mast wiring is usually invisible, we make the mast wiring sketch from the components on the mast and the wires and cables visible at the mast foot. There may be lights, instrument heads, and antennas with their wires and cables. Wind instruments and antennas usually have their own cables extending through the mast foot, but lights often use wire splices if two lights are located close together or have the same function: steaming light and deck light in the same fitting often use a common ground for wire for the two lamps, and two spreader lights may use both common plus and ground wires. There should never be any splice within the mast, and aluminum masts should never be used as the ground.

Start a sketch with the mast lights, and with a number for each separate wire at the mast foot. Exclude antenna cables and the normally thin instrument wires in cables. If you find six wires for three lamps on the mast, each apparently has its own plus and minus wire, shown in **Sketch 19**, rare. In most cases, there will be wires used for more than one light. **Sketch 20** shows a steaming light and deck light fitting with corresponding schematic, both lamps have a common ground wire and may be connected with three separate wires or a three conductor cable. **Sketch 21** shows the wiring diagram of two spreader lights with common plus and minus wire. To identify the wires, use a test light or voltmeter, and switch mast lights on individually. See the trouble shooting section about how to use test light or meter.

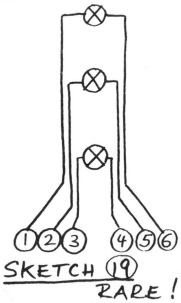

SKETCH 19
RARE !

36

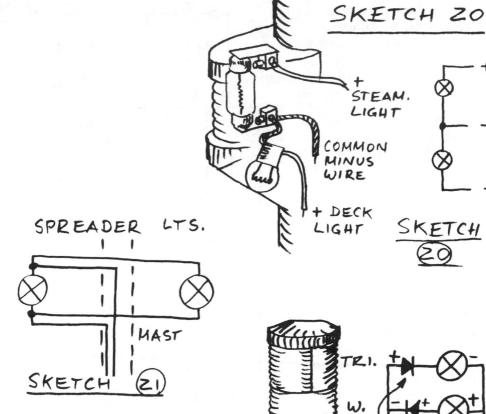

SKETCH 20

+ STEAM.
LIGHT

COMMON
MINUS
WIRE

+ DECK
LIGHT

SKETCH 20

SPREADER LTS.

MAST

SKETCH 21

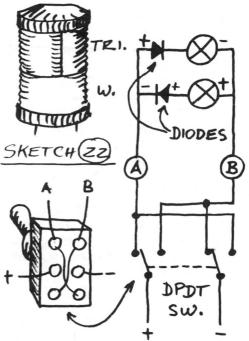

TRI.

W.

DIODES

SKETCH 22

A   B

A   B

+   —

DPDT
Sw.

+   —

Sketch 22 shows how the more recent tricolor running lights and white "anchor" lights can be operated from two wires. Each of the two lamps are wired in series with a diode, a check valve which lets current flow only in one direction. Note that the diodes are in different directions. If wire "A" is positive, the tricolor lamp will be on. If wire "B" is positive, the white masthead light will be on. Switching is done with a DPDT (double pole double throw) switch which reverses polarity. These lights are often installed in place of masthead lights and then use the two existing wires.

Other lights on the mast may include the red over green lights of COLREGS RULE 25-C which may have common plus and minus wires, strobe light which sometimes is combined with tricolor and white masthead lights in a common housing. You should include the mast wiring diagram in the terminal block or plus of any wind instruments. Note the type of cable, and the colors of wires with their location on the terminal block or in the plus. An example of a mast wiring diagram is shown in **Sketch 23**.

Deck

On sailboat masts, the white masthead light is often replaced with a combined tricolor running light and white light, see previous section on masts. When sailing, the tricolor running light with its single lamp saves electricity and makes the boat more visible than with the old running lights on cabin trunk or hull. Under engine though, with the steamer light

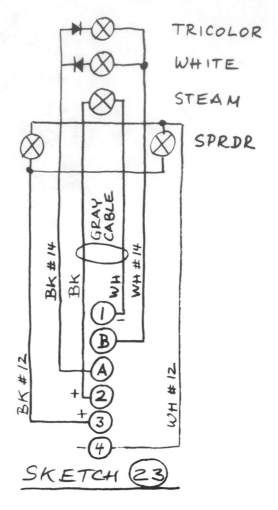

on, the red and green running lights are required below the steaming light. For this application, a switch is used to select tricolor masthead or running lights at deck level, steamer light, and masthead light combination (with its selector switch), as shown in **Sketch 24**. Two sets of running lights can be switched on at the same time. If the number of circuit breakers is limited, a similar arrangement with only one breaker (possibly labelled NAV.LTS.) is shown in **Sketch 25**. After the breaker, one SPDT switch selects running lights at deck or mast. With this switch at "DECK RUN. LTS.," a single pole switch can turn on the steamer light. In the "MAST" position, the switch feeds the polarity-reversing DPDT switch as in the previous sketches.

Other equipment which could be included in the "DECK" wiring diagram is the compass light, other instrument lights, outlet for hand held spotlight, and if not in a separate diagram, the knotmeter, log, depth sounder, auto-

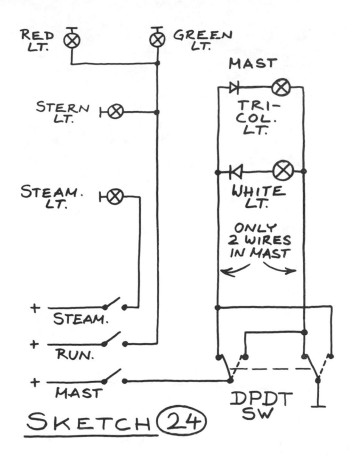

RED LT. ⊗   ⊗ GREEN LT.

MAST

STERN LT. ⊦⊗

STEAM. LT. ⊦⊗

TRI-COL. LT.

WHITE LT.

ONLY 2 WIRES IN MAST

+ ——— STEAM.

+ ——— RUN.

+ ——— MAST

DPDT SW

SKETCH (24)

pilot, windlass, deck wash pump, bilge pump. Most of these will only be shown with their positive and negative supply wires which you should locate and number. See **Sketch 9**. Only bilge pump and windlass will have more than a plain on-off switch. Bilge pumps are usually installed with a float switch which makes contact when bilge water rises, with a selector switch for manual or automatic operation. This is shown in **Sketch 26**. Note the joint of wires between selector switch, float switch, and pump: this splice is vulnerable because wires "2" and "3" are often not long enough to keep the splice out of the bilge. Locate and renumber the wires. The positive wire often incorporates a fuse, a nuisance worth noting if your boat otherwise has breakers.

Windlasses require much current and heavy wires which the main circuit breaker panel cannot handle. The heavy wires usually start at the battery main switch and engine block, and switching is by solenoid which is a relay or electromagnetic switch very similar to the starter solenoid. This solenoid is normally located near the windlass below deck and its coil switched on and off with a momentary switch on deck, as shown in **Sketch 27**.

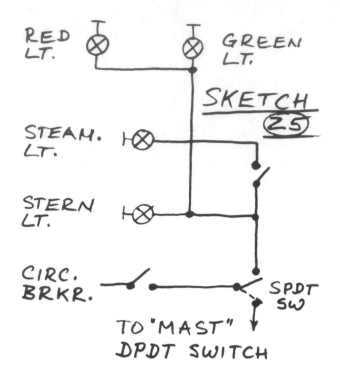

RED LT.

GREEN LT.

SKETCH (25)

STEAM. LT.

STERN LT.

CIRC. BRKR.

SPDT SW

TO "MAST" DPDT SWITCH

Pressure water system pumps are equipped with a pressure switch in series with the pump motor. The pressure switch contacts are closed until water pressure reaches the designed level. The pressure switch is often located on or near the pump. Some such pumps have another switch which opens if the pump is running but the water tank empty, this switch is also wired in series with the pump motor, as in **Sketch 28**.

Main Panel

This panel will consist mostly of circuit breakers or fuses with toggle switches. Most of these are already shown in the sketches for individual circuits such as running lights, cabin lights, pressure water system and so on, and the supply side of the panel which consists of a wire to the battery main switch is shown in **Sketches 10 and 12**. For your sketch, include all breakers on your panel and arrange them as on the panel, upper breaker at top of sketch. Label the breakers, and number the wires from the individual breakers but do not include details of individual circuits which you already have in separate wiring sketches. Include any voltmeter, ammeter, and their wiring if applicable, and any pilot lights. An example of a main panel is shown in **Sketch 29**. The battery main switch is included for better orientation.

Alternator, Battery Charger

Try to find your alternator and its wiring in the section on alternators. Keep in mind that at this point we want to sketch only the existing wiring.

Alternators always have one larger terminal stud which is the current output terminal, connected to battery main switch terminal "C" or to the starter solenoid terminal as shown in **Sketch 10** at "X." Battery chargers or converters often have diode-isolated output terminals for two or three separate batteries or battery banks and then have one wire connected to each battery plus terminal or the corresponding terminal at the battery main switch. Usually, one minus wire is connected to one of the minus terminals and serves all batteries.

110 Volt Wiring

If your boat has shore power wiring, safety requires that you survey this wiring and include a sketch in your wiring diagram file.

SHOCK HAZARD: Before anything else, disconnect the shore power cable at the boat's socket and screw down the cover. Do not use the dock end of your cable to disconnect since some helpful hand may plug your cable back in. Use tape or labels if necessary. Do not expose or touch any of the boat's electrical equipment if you are not thoroughly familiar with the hazards of 110 V. If necessary, have a professional electrician inspect your 110 Volt system to make certain that there is no 110 V wiring exposed at the electric panel, and that this wiring is distinctly separate from all 12 V wiring and can not be mistaken or inadvertently touched. At the same time, have the electrician tell you how your 110 V wiring is grounded: i.e. to the shore cable ground wire, to boat's ground, with ground fault interrupter.

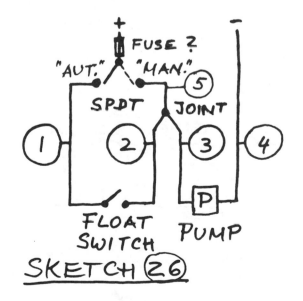

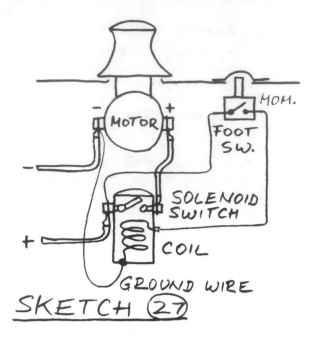

SKETCH 27

Most 110 V shore power wiring consists of a three conductor shore power cable, a male three prong connector on the boat, a metal circuit breaker box with one double pole main breaker and additional single pole circuit breakers, a pilot light and reverse polarity light or buzzer alarm, three conductor wiring to grounded outlets, water heater, battery charger, and other appliances. Wiring is to code, black wire is hot to short slots at outlets, white wire neutral to long slots at outlets below deck, green wire to ground terminals. A sample wiring diagram is shown in **Sketch 30** but is not intended as a trouble shooting guide and is otherwise beyond the range of this book.

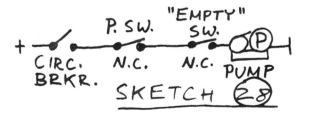

SKETCH 28

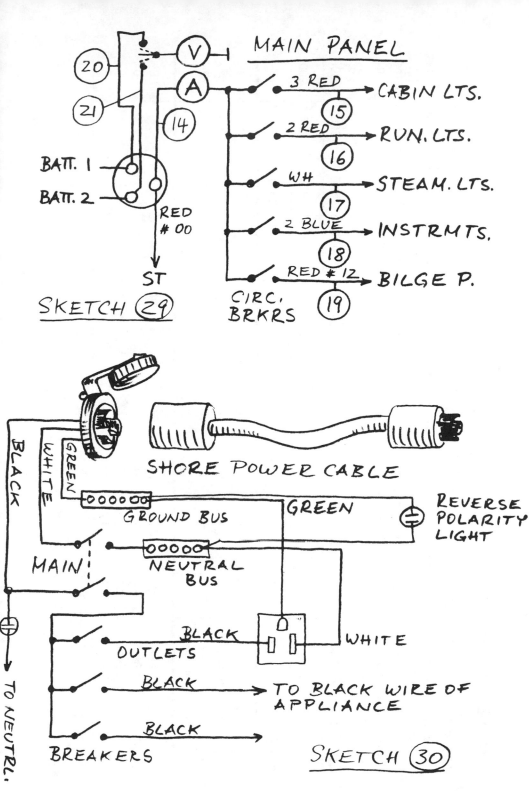

MAIN PANEL

20

21

V

A

14

3 RED → CABIN LTS.
15

2 RED → RUN. LTS.
16

WH → STEAM. LTS.
17

2 BLUE → INSTRMTS.
18

RED #12 → BILGE P.
19

BATT. 1

BATT. 2

RED #00

ST

SKETCH 29

CIRC.
BRKRS

SHORE POWER CABLE

BLACK

WHITE

GREEN

GROUND BUS

GREEN

REVERSE
POLARITY
LIGHT

MAIN

NEUTRAL
BUS

BLACK

OUTLETS

WHITE

BLACK → TO BLACK WIRE OF
APPLIANCE

BLACK

BREAKERS

TO NEUTRL.

SKETCH 30

43

Wire Size Table

Application Example.

You want to connect a bilge pump, rated 5 Ampere. You need 35 feet of wire, and you have decided that 5% loss of electric power in the wire is tolerable. What size wire is needed?

Find the LOAD column for 5 Amps/64 Watts, below it in the 5% section, wire size No. 18 AWG is listed for 20 feet of wire length, No. 14 AWG for 50 feet. Choose No. 14 wire, the value nearest the required 35 feet.

LOAD: Watts	1.3	6.4	13	26	64	130	260	640	1300	2600
Amps	.1	.5	1	2	5	10	20	50	100	200
Ohms	128	26	13	6.4	2.56	1.28	.64	.256	.128	.064
1% Loss — 10 feet	24	24	20	18	14	10	8	4	1	a
1% Loss — 20 feet	24	20	18	14	10	8	4	1	a	a
1% Loss — 50 feet	24	16	14	10	6	4	1	a	a	a
1% Loss — 100 feet	20	14	10	8	4	a	a	a	a	a
5% Loss — 10 feet	24	24	24	24	18*	14*	12*	8*	2*	0*
5% Loss — 20 feet	24	24	24	22	18*	14*	12*	8*	2*	0*
5% Loss — 50 feet	24	24	20	18	14	10	8	4	1	a
5% Loss — 100 feet	24	20	18	14	10	8	4	1	a	a

*Wire number reduced, wire thickness increased, to match N.E.C. Recommendation.
aApplication not practical in that % loss category.

Soldering

How to Solder, and Why

Many electrical wire connections are made by applying pressure on the copper wires to make electrical contact. The twisted wires under wire nuts in house wiring, wire wrapping connections in computers, crimped terminals, wires under pan head or set screws all rely on pressure, and normally work well. Many are favored because they are fast to make. On the boat however, moisture and salt tend to tarnish and corrode the surface of copper so that after some time the contacts become less perfect. Why such contact resistance can be ignored with low wattage is explained in the section on basic electricity. Some other connections however must be near perfect: The corrosion process never stops and any connection may be fine one season but fail the next.

Soldering is the best available compromise between speed and durability. It takes a little longer to make soldered connections but their reliability is outstanding and not affected by time.

When to Solder

On new boats or recently installed wiring the normally crimped connections are still clean and can easily be soldered. Since all of the wire on board is stranded, corrosive moisture is drawn into the wires by capillary force so that later soldering becomes difficult, even if some inches of the wire are first cut away. You should solder connections whenever there is an opportunity. The usual crimped terminals as shown in **Sketch 1** have the ends of the copper wire exposed which you solder to the lug terminal. The plastic insulation may come off, usually a minor problem. If the lug must be insulated, you could use a piece of shrinkable tubing shown in **Sketch 2**.

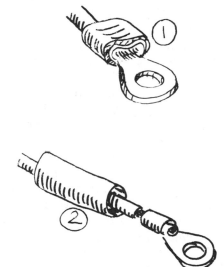

Materials and Tools

You need rosin core solder which is a very thin tube of solder alloy filled with rosin flux. The solder alloy should be 60% tin and 40% lead, the tin is the costly part and unspecified solders will contain less tin, will not wet copper as readily, and make less perfect connections. This solder is available in half- and one pound spools, and in thicknesses from less than .03 inch diameter to .125 or ⅛ inch diameter. To use the "no third hand" technique, below, the solder wire must be thick enough to stand a few inches on its own. The 1/16 or 1/18 inch diameters will do that.

An electric solder iron of about 50 Watt, or solder gun of at least 100 Watt will be useful if you have 110 V shore power on board. Irons for 12 V are available but guzzle battery power if they are suitably big. Instead, use these soldering tools:

For small solder connections, or where rarely needed, clamp a brass, bronze, copper, or iron bolt, or nail into the jaws of a self locking pair of pliers, heat on the galley stove, tin the end the moment it is hot enough by touching rosin core solder to the tip of the nail, then use and re-heat.

For more frequent soldering, twist a solid copper wire and clamp to the burner of a propane torch as shown in **Sketch 3**. With a very small flame, you solder with the tip of the twisted wire which must extend beyond the hot zone of the flame.

For massive solder connections, such as lugs on battery "cables," use the flame of the propane torch directly, touch the solder very briefly to lug or wire to test whether it will melt, and only then feed solder until the lug is completely filled. Before that happens, the excess rosin flux will overflow and probably burn. Such connections, as the **Sketch 4**, require wire and lug size to match.

To strip insulation from the ends of wires, use a sharp knife or single edge razor blade, roll the wire as shown in **Sketch 5** on a flat surface while cutting the insulation, to avoid injury. For thinner wires, use wire strippers, **Sketch 6**, or an automatic wire stripping tool if you do major wiring, **Sketch 7**. Other tools such as needle nose pliers you will have in your normal tool box.

"No Third Hand" Method

To make a solder joint, it must be heated first. Then, solder is applied which will melt on contact. To do that without a helper, arrange to have the end of the solder suspended near the twisted wires or other assembly which you hold in one hand, see **Sketch 8**. In your other hand, hold the solder iron or its substitute, and touch the hot tip to the wire joint. Then, to make the solder touch the work piece, you move it, with solder iron remaining in touch, toward the end of the solder. You will always find a

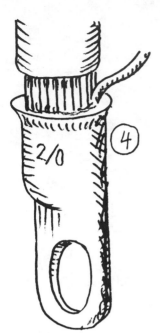

2/0

④

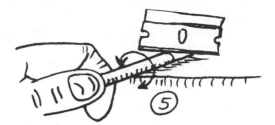

⑤

⑥

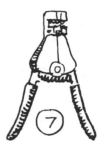

⑦

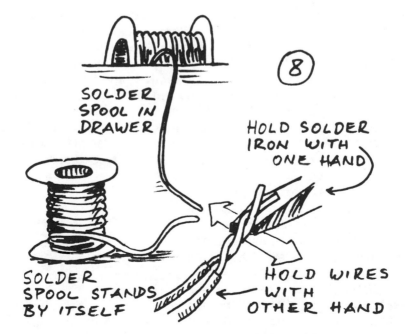

⑧

SOLDER
SPOOL IN
DRAWER

HOLD SOLDER
IRON WITH
ONE HAND

SOLDER
SPOOL STANDS
BY ITSELF

HOLD WIRES
WITH
OTHER HAND

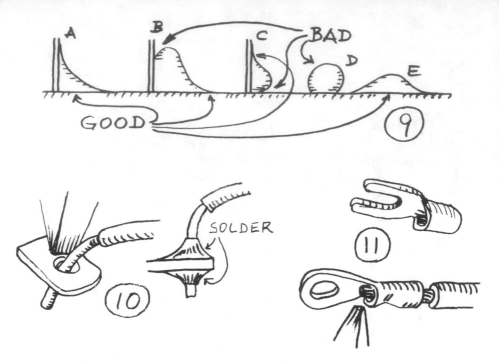

convenient place to stand or hang the solder spool and extend the solder, "no third hand needed," in tight places where no helper will find room.

All solder connections have in common that the solder alloy must wet the soldered metals. You can see good flow or good wetting at the outer edges of the solder as shown in **Sketch 9**. Note the different angles with good and bad wetting. At bad spots, more flux must be applied, simply by touching more rosin core solder to it. Sometimes more heat is needed.

When soldering a wire to a terminal as in **Sketch 10**, the hot solder iron must bring heat to both, best by squeezing it into the corner between the two. Apply a small amount of solder directly to the tip of the solder iron, this will improve the flow of heat to the two metal parts and will apply the first small amount of flux. The final connection is shown at right, note the angles at the solder. To connect ring or fork terminals or lugs, **Sketch 11**, pinch lightly to keep in place, then solder with the iron at the wire end. You may connect two or more wires into one lug, as needed at some crowded terminals.

Some switches have screw terminals as in **Sketch 12**. You can usually discard the screw and solder the wire directly into the hole of the terminal. Very rarely are there switches which will melt.

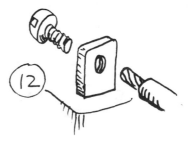

Terminals with pan head screws, **Sketch 13**, require that the stranded wire first be tinned, the strands soldered together. Bend clockwise, as shown, then pinch the wire loop close around the screw. Use lock washer if possible.

Set screw connections, **Sketch 14**, also require the wire end to be tinned. Otherwise the strands will be mashed and will break.

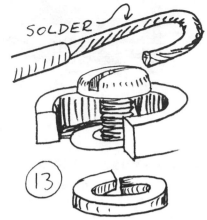

To connect one wire to another, do not twist end to end as in **Sketch 15** which is difficult to insulate. Rather twist the wires as in **Sketch 16**, with some excess length, solder, then cut the excess off and inspect the cut: it will show you if solder has completely penetrated. To insulate, use plastic molded "wire nuts," available in several color coded sizes, normally used in house wiring. They have sharp conical metal threads inside. They are not suitable to make connections without soldering but make durable insulation. Turn upward so that water will not collect in them. If many wires must be soldered together, as in "ground pigtails," you may hold them together by wrapping a single thin wire strand around them as in **Sketch 17**, then solder, cut off excess, and insulate. If more wires have to be connected to a terminal with pan head screw, such as a circuit breaker, you could make a connection as in **Sketch 18**, with one extra wire with lug terminal to the pan head screw.

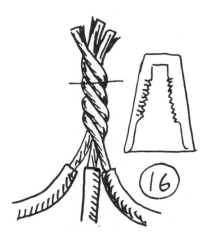

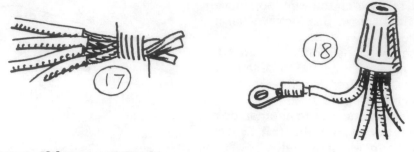

Some things not to do

You may be tempted to use the more aggressive acid fluxes or paste fluxes or acid core solder, to solder older tarnished or corroded wires. Such flux will soak into the stranded wires and will cause serious corrosion even though the solder joint itself may be a success. Neutralizing the flux does not solve the problem since a salt is formed in the process which will still corrode.

Plastic electrician's tape which normally is such handy insulating material does not work too well on board. While on land it appears to get harder and the adhesive less sticky with age, on the boat it tends to get soft, and the adhesive sticky as sirup, and then unravels. If it must be used, secure the end with a cable tie.

Finishing Touches

When you have planned to run a new wire from A to B, all that is left to do is to connect the wire to A and B. However, there are some mechanical details to be taken care of. Instead of letting the wire dangle freely from its terminals, it should be fastened somehow, the terminals insulated, made inconspicuous if it runs through the cabin area, and safe from being stepped on or torn loose if it runs in sail lockers or engine room. If you had to look for it, you want to be able to find it quickly if necessary. Here are some suggestions.

Run any new wires parallel to existing bundles of wire, pipe, tube, or hose to which you can fasten. Number the wire at the ends near the terminals, use adhesive wire numbers which are available in small books. Stick the number strips to the wire as in **Sketch 1**, the adhesive ends toward each other, instead of round-and-round. Enter in the appropriate wiring sketch. Use cable ties to lash new wires to existing wires or other supports. Nylon cable ties are offered in different lengths, and with eye for screw fastening, **Sketch 2**. If the available tie happens to be too short, you can connect two to each other as in **Sketch 3**. Black cable ties are necessary to secure wires at the mast top, the light ones do not resist sunlight for very long.

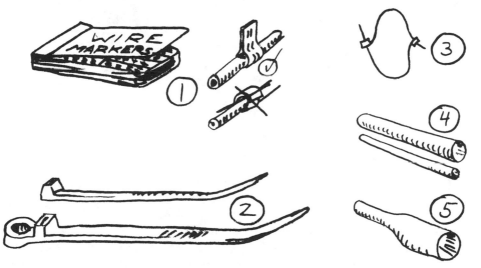

To insulate lugs or wire connections in crowded places, a piece of "spaghetti," thin wall plastic tubing, can be slipped over the ends of wires before fastening to terminals. Spaghetti, **Sketch 4**, comes in various diameters and colors. If you cannot find any, use clear vinyl tubing instead.

Shrinkable tubing is a kind of spaghetti which will shrink to about half of its original diameter when heated, **Sketch 5**. It can be made to cling tightly to wire and different sized terminals but will not exclude moisture. Heating it in confined places can be a nuisance. If you have to run wires along a new route and need fasteners, use cable clamps, **Sketch 6**, and very short pan head screws or oval head screws with finishing washers if dealing with thin panels or fiberglass inner liners. A useful screw size is number 8 stainless pan head screw of ½ inch length. If you want to conceal wires and cannot fish through spaces behind liners or in bilges, make teak channels as shown in **Sketch 7** which you mount on the surface with screws, along edges as in the lower sketch. To make, start with teak molding, about ¾ inches thick, and make repeated cuts on a table saw.

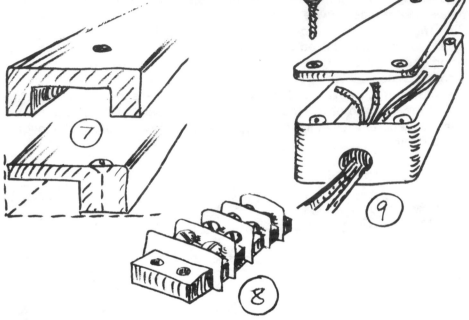

If several new wires must be interconnected, terminal- or barrier strips, **Sketch 8** are often used. If reliability rates higher than neatness, soldered connections under wire nuts as insulators are much to be preferred, see section on soldering. If necessary, the wires can be spliced inside a plastic box, **Sketch 9**, which you mount in a suitable place. Make a hole at each end for wires, tape a sketch into the lid of the box, discard the supplied screws and fasten the lid with stainless number 4 oval head screws instead.

Electricians tape, **Sketch 10**, was mentioned earlier, with the fact that its adhesive, on the boat, usually changes in a most unpleasant way.

For major wiring, consider installing plastic conduit, for example through the engine space or in sail lockers or storage spaces along the fiberglass hull. Use polyvinyl chloride (PVC) pipe available from plumbing suppliers. For curved runs along the hull, try to use bowed wood or plastic battens as shown in **Sketch 11**, which you brace against any opposite surface, all

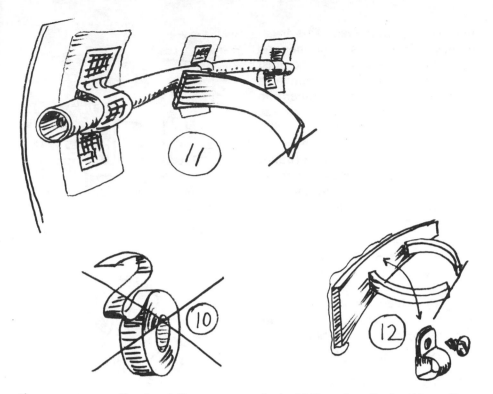

the way across the boat if necessary, to hold the pipe flush. When fiber-glassing as sketched, the hull must first be stripped of any paint: paint remover works well. Fasten with 2 to 5 layers of glass cloth and polyester resin.

Important: with near horizontal runs of conduit pipe, make one or more drain holes at low places, to avoid accumulating water. Similarly, you can fasten thin, bendable wood molding to the hull, **Sketch 12**. Again, use springy bows of wood or plastic to press in place, fasten with silicone rubber or polysulfide caulk or adhesives such as epoxy. Such wooden wiring support has the advantage over pipe that you can fasten any existing wires with the new wires.

Plugs and sockets are used where connections must be taken apart regularly. They are also used to ease the installation of electronic instruments. Problems are usually caused by poor contact when metal surfaces corrode or salt crystallizes between contacts. It helps to apply grease to both halves of a clean plug connection before assembly, so that 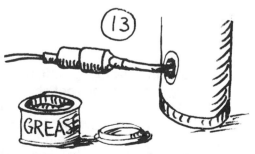 the spaces in the plug and around contacts are completely filled. Most greases including petroleum jelly will serve although some wash out and then must be replaced. This treatment, **Sketch 13**, is recommended if you must have a plug at the mast foot above deck. An alternative to such plug is the arrangement in **Sketch 14**: it consists of a bronze or white plastic through hull fitting installed through the deck near the foot of the mast, and a black rubber or silicone lab "stopper" permanently sealed around the end of a single mast cable or bundle of single wires. When the mast is unstepped, wire connections are freed below deck and the stopper with wires pushed up from below. The stopper may be sealed into the hull fitting lightly with silicone sealant, it should be almost flush with the fitting. Get stoppers from lab supply houses, ask college or high school science teacher.

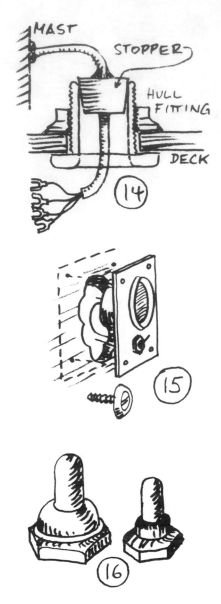

To install an additional meter, switch, or other component for which there is no room on the electric panel, do not try to make its cutout directly in the bulkhead or panel but instead, make a small new plastic panel, **Sketch 15**, from ⅛ inch colored Plexiglass, fit the new components, connect the wiring, then make the cutout on the boat: easier to make now because less accuracy is needed. Make relatively oversized mounting holes near the corners and use oval head screws with finishing washers.

If any of the standard or miniature toggle switches on the boat are exposed to the weather or otherwise likely to get wet, you could install a flexible silicone rubber boot shown in **Sketch 16**, by removing the thin retaining nut and threading the boot on. It has its own nut molded into the base. "Standard" toggle switches are mounted in holes of approximately ½ inch diameter, their thread is ¹⁵⁄₃₂ by 32. "Miniature" toggle switches, mounted in approximately ¼ inch holes, have a ¼ by 40 thread. Boot seals are made by Hexseal Division, APM Corporation, Englewood, N.J. It should be noted that switches on pedestals may get wet from the inside, and this boot then would not help at all.

54

Switch On Here, Off There

If you come back on board after dark, you may want to switch the cabin lights on with a switch near the companionway. You can do that, have two switches at different locations, switch the same light or groups of lights on with one switch, off with the other switch, with both switches in full control.

The **Sketch 1** shows how to do it: the two switches must be SPDT types, and there must be two wires between the switches. The switches are sketched with the light off. If you switched either of the switches, the light would go on. Then, it could be turned off again at either switch. Not earth shaking, but sometimes very nice to have.

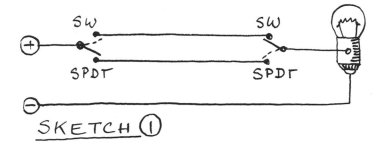

SKETCH ①

For your notes:

Trouble Shooting

In this section, you don't want to learn about electricity as much as you want to fix a problem. Trouble shooting could be made scientific and systematic, it sometimes, rarely, has to be that. But more often, it is the art of testing first where the problem is most likely to be, and to fix it in ways which fit the circumstances.

If you are looking for a trouble spot, be suspicious if you appear to find two problems. Only one of them caused the current trouble, the other may contribute but probably existed before. It is extremely unlikely that two unrelated things go wrong at the same time. You are therefore always looking for one major, clearly responsible cause for your immediate trouble.

While trouble shooting, you may see things which need overhauling, but keep in mind the difference between the two: while trouble shooting, you want to make things work again quickly, perhaps while at sea. Later, over-hauling is probably a good idea as you cure potential trouble spots which had not happened yet, in a program of preventive maintenance.

The trouble shooting tests will start with those which are both simple to carry out and most likely to pinpoint the problem. Then, as you did not find the problem, tests must look at additional details more closely. If at any point it occurs to you to test any particular detail because you are suspicious of it, do so and find it by the heading of its paragraph, in the sketches, or in the index. To prevent you from overlooking a test and, instead, doing other tests over and over, make a sketch or use a wiring diagram, and sketch in what and where you have tested.

A test light (TL) is a great tool for this type of trouble shooting because it is so relatively crude. A sensitive VOM (Volt Ohm Meter) may show 12 V through a hopelessly corroded switch contact while there is no other load. A test light draws enough current to light, to avoid some possible wrong conclusions. If you are using a VOM, be aware that it may be so sensitive to show you voltage through a wet timber.

Engine Starting

If you cannot start the engine, switch the battery main or selector switch to ALL or BOTH even if you are connecting to a battery which is nearly empty. As long as it still has more than about 10 Volts it will contribute starting current. Switch the battery main switch back and forth between the OFF and "2" position several times while no electricity is being drawn. We call this "exercising" the switch: the action tends to clean the contacts as they are wiped against each other.

Main Switch Test

Switch several cabin lights on, then move the main switch handle slightly back and forth. Less than perfect contact is indicated by flickering of the cabin lights. Switch from one battery through the ALL or BOTH position to the other battery. Again, the cabin lights will flicker (slight changes in

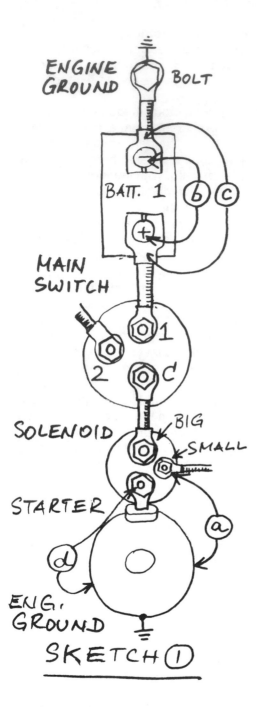

ENGINE GROUND **BOLT**

BATT. 1 (b) (c)

MAIN SWITCH

1

2 C

SOLENOID

BIG

SMALL

STARTER

(a)

(d)

ENG. GROUND

SKETCH ①

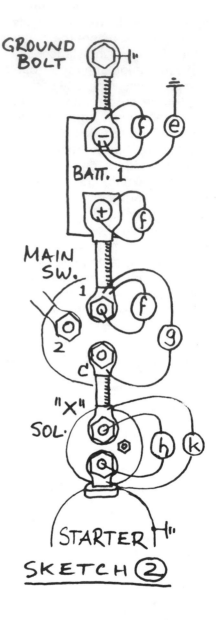

GROUND BOLT |"

(f) (e)

BATT. 1

(f)

MAIN SW.

1

2

C'

(f)

(g)

"X"
SOL.

(h) (k)

STARTER |"

SKETCH ②

58

brightness) if the contacts are less than perfect. (A permanent difference in brightness may be due to different charge levels of the batteries, the cabin lights will be consistently darker on one battery). Next chance, try the flicker test at night.

Starter Current Path: First Test

If there is a distinct response when you push the start button or turn the key, the clicking sound of the starter solenoid, the groaning of the starter motor, or the engine being turned, hold the starter button down for about three seconds, then quickly feel all terminals shown in **Sketch 1** by hand. Determine if any of them have become warm. Touch the battery posts with terminal hardware on both batteries, plus and minus, try the grounding bolt where the minus terminals are connected to engine ground, the terminals at the back of the battery main or selector switch, and the terminals of the starter solenoid which is located directly on or near the starter motor. If you find any of these to be warm, clean and re-tighten the connection.

In the case of battery post terminals, see the details later in this section.

If the only response to pressing the start button is the click of the starter solenoid, or if there is no audible response at all, switch on any cabin light, then press the start button again. If the cabin lights are dim to begin with, and become dark when you push the start button, a low battery is likely. Switch to all batteries as recommended earlier in this section.

However, if the cabin lights remain bright when start button is pressed, there is a poor contact in the starter current path, with too little current flowing to detect it by hand through generated heat.

In this case, test with a test light at **d** in **Sketch 1** while someone pushes the start button, with power switched on at the main switch. If the test light remains dark, or VOM does not show 12 V, go to *"Solenoid Contact Problem"* and **Sketch 3**. Should the TL light up while the start button is pushed, power reaches the starter motor "plus" terminal. Test between starter motor housing and engine ground bolt shown in **Sketch 1**: with start button pushed, TL should remain dark, VOM should not show any voltage and if that is the case, problem is in the starter motor, difficult to correct on the spot. Other trouble spots are much more likely.

Starter Current Path: More Tests

Have someone stationed at the start button or key switch and, after making certain that the engine indeed will not start when the button is pushed, that the cabin lights remain bright touch the test wires of the test light (TL) as sketched at the letters in small circles in **Sketch 1**. Then have the start button pushed while you observe the TL:

a: TL lights, indicating that power reaches the solenoid coil and makes the solenoid click. If not, problem is not in the starter current path of this sketch but at the engine panel, or the batteries are not turned on.

If the TL lights up but the solenoid does not click, search for another second small terminal on the solenoid which may be a grounding terminal for the coil. If it has a wire to any ground terminal, then have start button pushed. If TL lights up, poor ground connection is somewhere between the two points. Correct by remaking the wire connections after first switching battery power off.

b: test directly at the two lead battery posts, not at the terminals clamped to them, battery main switch turned on to this battery, start button pressed, TL should get slightly dimmed (full battery) when things are normal, or become dark (low battery). If it remains bright, continue:

c: hold TL wires to the terminals as shown, not to the battery posts as in **b**. If results are different from **b**, for example bright at **b**, but dimmed at **c** while the start button is pushed, there is a poor connection at one of the battery post terminals. Use tests **e** and **f** in **Sketch 2** to identify the trouble spot. See the battery post sketch in this section and note that tightening the bolt and ½ inch nut may not improve contact.

d: if the TL becomes bright while the start button is pushed, problem is in the starter motor, hard to correct but not likely. If no help is available, you could try to see the brushes if you can remove the steel band covering the brushes. On most engines, this will be hard to do because of limited access.

Starter Current Path: Search for Poor Contacts

Sketch 2 shows the places for the test light (TL) wires, hold them firmly in place, then have a helper push the start button, with battery main switch turned to the battery which you are testing.

CAUTION: protect yourself in case the engine should start unexpectedly. Do not ground any terminals accidently which could generate sparks and heat.

While start button is pushed:

e: overrides the ground connection. Bright TL indicates poor contact between battery minus post and engine ground.

Keep notes of what you have tested.

f: bright TL shows poor contact at this terminal which you should refasten.

Note: Only one battery is shown in the sketches. Use the same tests for other batteries, switch the main switch accordingly.

g: bright test light (TL) indicates poor contact at the switch. Make sure that the switch was actually turned on, test with **f** to make certain poor contact is not at the switch terminal studs, exercise the switch, see details in this section. If the switch is at fault and cannot be repaired, an emergency repair is to remove the nuts and fasten one or both battery cables from terminals "1" and "2" to terminal "C," or to each other, by using a ⅜ inch bolt.

CAUTION: Do not touch any of these to ground: sparks and much heat, fire hazard. If you make this connection, do not take it apart again while the engine is running. Keep notes of what you have tested.

h: bright TL (while starter button is pushed!) indicates poor contact at solenoid. Test again and hold wires to **k**: if different from **h**, use test **f** directly at each terminal and tighten if you have a bright TL with test **f**. If you have pinned the problem to the solenoid internal contact, namely bright TL with **h** and **k** but not with **f** at these terminals, proceed to **Sketch 3**.

Starter Solenoid Contact Problem

Sketch 3 shows the starter solenoid with its big terminals and with the start button. The solenoid connects the two heavy terminals to each other when the start button is pressed. If your engine will not start, starter motor not turn, but starter solenoid clicks when you push the button, and cabin lights then do not dim, the contact within the solenoid maybe poor. That happens relatively often and is fairly easy to correct.

BATTERY MAIN SWITCH MUST BE OFF.

Connect a wire to the plus terminal of a battery, or to the "1" or "2" terminal of the main switch, then touch the other end of the wire to the starter button terminal as shown, or to the small terminal on the starter solenoid. The battery main switch must be off so that there will be no current flowing through the solenoid, and the starter will not turn. The wire with plus 12 Volt must be touched firmly, some sparks will form: protect your eyes. If the start button terminals are more accessible,

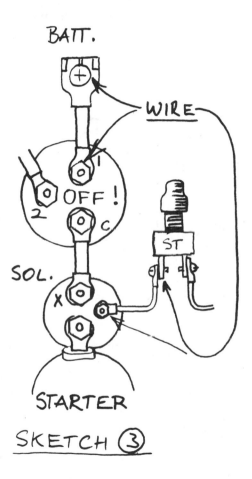

touch the wire there, try either terminal, only the correct one will respond. Or, if easier to reach, touch to the small solenoid terminal which will respond with a sharp click as the electromagnet closes contact. This contact usually consists of a large copper ring pulled against two bolt heads which are the inner end of the big terminal studs. Since very large currents are switched, the copper ring, develops burn marks around its edge. This ring is free to rotate, and not enough current can flow if a pitted place happens to make contact. Touch the wire ten or more times and let the solenoid click. You are only using a few Ampere for its coil since power to the starter is turned off at the battery main switch. Remove the wire first, then try the starter.

If this problem has ever happened to you, especially when you were approaching an inlet and wanted the engine, you may be inclined to make up a wire for this purpose. Use a clip as in **Sketch 4** which is able to clamp to larger terminals, solder a wire number 12 to it, tin the other exposed end of the wire, and pack it in a plastic bag with instructions.

Battery Terminals

Battery posts are slightly conical. Inspect yours and see if the bolts at the clamp type terminals are tight, and if the ends of the clamps touch, as in **Sketch 5**. If so, additional bolt tension will tend to further deform the terminal but may not increase pressure on the battery post. To remedy, the terminal may have to be moved further down on the conical battery post. To do that, take the bolt out, then bend the terminal, for example as in **Sketch 6** with a large flat screwdriver.

DO NOT SHORT! HAZARD OF SPARKS AND HEAT.

Reset the terminal low on the battery post, install the bolt with lockwasher, and tighten. Do this with both positive and negative terminals. If you have to tap the terminal down in place, use a light tool, not a massive hammer, to avoid damage to the battery. With a piece of wood in between, tap alternate places, **Sketch 7**, lightly.

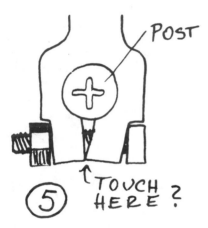

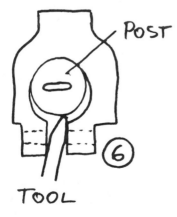

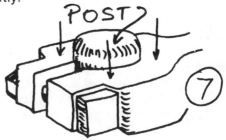

More Complicated Starter Wiring

More than one wire connected to the heavy solenoid terminal: Very often, plus 12 V electricity for engine related uses is taken from the upper or outer of the two heavy solenoid terminals. This is the terminal which is connected directly to the battery main switch "C" Common terminal, and wires are connected to the solenoid rather than the main switch out of convenience, or before the engine was installed on the boat.

There is always only one connection between the other heavy solenoid terminal and the starter motor. This connection often is a flat copper strap. It may be very short and sometimes invisible, under the body of the solenoid. There is no need to connect test wires to it, its Ohm measurement to ground is zero, it is at plus 8 to 10 Volt while the starter is cranking.

More than one small terminal on the solenoid: The coil in the solenoid has two ends. One of these is always connected to a small terminal on the outside, the other is usually connected to the solenoid housing and thus connected to engine ground without any other wiring. Sometimes, though, the other end of the coil is also fitted with a terminal at the outside. It is then connected with a wire to engine ground, at a bold or stud on engine, starter motor, or ground terminal, and this connection deserves close inspection. Solenoids with this arrangement are sometimes made for installation separate from starter motor, and may then not get reliable grounding by their fastenings. Sometimes, see below, the solenoid coil is switched by a relay which looks, and is, another solenoid. To test solenoid coils with two terminals, connect test light (TL) between each of the small terminals and engine ground. At one of them, the TL lights when starter button is pressed, this is the positive terminal as in all earlier sketches. At the other, the TL remains dark when the starter button is pressed. If it lights, and the solenoid not respond with its click, that terminal is not properly grounded. Trace its wiring, clean and fasten.

More than one solenoid: On larger engines and starter motors, the solenoid current is switched with an additional relay, rather than directly from the start button. Such relay is shown in **Sketch 8**. Sometimes, one of these is used even on small auxiliary sailboat engines and then may cause confusion. Inspect the starter side of the engine, to see if your starter has its solenoid, plus the additional relay mounted in the vicinity: you will find it by tracing solenoid wires.

Sketch 9 shows the arrangement of starter solenoid with the extra relay. Its wiring diagram is in **Sketch 10** and shows how the start button sends power to the relay coil, the relay sends power to the solenoid coil, and the solenoid sends power to the starter motor. On sailboat auxiliary engines, the reason for this extra relay is worry that the start button wiring may be too thin and long, its terminals vulnerable to corrosion and high contact resistance, or the switch contact rating marginal. All trouble shooting steps of the earlier **Sketch 1** and **2** apply here. In addition, a poor contact in the (main, big) solenoid can be treated by exercising the solenoids as in **Sketch 3** as long as the engine is no larger than about 50 horsepower. You can bring the wire described in **Sketch 3** directly to the small solenoid terminal, or to the corresponding relay terminal labeled "C" in **Sketch 9**. As outlined, *battery main switch must be OFF,* and you should guard against sparks.

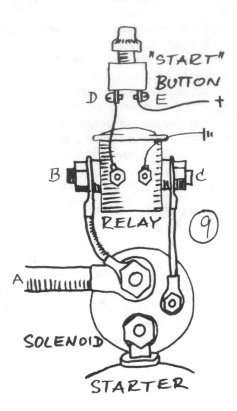

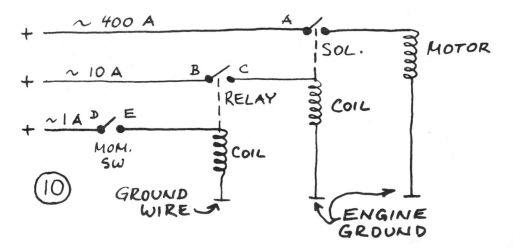

64

The contacts between "B" and "C" in the extra relay are not likely to be pitted by high currents but may still cause trouble by contact resistance from corrosion. To exercise these contacts, have battery main switch turned off, then touch the wire of **Sketch 3** repeatedly to terminal "D" of the start button, see **Sketch 9**. You will easily find which terminal that is: if you touch terminal "E" instead, no harm, but no action either. If the relay does not respond, test its ground terminal, the right small terminal in **Sketch 9**. A TL (test light) between it and engine ground should not light.

If this relay fails and cannot be repaired, start the engine by momentarily connecting terminal "B" to terminal "C," **Sketch 9**, or by connecting the heavy terminal at cable "A" to the small terminal on the solenoid. In either case, a suitable metal conductor must first be found and must not short any of these terminals to ground. Be prepared for sparks, and protect your eyes. To make such jumper connection at the solenoid, a heavy screwdriver may work.

For your notes:

Electrical Leaks

While this is a trouble shooting subject, searching for leaks is something you will not have to do under pressure of time, if at all. Leaks are often blamed but only rarely searched for, and then hardly ever exist. They make great excuses for low batteries but to search for one means actually believing that there is one. If you insist, here are two tests, both to be done with a Volt Ohm Meter (VOM), switched to measure 12 VDC. One test is slightly more troublesome but will detect absolutely every leak, the other test is extremely easy to carry out but assumes that there are no leaks upstream of the battery main switch, between battery plus terminal and the main switch terminals. A reasonable assumption.

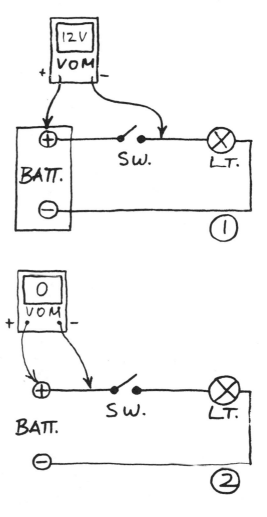

Background: Sketch 1 shows a battery and a simple circuit of a switch and a lamp with its wiring. With the switch open, touching the VOM wires as shown will have the meter needle show 12 V, or whatever the battery voltage happens to be. The reason is that any lamp filament will be conductive enough to make a connection of the black VOM wire to ground and battery minus terminal, to have the VOM show the battery voltage. In comparison, the tests light would require a path to ground which would allow about ½ Ampere to flow, or the TL would not light up. VOMs usually only require about ¹⁄₁₀₀₀ of one Ampere to move the meter needle.

In practice, no switch is located conveniently close enough to the battery terminals, and touching the VOM as in **Sketch 2** will not work. We have to first have an interruption in the wire, as in **Sketch 1**, but near the battery. That is shown in **Sketch 3**: The meter will show 12 V when the switch is closed, or when a leak provides a path which connects the black negative meter wire to ground and the battery minus terminal. If you take off the positive battery cable from the terminal of the battery as in **Sketch 4**, and then touch the meter wires as shown, with meter switched to 15 VDC or 50 VDC, meter needle at zero tells that there is no leak or drain from that battery greater than one thousandth of an amp. Verify that the meter actually works by switching a cabin light on (meter shows battery voltage but cabin light remains dark), or by touching the black minus meter wire to the battery minus terminal, directly on hand (meter shows battery voltage).

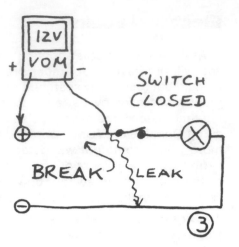

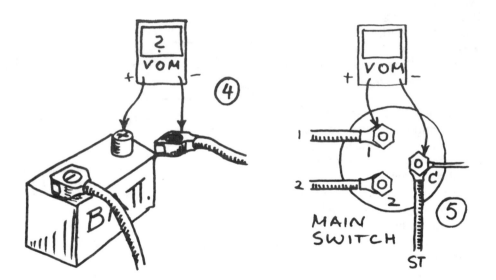

A much simpler leak test is shown in **Sketch 5**. With the VOM range for 12 VDC, touch the test wires to the battery main switch terminals "1" and "C," or "2" and "C." The main switch must be turned off and all other circuits as well, since you are looking for an unintentional current drain, not a light left on. Any leak of about $\frac{1}{1000}$ A will make the meter needle show 12 V.

You can test the meter by having a cabin light and its circuit breaker switched on while the main switch remains off. The meter will show 12 V but the cabin light remains dark. In this test, leaks from the "1" and "2" battery cables to ground remain undetected. For all tests, the battery must have some minimal charge.

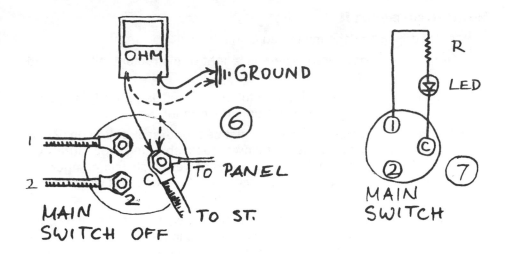

With leakage within the main switch you might conceivably get a meter reading when current from a well charged battery tries to flow into a lower battery. This reading would decrease after the main switch had been in the ALL position for a few minutes.

How big a leak?

Two limits are easily established: touch a test light in place of the VOM. If it lights up, or even barely glows, the leak is massive and would drain a battery in a week. Did it do that? If not, you are looking not at a leak but at something still switched on.

If the VOM is relatively sensitive, it might have a rating of 20,000 Ohm per Volt and, if its needle only moves to less than full battery voltage, or only indicates when switched to a 10 VDC or 2 VDC range, it tells you of a leak of only a few milliamp. Anything in between should be measured with Ohm meter: The VOM is switched to one of the Ohm ranges, the test wires plugged into the proper sockets, their ends held to each other, and the Ohm adjustment turned until the needle points to the zero on the Ohm scale, usually at the far right end. (Internal battery!) Then, touch the test wire to the separated battery cable in **Sketch 4**; other wire to ground, or to battery main switch terminal "C" and other wire to ground, the main switch turned off **Sketch 6**. Measure with test wires in both directions. Since a leak is likely to encounter some conduction through salty wetness and dissimilar metals, readings in two directions are likely to give different results. Switch to the Ohm range which will give the reading nearest the middle of the scale.

What to do about it:

Action will depend on the measured Ohms.

0-10 Ohm: not a leak. There is a light or instrument still switched on.

10-100 Ohm: still something switched on, such as a pilot light, instrument light, electronic instrument.

100-1000 Ohm: a significant leak, must be found, see section on wiring diagrams, then follow trouble shooting procedures. Or could still point to a low power electronic component such as a liquid crystal display clock, not wired with a switch, to remain on at all times.

1000-10,000 Ohm: measure again on a very dry day, or after spraying "penetrating oil" or moisture repellants on suspicious electrical components (but not into electronics or on plastic housings which may be damaged). Keep an eye out for an explanation, make sure this reading does not change to lower Ohms.

10,000 + Ohm: insignificant. Measure again on a very wet day, in humid weather, or after some rough ocean passage, and always keep electrolytic corrosion in mind. Action only if measurement decreases significantly.

Leak Detector Light

When leaks or forgotten lights are suspected to cause low batteries, install a leak detector light, like the VOM in **Sketch 5**, but permanently connected to the main switch terminals, and mounted next to the main switch, or at any distance from it, on the main electric panel or circuit breaker panel. Such light must become visible with only a few milliampere of current, and must be able to withstand full 12 Volt. Such a light can be made from a light emitting diode and series resistor **Sketch 7**. A red light emitting diode (LED) with series resistor of 470 Ohm, ½ Watt, will tell that some equipment was left on or that there is a leak of as little as 5 milliampere. To test, the main switch is turned off. If the light then becomes bright, something is drawing current.

Sketch 8 shows an LED mounted in a small plastic panel for easy installation in a ¼ inch hole. The resistor is soldered to the LED and covered with a piece of spaghetti. Horseshoe shaped large lugs can be slipped under the terminal nuts of the main switch.

Electrolytic Corrosion

Most solid materials are subject to corrosion, to the gradual wearing away of material from the surface. Whether metals or non-metals corrode depends on their surroundings which may leave them perfectly unchanged or cause them damage. Some materials corrode by dissolving, such as the lollipop in a child's mouth. Other materials corrode by changing their molecules, such as nylon sailcloth when exposed to the high energy in ultraviolet sunlight. Most materials corrode by reacting with others in their surroundings. They form a new material by chemical reaction. Marble statues corrode when their calcium carbonate reacts with the sulfuric acid in "acid rain." Or a silver spoon turns black from silver sulfide at its surface when reacting with sulfur in eggs. Most important to us are the reactions of metals with oxygen. There is oxygen in the air, and oxygen dissolved in water: fish live by it. Many metals and alloys will not react with oxygen alone but need water present also, and the corrosion product often incorporates water. To us boat owners water is always close at hand, if only as humidity, water, dissolved in air.

Table 1	
Metals arranged in the order of increasing drive to react with oxygen:	
Platinum	NOBLE
Gold	
Silver	
Nickel	
Copper	
Tin	
Lead	
Iron	
Zinc	LEAST
Magnesium	NOBLE

The pure metals can be arranged in the order of their urge, drive, or tendency to react, for example with oxygen, **Table 1**. In reality, there are several factors which can either accelerate or prevent corrosion of most metals.

Important is that we are never dealing with pure metals. Rather, the metal parts on the boat are made from alloys which consist of two or more pure metals, either because they were "alloyed" on purpose, or because small percentages of one or another pure metal were left in as impurities: too difficult or too unimportant to remove.

Another important factor is that most metal parts do not exist in isolation. Often, metal parts are intentionally or accidentally connected to each other: you have likely heard of the term "dissimilar metals" used in connection with electrolytic corrosion. We will see how dissimilar metals cause corrosion both on a large scale when obviously different metal parts are interconnected, and on a microscopic scale when dissimilar regions of the same piece react.

Dissimilarity can also be created by the surroundings: we will discuss why one area of a piece of otherwise uniform or homogeneous metal will behave as though it were a different metal from the rest of that piece's surface. The difference can be caused by the surroundings and we will see how water flow rate over the metal surface, or temperature of water and metal, or closeness to air, dissolved oxygen, saltiness, can make one area of a piece of metal become dissimilar from the rest.

Finally, the most troublesome contribution from the surroundings is stray electricity: the flow of electric current through the water in which your boat floats. To explain how and why electric current causes corrosion, and why it is called "electrolytic" to begin with, requires a closer look at a corroding metal surface.

The basic corrosion process

Do you remember atoms? Made up from electrons in orbit around a center called nucleus? **Sketch 1** shows metal at left, water at right, and one metal atom which has just reacted and formed a metal ion. In the

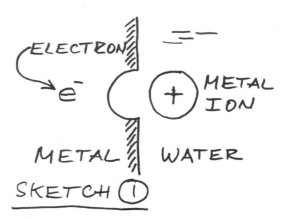

process, the metal atom has released one electron which is also shown. The electron has a negative charge and the metal atom now has one electron less so that its positive charges now have a majority of one. This gives the metal an overall positive charge and we call it a metal ion. This metal ion with its positive charge can now attract negative ions to form an oxide, hydroxide, chloride, or whatever its individual natural chemical inclination might be. Important to us is the electron. It can flow through metal with ease, at the speed of light. Such travelling electrons we call a current. And that there is a current generated where metals are corroding is easily demonstrated. Just pick two metals from **Table 1**, one near the bottom and a different one higher up the list. Connect them as in **Sketch 1** and let the current flow: you have a battery.

All primary batteries work in this way (secondary batteries are the ones which can be recharged). In a "zinc carbon" flashlight battery, a cup made from sheet zinc corrodes away to make the electric current, **Sketch 2**. Instead of a noble metal, a carbon rod happens to work as an inexpensive substitute. The amount of electricity is limited by the amount of zinc metal. You wonder how much electricity? It happens that some metals give up only one electron, while others give up two or three. The metal ions then have one, two or three positive charges called valences. Zinc happens to be two valent: zinc atoms give up two electrons and form ions with two positive charges.

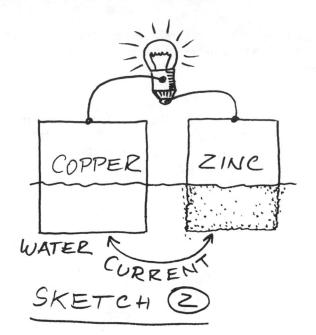

WATER CURRENT

SKETCH ②

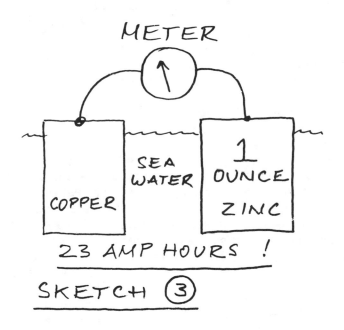

METER

SEA WATER

1 OUNCE ZINC

COPPER

23 AMP HOURS !

SKETCH ③

One ounce of zinc generates electrons equivalent to 23 Ampere hours. In **Sketch 3**, zinc and copper are shown connected by a meter which would, for example, show a current of 0.023 Ampere for 1000 hours which would be 0.023 A times 1000 h = 23 Ah (Ampere hours). There is one important requirement: the water must be electrically conductive. If it is, it will allow a current to flow between the two metals. This current will be of exactly the same size as the current through the meter.

Electric Current in Water

If we changed the experiment of **Sketch 3** and placed the two pieces of metal each into its own beaker with corrosive salt water as in **Sketch 4**, no current would flow through the meter no matter how sensitive we made

the meter. The reason is that our electric circuit is incomplete: the circuit is open between the two beakers and no current can flow.

Will the metals corrode? Both are in corrosive salt water and, yes, both copper and zinc will corrode according to their position in **Table 1**. Copper will corrode only slightly because of its relatively noble metal characteristic, and zinc will corrode faster because it is more reactive as indicated by its position in the table. Both will corrode as though they were completely isolated from each other. The wire connection will have no effect at all. But the piece of zinc will corrode slower than the zinc **Sketch 3**, and that has to do with the conductivity through the water.

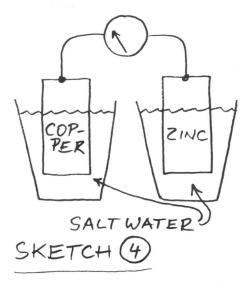

SKETCH ④

For all practical purposes you can assume that all water, from sea water to brackish river water to the clearest inland lakes is electrically conductive. That includes all drinking water, as you can easily test with an ohmmeter. However, electric current is conducted much differently in water than in metals. We have talked about electrical current being a stream of flowing electrons. Metal conductors such as a copper wire consist of copper atoms each with a cloud of orbiting electrons. To conduct an electron through

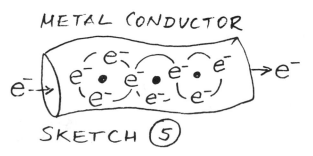

such wire, see **Sketch 5**, it is only necessary to push the electron in at one end, to have another come out at the other end. Not the same electron. Instead, musical chairs style, electrons hop over, create room for the electron at the left, and cause one to overflow at the right. Because in metals electrons are so extremely mobile, metals have such high electrical conductivity. That is much different in water. In order to have current flow in water, an electron must hitch a ride. It must find a compatible ion in the water which will pick up the electron. As in **Sketch 6**, such ion must have a positive charge which means that it has a vacancy for an electron.

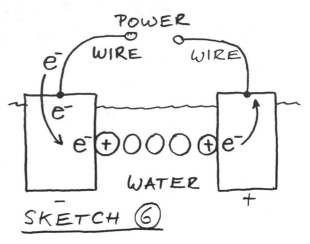

SKETCH ⑥

To complete the circuit, somewhere else in the water, electrons must be unloaded from water to another metal conductor, the one on the right. If you compare this sketch with **Sketch 1**, you can see that there are two different processes possible at the interface between metal and water. Water is conductive if it contains ions which can offer electrons a mode of transportation. Water then is also corrosive: ions are involved in the process in **Sketch 1**. Physical and chemical processes determine which route is taken. Since water itself forms ions, one OH^- and one H^+ from each H_2O molecule, quite a number of chemical reactions can take place at the metal surfaces, all of them taking part in conducting current through water, but some not corroding the metal. All of these reactions need a driving force to proceed. That force can be the natural characteristic of zinc to react and corrode, or it can be an electric potential applied to the wires in **Sketch 6**, or the forces which drive chemical reactions to proceed. With this in mind, we have to look again at the corrosion of pure metals, and of dissimilar interconnected metals.

The first observation here is that metals by themselves in sea water do not corrode very much at all. Even the metals at the bottom of **Table 1** have relatively modest corrosion rates as shown by the values for the corrosion rate in inches per year (ipy) in **Table 2**. This table gives approximate values only since it considers the corrosion to occur evenly. In reality, corrosion damage is more often caused by pitting, by loss of metal in small areas where small but deep holes are generated.

Table 2

Corrosion rate of pure metals in sea water, inches per year.

Metal	ipy
Platinum	0.0000
Gold	0.0000
Silver	0.000
Nickel	less than 0.0003
Copper	about 0.001
Tin	less than 0.001
Lead	less than 0.001
Iron	about 0.001
Zinc	about 0.001
Magnesium	about 0.001

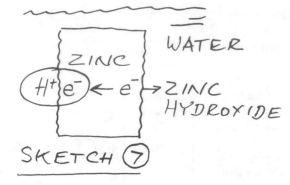

SKETCH ⑦

In comparison, the corrosion rate of zinc in **Sketch 2** or **Sketch 3** is much greater since zinc is connected by wire to another electrode, the piece of copper, which accepts and disposes of the electrons which the zinc is generating. The noble metals or graphite or the carbon rod in a flashlight battery can do that better than zinc or other reactive, "base" metals. Here is what must happen: a piece of zinc, by itself in sea water, **Sketch 7**, corrodes and generates free electrons. The increasing excess of electrons will slow and eventually stop the corrosion reaction unless there is another reaction going on at the surface of the zinc which will use up the free electrons. One possibility is sketched here: electrons could combine with hydrogen ions, H^+, to form hydrogen gas bubbles. Or they could combine with other positive ions which, after a while, would get scarce in the neighborhood of the zinc and the whole corrosion process would slow or halt. We can easily prove that by connecting a wire to the zinc and feeding extra electrons to the zinc, for example from a battery. Electrons, e^-, are negative, and if we connect the negative wire to the zinc and the positive wire to another electrode to complete the circuit, **Sketch 8**, we would stop all corrosion at the zinc. Never mind what happens at the other electrode: you can figure that out in a moment.

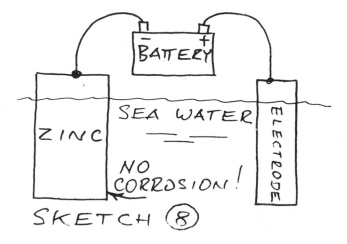

SKETCH ⑧

Here we have the explanation why electrolytic corrosion is so often related to dissimilar metals, and why the term "dissimilar metals" is associated with often vague but threatening worries. On the one hand, there are such metal couples like copper and zinc which can readily generate electric currents. We use some of them and turn such currents to our advantage, as in electrolytic protection with so called sacrificial anodes of zinc on boats, or of magnesium or aluminum in other applications. On the other hand, there are conditions which can make a limited area of a piece of metal become "dissimilar" to other areas of the same metal or alloy. A current begins to flow and electrolytic corrosion sets in.

Dissimilar Metals

Before we look at these microscopic dissimilar metal cells on a piece of metal, let us arrange some metals and alloys by their relative behavior toward each other. Unless two pieces of metal are exactly alike, an electrolytic current will develop between them if electrically connected and immersed in an electrolyte such as sea water. As in **Sketch 3**, one would corrode, become the anode, and reveal its character as the more active base metal, while the other would be more passive, more noble, and become the cathode. Note that a given piece of metal can be the anode to one metal and the cathode to another. Only platinum and gold are difficult to surpass as cathodes, and magnesium will always be an anode since we will not discuss any more reactive metals. For example, if a piece of iron or steel were connected to a piece of copper and the two placed in salt water, iron would be the anode. If the same piece of iron were connected to a piece of zinc, the iron would here be the cathode, **Sketch 9**. Such experiments have been made with most commercial alloys and commercial grades of "pure" metals. **Table 3** gives the so called galvanic series of metals and alloys in sea water. The metals are shown in groups and are most cathodic or passive at the top of the list and become progressively more reactive toward the bottom. Any metal in the list will be an anode to a metal higher in the list, and a cathode to a metal lower in the list, if connected as in **Sketch 9**, in sea water. Only metals within a group, such as the group of cast iron,

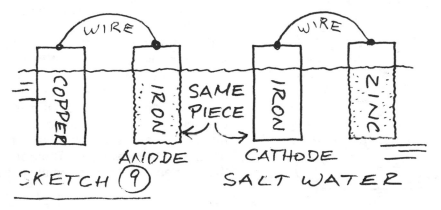

wrought iron, and steel, are so close in activity that no difference in electrical potential develops and, in this example, all corrode evenly as long as conditions remain equal.

Most striking is that some metals are listed twice: once passive and once active. Nickel, for example, is more noble than all bronzes when in its passive state, but much more corrosive when it is active. Chromium behaves similarly, and stainless steels (note that there are different types) which are alloys of iron with mostly nickel and chromium, show the most notorious difference between active and passive state. Type 316 stainless steel, for example, is used to make the most corrosion resistant bolts and hardware normally available in marine stores. This grade performs much like a noble metal, is listed close to the top in **Table 3**, hardware made from it remains brightly shiny on board, but only when passive. The same metal active behaves just like its major ingredient iron. It rusts, and is listed far down the list in **Table 3**.

There are two theories for the explanation of passive/active behavior of these metals. We do not have to choose because both have to do with oxygen which is adsorbed on the metal surface, or forms oxides which form a film on the metal surface. An abundance of oxygen helps to maintain the "passivity" of stainless steel. Stainless fittings at deck or rig perform very well even when sprayed with sea water. When stainless steel is immersed in sea water for limited lengths of time, the surface remains shiny and free from corrosion: it remains passive. The same applies to the nickel plating which is the visible surface of many (most ?) pieces of commercial stainless marine hardware. But have anything cut off the supply of oxygen and stainless steel will revert back to the behavior of iron: it will rust as it becomes active. The first signs of that you can see where a part of a stainless fitting is covered as in **Sketch 10**. Where the deck material, resin in a fiberglass boat, or paint, caulk, cover the stainless, a small edge of rust will become visible if there is any water. Some of the stainless surface under the paint cover will become active and will then, whenever there is an "electrolyte" such as sea water spray, become the anode to the other, still passive areas of the same fitting.

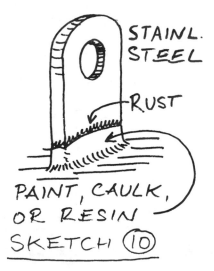

STAINL. STEEL

RUST

PAINT, CAULK, OR RESIN

SKETCH ⑩

If the fitting is nearer the water such as the dinghy towing eye in **Sketch 11**, there will be water "electrolyte" almost all the time, and a narrow brown edge of rust will develop and sometimes stain the nearby gelcoat. It would be unfortunate to have stainless steel fittings permanently under water. Theoretically, the stainless steel would remain passive

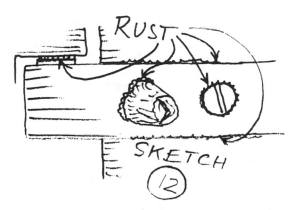

STAINL STEEL

RUST STAIN

ACTIVE

PASSIVE

DINGHY TOW FITTING

SKETCH 11

near the surface where the surface water usually contains enough dissolved oxygen. However, in reality such fitting will get covered by fouling, oil, floating surface dirt, or paint which cause "oxygen starvation" and make stainless steel become active. At that point, we have two decidedly dissimilar metals in the sea water electrolyte. The active surface will get additional cover from loose, porous rust which makes it quite impossible to revert back to the protected passive state. **Sketch 12** shows a rudder gudgeon fitting which you will occasionally see made from stainless steel. Rust will first develop at the narrow gaps around screws or bolt heads, at the edges along the hull or the bedding compound, and at the bearing surface near the pintle, and around the barnacle which may not remain alone for very long. At these places, the stainless steel is most likely starved of oxygen and turned active. With electrolyte present, dissimilar metal corrosion can then start between the active area as anode and the passive areas as cathode. We will discuss further on how to protect such stainless fittings. Traces of rust on stainless steel, as for example on lifeline stanchions and other deck hardware usually tell you that there is a film of oil, grease, wax, grime, or air pollution deposits which keep the air away. Cleaning such surfaces will normally restore the passive character.

RUST

SKETCH 12

Another cause for dissimilar metal corrosion on one single, otherwise uniform piece of metal can be caused by differences in the electrolyte. We have seen how low oxygen content in the surroundings can make stainless steel loose its passivity. The corrosion reactions of other metals can often be accelerated or retarded by differences in the composition of the electrolyte. If the same piece of metal is exposed to different electrolytes at the same

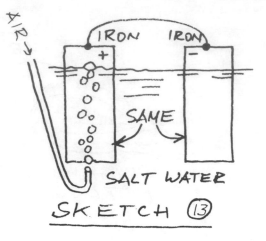

SKETCH 13

time, a dissimilar metal "cell" may be formed: in **Sketch 13**, air is bubbled over one piece of iron while the other is in more or less quiet, non-gerated salt water. The left piece will become an anode, corrode faster, and actually reduce the corrosion rate of the right piece. In this experiment, that may be due both to the extra supply of oxygen and the extra agitation at the left

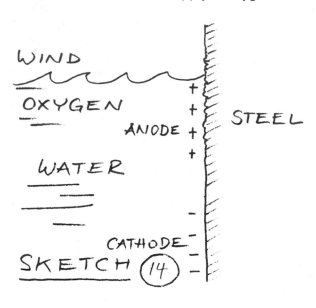

SKETCH 14

piece. Iron is unable to form any protective passivating film and here, more oxygen means faster corrosion. In practice, a similar case can be seen at steel pilings which become anodic near surface water, **Sketch 14**, and cathodic deeper down. Here again we are looking at two factors at work at the same time: there is the difference in oxygen concentration and the difference in flow rate. The surface water is stirred much more by waves, and flows faster over the metal surface.

Finally, differences in temperature also can cause dissimilar metal corrosion on one single piece of metal. At the higher temperature, any possible corrosion reaction will be accelerated and, all other conditions being the same, the warmer end of, for example, a pipe, will become the anode, **Sketch 15**. Keep in mind that we are looking only at the behavior of a single, isolated

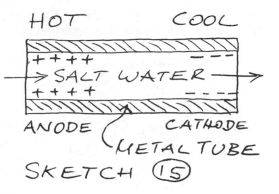

SKETCH (15)

piece of metal. In most cases, there will be other influences, for example from additional metals in contact, and from the flow of electric currents, intentional or accidental.

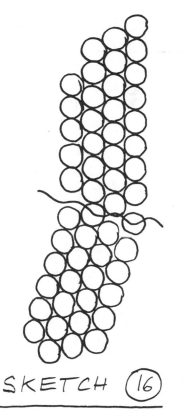

SKETCH (16)

Dissimilar metal corrosion also coccurs at pieces which appear to be uniform or homogeneous but in reality are not. You may have heard the term "stress corrosion." Uniform pieces of metal may have been formed or altered by cold working, bending, or other forces, and can then develop localized places where an arrangement of atoms in a crystal structure was interrupted, something not visible to the eye, and certainly not an actual crack as **Sketch 16** might falsely imply. But think of a discontinuity of a pattern which can then behave differently toward an electrolyte and start an electrolytic corrosion cell.

Much more visible, and easier to understand is the type of dissimilar metal corrosion which can seriously affect alloys with a crystalline structure. Some alloys are solutions of one metal in another molten metal which, when cooled, remain "solid solutions." Other alloys, and many pure metals, grow crystals as they solidify during their manufacturer, or during sometimes elaborate separate heat treatments. The crystals are very often desireable in order to reach some of the physical properties of the metals. But some metals develop electrolytic corrosion between crystals which are oriented differently **Sketch 17**, or between crystals and other regions in the metals which have different composition and then are a cases of dissimilar metals on a small scale. As we will discuss later, brasses show this corrosion and you may find a brass casting which, after some fine sanding, might show both crystal patterns and corrosion traces.

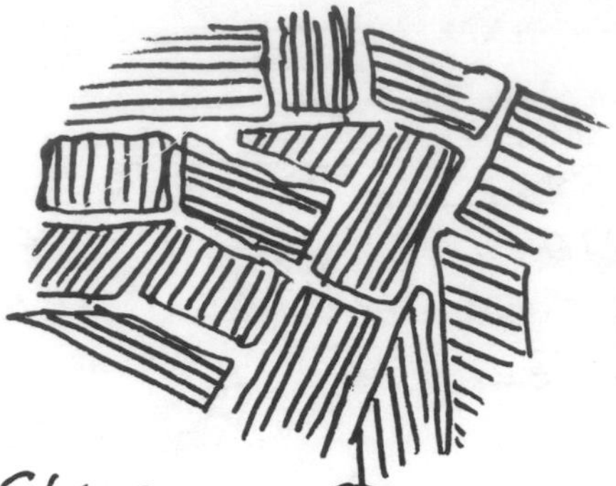

SKETCH 17

In comparison to the relatively complicated circumstances with active and passive areas on the same piece of metal, loss of passivity, oxygen concentration cells, intercrystalline electrolysis, electrolyte temperature and flow, all other cases of dissimilar metal corrosion are simple. Have another look at the list in **Table 3**. Whenever a metal on the list is in electrical contact with another metal and the two are in an electrolyte (anything from rain water

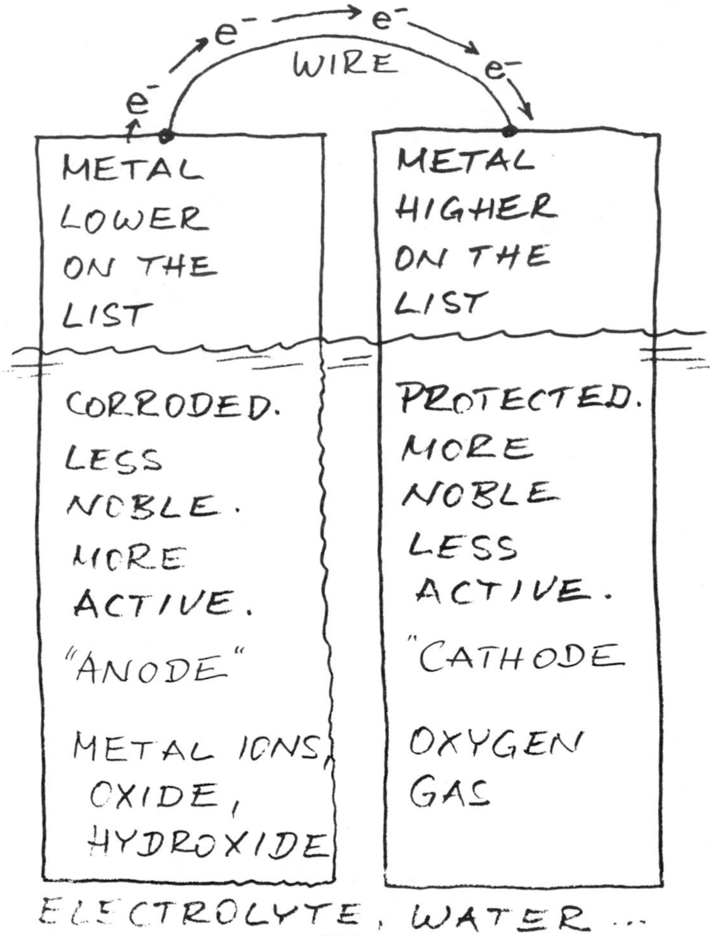

WIRE

METAL LOWER ON THE LIST	METAL HIGHER ON THE LIST
CORRODED. LESS NOBLE. MORE ACTIVE. "ANODE" METAL IONS, OXIDE, HYDROXIDE	PROTECTED. MORE NOBLE LESS ACTIVE. "CATHODE OXYGEN GAS

ELECTROLYTE, WATER ...

SKETCH 18

to battery acid) the two will form an electrolytic couple and will do some or all of the things noted in **Sketch 18**. We will now apply this mechanism of dissimilar metal electrolysis to concrete cases and specific metals on the boat. An then, of course, you want to know how to protect against electrolysis. Easy except for one point which we should clarify:

Plus and Minus: Electric Current

As we keep talking about anodes and cathodes, electrons, and flow of current, we have avoided the subject of the direction of currents. Before we get deeper into the subject, let us look at an example, name things, and try to avoid possible terrific confusion. In **Sketch 19**, an oldfashioned zinc carbon flashlight battery powers a lamp. The battery generates electricity from two members of our list in **Table 3**: zinc is the anode and dissolves, freeing electrons, and the carbon rod is the cathode and stands in for more expensive noble metals. The carbon is the plus or positive pole of the battery, the zinc beaker the minus or negative pole. The term "plus" implies plenty, an excess, and *conventional electric current flows from plus to minus.* However, electrons each have one negative charge, and it is electrons travelling through our wires. The flow of electrons in **Sketch 19** is from minus to plus, *electron current is in the opposite direction of conventional current.* This distinction is very important when we discuss electrolytic corrosion but is totally irrelevant and potentially confusing in all other sectons of this book. We therefore want to acknoweldge the facts, stick with conventional current throughout the book, but note electron flow in all electrolysis sketches where that information is important. In the following section on cathodic protection and the workings of zincs, electric currents are used and **Sketch 20** shows another flashlight zinc carbon battery

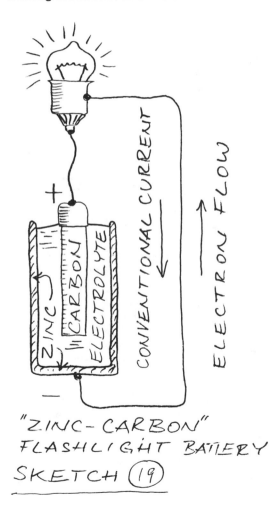

"ZINC-CARBON"
FLASHLIGHT BATTERY
SKETCH (19)

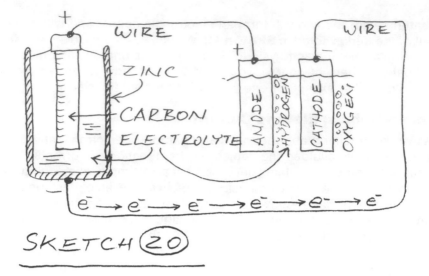

SKETCH 20

connected to two metals in an electrolyte. You think that the naming of anodes and cathodes is confusing? Sorry. But once we get to the essence and apply it to our boats, much of the details may be put on a high shelf again and be forgotten.

Zinc

As you can see in **Table 3**, zinc is one of the most active or reactive, eager to oxidize or corrode, least noble metals on the list. Although there are some very unsatisfactory fittings made from a zinc alloy, camouflaged under chrome plating, the only use for zinc on board is as a corrosion fighter. Zinc is silver white but in air coats itself with a thin layer of zinc oxide which protects it from further oxidation and gives it the typical gray appearance of, for example, your galvanized zinc coated anchors. Zinc oxide is used as a white pigment, for example in sun shielding ointment. Under water, a more voluminous white material called zinc hydroxide forms which does not protect the zinc metal underneath. As zinc metal reacts or corrodes, each of its atoms releases two electrons and forms a "two valent" ion. One ounce of zinc can generate a stream of electrons equivalent to 23 Ampere hours, **Sketch 21**.

SKETCH 21

In practice, the size of the piece of zinc (surface area), average distance to the surface of the protected propeller in the sketch, and conductivity or corrosiveness of the water will mainly determine how much current, for example in milliampere, will flow. That current, multiplied by the hours it takes for one ounce to be used up, will give the actual amount of current in Ampere hours. Since zinc corrodes in sea water no matter whether it is connected by the wire or not, less than the theoretical 23 Ampere hours will be measured.

Zinc Anodes

Pieces of zinc are used as so called sacrificial anodes to protect other metals from electrolytic corrosion. The zinc must be connected to the protected metal by an electrical conductor, or the two metals must make direct electrical contact. When the two are under water, the two metals make a dissimilar metal electrolysis cell in which the zinc is the anode. Zinc corrodes and is consumed, its electrons travel through the electrical conductor to the other metal and create conditions on the protected metal which discourage corrosion reactions there. As discussed earlier, the electrical circuit is being completed by the conductive lake, river, or sea water which contains enough ions from dissolved salts to accept electrons at the protected metal surface.

Zinc anodes are available in many rectangular block, oval, domed round, and tear drop shapes with flat surfaces to be fastened to hull, keel, propeller, shaft, hang or rudder, in large sizes for mounting on steel hulls, in phantasy shapes with cast-in-place wire conductor such as the zinc "guppy" and "grouper" which you hang over the side, and specially shaped zinc fittings for outboard motors and outdrives. The shape of all these may have some effect on the drag of the boat but otherwise is unimportant, only surface area is important.

Which Metals Protected?

Zinc anodes can be used to protect any other metal which on the list in **Table 3** is more noble than zinc. Surprisingly, aluminum which is so close to zinc on the list is protected with zinc anodes. As you know, aluminum in air is always covered with a protective film of oxide. Under water, aluminum corrosion is started or greatly accelerated by some trace metals in the aluminum. Iron, cobalt, copper, and nickel are such culprits. Copper dissolved in the sea water, for example from antifouling paint nearby, causes increased aluminum corrosion. Zinc anodes, on the other hand, are able to keep these corrosion causing impurities on the aluminum surface inactive and thus protect the aluminum, if only indirectly. You may wonder why magnesium is not used instead of zinc to protect aluminum. Magnesium is located one step further down in **Table 3** and would generate a more powerful stream of electrons than zinc. But aluminum can be dissolved in both acids and bases or alkali. The protective aluminum oxide

Table 3

Galvanic Series of Metals and Alloys in Sea Water

Cathodic **Noble** **Passive**	Platinum		76 Ni-16 Cr-7 Fe alloy, active
	Gold		Nickel, active
	Graphite		Naval Brass
	Silver		Manganeze Bronze
	Type 316 Stainless Steel, passive		Muntz Metal
	Type 304 Stainless steel, passive		Tin
	Titanium		Lead
	Type 410 Stainless Steel (13% Cr) passive		Type 316 Stainless Steel, active
			Type 304 Stainless Steel, active
	67 Ni-33Cu alloy		Type 410 Stainless Steel, active
	76 Ni-16 Cr-7 Fe alloy, passive		Cast Iron
	Nickel, passive		Wrought Iron
	Silver solder		Mild Steel
	M bronze		Aluminum 2024
	G Bronze		
	70-30 Cupronickel		Cadmium
	Silicon bronze		Alclad
	Copper		Aluminum 6053
	Red Brass		
	Aluminum brass	**Anodic**	Galvanized Steel
	Admiralty Brass	**Active**	Zinc
	Yellow Brass		Magnesium alloys
			Magnesium

LaQue & Cox

film dissolves in acids as well as in bases or alkaline solutions, and aluminum is most resistant to corrosion in near neutral solutions. The protective current generated by a zinc anode flows through the electrolyte, the sea water. If the current is greater than necessary, the balance between ions is upset near the aluminum and the water becomes alkaline. This destroys the protective film of the aluminum and causes corrosion. Magnesium is likely to generate such overprotection on places on the aluminum which are near the sacrificial anodes, see "Aluminum."

Metals further distant from zinc in **Table 3** will also be more noble than zinc. Zinc anodes will be able to protect these metals better the further up from zinc they are on the list. First, they will be more dissimilar toward zinc and therefore generate increasingly forceful currents with zinc, and secondly these metals are more noble and by themselves less inclined to corrode. Steel, see **Table 3**, is being protected with zinc anodes. Steel hulls are normally coated with epoxy based resins, both to reduce corrosion and to allow the use of copper containing antifouling paints. Large zinc

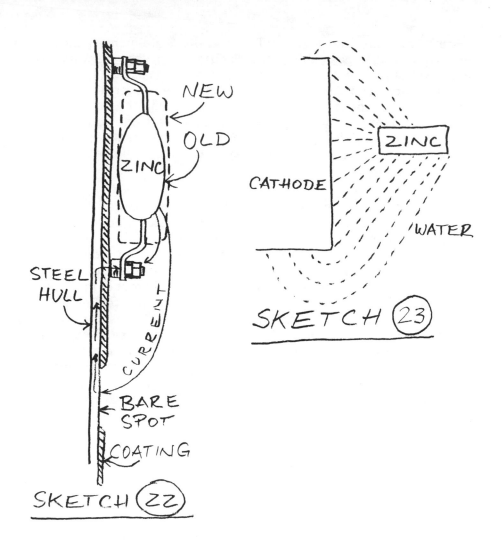

NEW

OLD

ZINC

STEEL HULL

CURRENT

BARE SPOT

COATING

SKETCH 22

CATHODE

ZINC

WATER

SKETCH 23

anodes with cast-in brackets are bolted to the hull and protective current then flows between zinc and any exposed steel surface on the hull, **Sketch 22**.

Nearby in the list of **Table 3** are the active forms of stainless steel which are stainless surfaces which have lost their passivating film of oxides. Such stainless steel can be protected with a zinc anode as long as the protective current can flow. In most cases, the stainless steel will have lost its passivity, as explained earlier, because access of oxygen had been cut off. Often, the same cause which cut off oxygen will also prevent protective current. A zinc anode then will be of little use.

Next on the list is a large number of copper alloys which we will discuss later. All of these can be protected with zinc anodes although, as we will see, some are resistive enough to not need the extra protection. Zincs are then only needed to protect against stray electricity, also discussed later.

The more noble metals on our list of **Table 3** are increasingly able to generate hydrogen gas bubbles and dispose of the electrons which a zinc anode will send their way. Since many of these metals and alloys by themselves do not need zinc anode protection in sea water, they may only consume zinc anodes rapidly. If you are protecting the normal crop of propeller and through hull alloys with zincs and have one part or fitting of a more noble metal, it will be worth while to keep it insulated if possible, instead of connecting it to a bonding system with zinc anodes.

How Big a Zinc?

We have to make clear what we expect of the zinc. We want it to generate a current which flows between the zinc and the protected metal surface. While the current flows in the right direction, the corrosion reactions at the protected metal are being discouraged because they, too, would generate currents which we are opposing. The term "current density" is used to describe how many Amps are flowing at each square foot of the protected metal surface or, more realistically, how many milliampere. For any given metal in a corrosive salt solution there is one current density which is just capable of stopping corrosion. For a brass propeller in sea water the recommended current densities range from just a few to as much as 20 milliampere per square foot. But that information by itself is not much help yet. We have to look at the way electric current flows through water. If a piece of zinc would distribute its current evenly as in **Sketch 23**, things

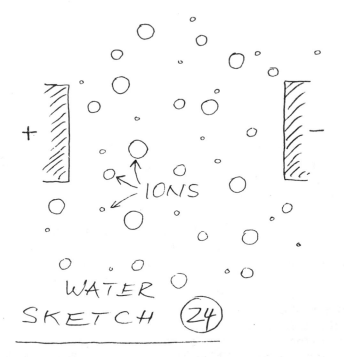

WATER

SKETCH 24

would be simple. In reality, the current, the electrons, travel with the help of charged ions as crudely shown in **Sketch 24**. These ions are evenly distributed through the water but are relatively scarce so that the water is not nearly as conductive as the metals. The ions have different sizes and different mobility which is extremely slow compared to that of the electrons in metal. Current therefore flows best where the distance through the water is shortest. But since the mode of travel there is quickly sold out, the next best routes along greater detours also are used, and current in **Sketch 23** would probably flow in a pattern similar to that in **Sketch 25**. Current would be greatest at the shortest route, much less at the longer detours. With a small piece of zinc distributing its current over a relatively large protected cathode area, the current densities will greatly vary with distance and most of the current will flow to the nearest area of the protected metal. In **Sketch 26**, a piece

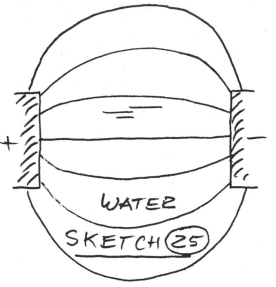

of zinc is shown. Imagine that you are looking down on a flat metal surface to which the zinc is electrically connected, and that both metals are under water. Along the lines in the sketch, currents are flowing which are greatest at the shortest distance. If the desired current density were 1.0 as on one of the lines in the middle, a current of 7.0 would flow at the shortest path, giving considerable overprotection and wasting zinc, while at the longer paths only small fractions of the desired current would flow, as indicated by the values of 0.3, 0.1, and 0.06. The values were calculated with the sketch made to scale.

In practice this means that a zinc nut on a propeller, **Sketch 27**, will mostly, if not only, protect the aft surfaces of the propeller. In addition, the closeness of the inner surfaces of the propeller to the zinc anode will help to consume the zinc fairly rapidly due to the large current which can flow there. Similarly, a zinc collar on a shaft as in **Sketch 28** will generate high currents to the nearest areas on the shaft which will accelerate use of zinc. There will be much less current to the more distant places on the shaft where protection will be marginal.

Why a zinc anode directly on shaft or propeller may still be a good idea will be discussed in the following part on stray electricity. For boats on moorings, private docks known to be free from stray currents, and for propellers and shafts made from corrosion resistant alloys, a zinc mounted on the nonmetallic hull as in **Sketch 29** would distribute current more evenly if located above the propeller, one zinc on either side of the boat, and with a wire connected to the engine, or to a wiper which touches the propeller shaft. A similar arrangement results if you hang zinc anodes over the sides of the boat as in **Sketch 30**. Use a length of stainless steel welding electrode wire which you bend through the holes of a piece of zinc. Above the water line, solder with acid flux to a copper wire which you connect to grounded chain plate or deck fitting, or directly to engine or propeller shaft. In these cases, the longest distance to a place on the protected metals is not much different to the shortest distance, so that you will have more even current distribution.

A recommended current density of 1 mA (milliampere) per square foot corresponds to 0.024 Ah per day which would consume one ounce of zinc in 2.6 years if we disregard that some zinc is lost by direct corrosion. If we assume that the efficiency of the zinc to generate current is only 50%, then one ounce of zinc would be consumed to protect one square foot of metal surface for 1.3 years. A current density of only 1 mA is the lowest value mentioned anywhere in the technical literature. A comparatively very high current density of 15 mA per square foot is recommended to protect corrosion prone metals. Let us take that value to estimate the upper limit of a practical current density range:

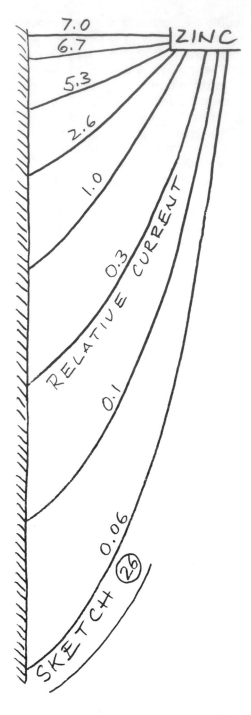

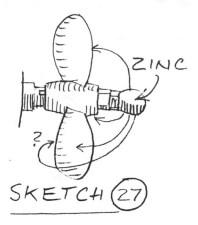

ZINC

SKETCH (27)

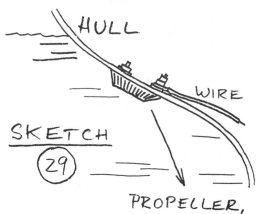

HULL

WIRE

SKETCH
(29)

PROPELLER,
SHAFT, RUDDER
FITTINGS.

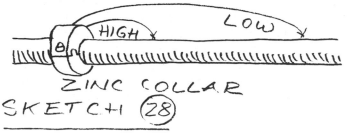

LOW

HIGH

ZINC COLLAR

SKETCH (28)

A current density of 15 mA per square foot corresponds to a zinc consumption of one ounce per month, assuming 50% efficiency of the zinc.

As a reasonable estimate for all common copper based alloys in sea water, a current density of 3 mA per square foot will give us a safe guideline. This current density will consume 0.072 Ampere hours per day on one square foot of protected metal surface area, or about 26 Ah per year. This corresponds to a little over an ounce of zinc per year.

Obviously, just before a one-ounce piece of zinc would be completely consumed, the remaining zinc would be very small,

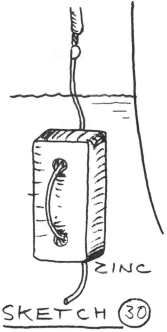

ZINC

SKETCH (30)

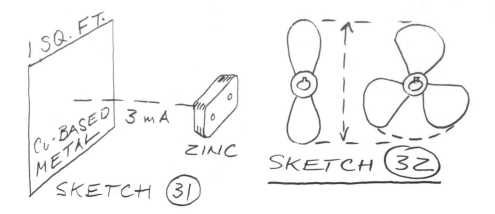

SKETCH 31

SKETCH 32

with very little surface area which would generate only a small fraction of the original current. In addition, zincs tend to loose the electrical contact through their fastening bolts when they have worn to some extent. From then on, they would continue to corrode but fail to send their current to the metal which was to be protected. For a zinc which is expected to supply electric current equivalent to one ounce of zinc, we should use at least two ounces so that a large enough zinc remains toward the end of its expected life. We should double it again to allow for the amount of zinc which would corrode away if the zinc were in the water by itself, not connected to supply

Table 4
Approximate Surface Area in Square Feet, two and three blade propellers.

Two blade propellers:

Diameter in inches	Surface area, square feet
10	1.2
12	1.4
14	1.6
16	1.9

Three blade propellers:

Diameter in inches	Surface area, square feet
10	2.1
12	2.5
14	2.9
16	3.3
18	3.7

Table 5
Surface Area of Propeller Shafts: surface area in square feet for one foot of length.

Diameter in inches	Surface area, sq. ft. per foot
7/8	0.23
1	0.26
1 1/8	0.29
1 1/4	0.33
1 3/8	0.36
1 1/2	0.39

current: this could be called the anode efficiency which we assume to be about 50%. The zinc in this example should be at least of 4 ounce size if it is expected to last for one year. If any stray electricity is suspected around your boat, read about it and consider that stray currents may consume the major portion of the zincs on your boat.

Approximate surface areas for propellers are given in **Table 4**, and the surface area for one foot of propeller shaft is given in **Table 5**.
Since you might at this point take a close look at your propeller shaft, make certain that you have its material identified. Then compare its position on the list of **Table 3**.

Brass: Dezincification

Brass is the name for alloys of copper and zinc. Since these two constituents are a good distance apart on our active—passive list of metals, **Table 3**, you might expect that, given any chance, the two would react as a dissimilar metal couple. Such chances apparently exist, at grain boundaries or between crystals in the metal as mentioned earlier. Typically, zinc is lost from the alloy which changes appearance from the normal golden yellow to pink or copper—red. A brass wood screw,

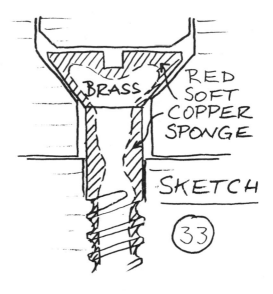

BRASS
RED SOFT COPPER SPONGE

SKETCH
(33)

93

for example, might suffer from dezincification as shown in **Sketch 33**. If water has access, the outer material, shaded in the sketch, looses its zinc content and does not protect deeper regions since the remaining copper is porous, sponge like, and allows water as electrolyte to diffuse in. Although the outer dimensions of the screw remain the same, the dezincified material has lost most of its strength and typically can be cut with a knife or scraper, sometimes even with a fingernail. Only when the zinc content in brass is less than 15% or if 1% or more of tin is added to the alloy is the rate of dezincification reduced. Alloy names and compositions follow in the section on copper alloys.

Copper and Alloys

Since the great majority of fittings below water on the boat are made from copper alloys, we will make a list here and mention the main advantages and disadvantages related to corrosion. We have to keep in mind that in addition to the simple even surface corrosion which wears away measurable layers of metal at the surface, there is so called pitting corrosion which we will discuss in connection with stainless steel and which causes pits or localized holes in otherwise uncorroded surfaces, **Sketch 34**. There is impingement·attack which is corrosion caused by fast flowing water which greatly accelerates corrosion attack in local areas as, for example, in pumps, or pipes, **Sketch 35**, and cavitation attack which is non-electrolytic, purely mechanical deterioration found on fast turning propellers. The special problem of dezincification corrosion of copper zinc alloys has been discussed earlier, and in all of these cases, corrosion rate expressed in loss of surface material with an "inches per year" rate would give a false picture. Sometimes, no loss of surface material occurs and the outer dimensions of a piece of metal remain constant as with dezincified brass. But the strength of such metal may suffer greatly from these special corrosion mechanisms including pitting and dezincification.

Copper: Plain pure copper itself is quite nicely corrosion resistant against both hot and cold sea water and, of course, is immune to dezincification. The rate of corrosion in sea water is 0.001 to 0.003 inches per year (ipy).

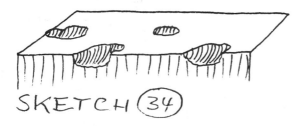

SKETCH (34)

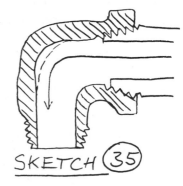

SKETCH (35)

However, it has low resistance against impingement attack and is not used for propellers or hull fittings since, as we will see in a moment, small additions of other metals are made to improve copper quite impressively. Copper by itself in sea water is resistant against fouling. Enough copper ions find their way into the sea water near the copper surface to prevent marine growth.

Brass: The name for mainly copper zinc alloys. Up to 37% zinc can be added to copper to obtain a wide range of brasses called alpha brass. When more zinc is added, some interesting mechanical properties can result in the alloy which can then be rolled, forged, extruded, hardened and so on. All of these alloys may show only very low corrosion rates in inches per year of material loss, however much more significant is that all suffer from loss of strength through dezincification. The rate of dezincification can be slowed down by the addition of small amounts of arsenic, antimony, or phosphorus to the alloy. Through the addition of some tin, aluminum, iron, or manganese, strong alloys can be made which are used in propellers.

Bronze: A name originally reserved for alloys of copper and tin. Now, all kinds of copper based alloys are referred to as being "bronze" and there is considerable confusion. The term has become almost meaningless by itself, and it is necessary to state exactly which "bronze" is meant. Tin, as you can see in **Table 3**, is considerably more noble than zinc and, unfortunately also more expensive than both zinc and copper. It imparts very desirable properties in the bronzes, and there is no parallel process to dezincification which would remove tin from the bronze alloy. Tin content of 5% is considered high, 10% is the maximum. There are a number of alloys which contain small amounts of tin, and there are a number of "bronzes" which contain no tin at all, listed with some of their properties in **Table 6**.

These bronzes make use of alloying metals other than tin and are also free from zinc.

Phosphor bronze appears to be the only copper-tin bronze free from zinc. It consists of copper, 5 to 8% tin, and small amounts of phosphorus, its corrosion rate is 0.0006 to 0.0012 inches per year, it is resistant to impingement attack and pitting, and of course immune to dezincification. Types "E" only 1.25% tin; "A" 5%, "C" 8%, "D" 10% tin.

Silicon bronze consists of copper and about 3% silicon, its corrosion resistance is much like that of copper.

Aluminum bronze is an alloy of copper with 4 to 7% aluminum and sometimes small amounts of nickel, arsenic, iron, or tin. This bronze shows sea water resistance enhanced apparently through a surface film of aluminum oxide which protects the metal and which forms again quickly where damaged. (There is an alloy called aluminum brass which contains about 22% zinc and 2% aluminum and which is subject to dezincification pitting and loss of strength from corrosion.)

Manganese bronze in one example consists of 40% zinc and 2% manganese, *is not a bronze* in the original sense but rather, brass. Its corrosion resistance is not nearly that of the tin, silicon, or aluminum based bronzes, it suffers from dezincification and the associated loss of strength, but has considerable resistance to impingement or water flow corrosion.

Copper nickel alloys: a wide range of compositions is in commercial use, often called cupro nickel. Alloys with nickel content of up to 40% nickel corrode in sea water approximately at the same rate as pure copper with the result that such metal surfaces are resistant to fouling. Above 40% nickel, not enough copper is dissolved and such alloys will foul. Compositions with higher nickel content show the ability of nickel and the stainless steels to become passive. Similarly also, these alloys are subject to pitting corrosion where the passive layer fails, for example under fouling or where access of oxygen containing sea water is interrupted.

Table 6
Copper and Alloys

All consist of copper, listed additional major ingredients, and sometimes other minor ingredients. Composition ranges or typical composition examples. It means: "dezinc," prone to dezincification and associated loss of strength, "pitting" tendency to pitting corrosion, for example where passivity is lost under fouling, "flow corrosion" is the corrosion of flowing sea water which can affect an otherwise corrosion resistant metal, "ipy" inches per year loss of metal corrosion rate usually measured with non flowing sea water, this value may not be significant if dezincification or localized pitting are causes of damage. Note that some alloys have several names.

Admiralty Brass: copper with 27 to 29% zinc, about 1% tin, dezinc, "inhibited" grade better dezincification resistance, 0.002 ipy.

Alpha-Beta Brass: copper with more than 37.5% zinc, dezinc, but some good physical properties.

Alpha Brass: copper with 21 to 22% zinc, 2% aluminum, dezinc.

Aluminum Brass: copper with 4 to 10% aluminum, 0.0015 ipy or less, good performance in sea water.

Arsenic in Alpha Brasses: used to reduce dezincification.

Bronze: copper with up to 10% tin, now also used for other alloys including some brasses.

Beta Brass: copper with more than 50% zinc, a phase constituent of alpha-beta brass, not used as such by itself.

Cast Red Brass: copper with 5% tin, 5% zinc, 5% lead, see Ounce Metal.

Commercial Brass: copper with 35% zinc, dezinc.

Commercial Bronze: copper with 10% zinc.

Common Brass: same as Commercial Brass

Constantan: copper with 45% nickel, used as thermocouple wire to measure temperatures. Very useful corrosion resistant wire.

Copper: resistant to sea water, 0.001 to 0.003 ipy, corroded by fast flowing sea water, ammonia, soft fresh water.

Copper Nickel Alloys: copper with 5 to 30% nickel 0.0003 to 0.002 ipy, corrosion behavior similar to copper. Above 45% nickel behavior similar to nickel, passive. Pitting when starved of oxygen.

Cupro-Nickel: see Copper Nickel Alloys above.

Everdur: copper with 3% silicon

G-Bronze: copper with 10% tin, 2% zinc.

German Silver: copper with 18% zinc, 18% nickel. Mostly replaced by stainless steel. Tarnishes easily.

Government Bronze: copper with 10% tin, 2% zinc, good performance in sea water, see Gunmetal below.

Gunmetal: copper with 10% tin, 2% zinc, also copper with 5% tin, 5% nickel, 2% zinc.

Hardware Bronze: copper with 9% zinc, 2% lead.

High Brass: copper with 35% zinc, dezinc.

Leaded High Brass: copper with 34% zinc, 1% lead, dezinc.

Low Brass: copper with 20% zinc, dezinc.

M-Bronze: copper with 6.5% tin, 3% zinc, 1.5% lead, not to be confused with Manganese Bronze. Good performance in sea water.

Manganese Bronze: copper with 40% zinc, 2 to 3.5% manganese, this is a brass, dezinc.

Monel: copper with 66% or more of nickel. See Copper Nickel Alloys. Propeller shafts. Some pitting under fouling.

Muntz Metal: copper with 40% zinc, dezinc.

Naval Brass: copper with 39% zinc, 1% tin, dezinc. Misleading name, not for marine use.

Nickel Aluminum Bronze: copper with 4% aluminum, 4% nickel.

Nickel Bronze: copper with 5% tin, 5% nickel, 2% tin. See Gunmetal.

Nickel Silver: copper with 18% zinc, 18% nickel. Mostly replaced by stainless steel. Tarnishes easily.

Olympic Bronze: copper with 2.75% silicon, 1% zinc.

Ounce Metal: copper with 5% zinc, 5% tin, 5% lead.

Phosphor Bronze: copper with 1 to 10% tin, small amounts of phosphorus, very good all around corrosion resistance.

Propeller Bronze: probably Aluminum Bronze, or Alpha-Beta Brass inhibited, with small amounts of tin, aluminum, iron, manganese.

Red Brass: copper with 10 to 25% zinc. Under 15% relatively resistant to dezinc, higher zinc content: dezinc, pitting.

Silicon Bronze: copper with 3% silicon

Silver Tobin Bronze: copper with 39% zinc, 1% tin, dezinc.

Yellow Brass: copper with 35% zinc, dezinc.

Aluminum

Aluminum is highly reactive as you can see by its position in the list of **Table 3**, but is protected from corrosion by a layer of oxide. This film can be artificially increased in thickness, modified for increased strength, and colored by processes referred to as anodizing. The oxide film is soluble in both acids and alkalies. This is different from many other metals and their corrosion products which can be dissolved by acids but not alkali. Rust, for example, is resistant to strong alkali solutions.

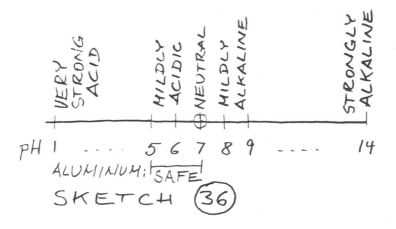

The aluminum oxide film is most stable, and aluminum most corrosion resistant, when the water around it is approximately neutral. In chemical terms, neutral means a "pH" value of 7, lower values correspond to acid and higher values to alkaline solutions, **Sketch 36**. Aluminum is most resistant at pH 6 and safe between pH 5 and 7. Sea water, on the other hand, has a pH of about 8, meaning that aluminum is most corrosion resistant in water which is very slightly acidic while sea water is very slightly alkaline. This is important for the cathodic protection of aluminum hulls where overprotection generates alkaline conditions of the aluminum surface and allows the aluminum oxide film to dissolve. Protection with zinc anodes has been discussed as relatively safe, but use of impressed current from a power supply instead of zinc, or use of more electronegative anodes such as magnesium, can "overprotect" and significantly increase the pH value of the sea water at the hull surface.

The position of aluminum in **Table 3** also indicates that most other metals in contact with aluminum will develop dissimilar metal electrolysis cells which, if there is an electrolyte, will have the aluminum corrode as the anode. Where stronger fasteners are needed on aluminum spars, deck fittings, boarding ladders, metals are used which are themselves covered with passivating films, such as the stainless steels or nickel alloys. The aluminum then tends to keep these fittings passive.

Other metals such as copper, iron, cobalt, and nickel tend to cause corrosion if contained in the aluminum alloy. Unfortunately, some of these are added to aluminum to improve its strength. Most aluminum extrusions such as masts, spars, moldings contain between 0.3 and 1% iron, up to 2% copper, and some chromium or nickel which will make its corrosion resistance worse than that of pure aluminum. Some casting alloys contain even greater contents of copper while even traces of copper dissolved in the water at an aluminum surface can start corrosion. Such copper may be released by nearby antifouling paint.

Graphite, which is carbon and behaves like a noble metal, see **Table 3**, is contained in pencil lead. Pencil marks on aluminum can cause etching of the aluminum when wetted with salt water. Finally, mercury, used in some thermometers, will dissolve aluminum and form a liquid "amalgam" solution. Since the dissolved aluminum in turn quickly forms a fluffy white oxide with air, the mercury is free to dissolve more aluminum and the process continues, so that a drop of mercury from a broken thermometer can do appreciable damage.

With fastenings on aluminum, the anode to cathode area is important. A stainless steel rivet in an aluminum mast will last nicely even if some aluminum is occasionally used to protect the stainless steel. In comparison, an aluminum rivet in stainless steel would have a very short life if any salt spray could reach it. Threaded screws or bolts of stainless steel in aluminum castings are similarly protected by the aluminum. However, the generated aluminum oxide or hydroxide tends to freeze such bolts quickly. Stainless or monel fasteners in, for example, aluminum self steering gear castings or outboard motor lower units can become tightly imbedded in little more than one season. In such cases, corrosion at the threaded surface can only be prevented when the electrolyte, water, is excluded by grease.

Galvanized Steel

Steel anchors, chain, shackles, thimbles, and some other hardware are made corrosion resistant by a cover of zinc. The zinc is applied by hot dipping, meaning that the steel articles are immersed in molten zinc which leaves a relatively uneven but thick coating. Some steel hardware is electroplated with zinc and called galvanized, and more often also electroplated with cadmium which has similar properties to zinc but makes a shinier, bluish mirror finish on steel hardware. These electroplatings only keep their good looks while in the hardware store and offer very little additional corrosion protection.

The hot dipped zinc on anchors quickly covers itself with a thin film of zinc oxide (hydroxide) when first under water. This thin white film gives galvanized anchors their typical dull gray appearance and substantially reduces the inherent corrosion of zinc in sea water. In addition, holes in the zinc coating from wear, for example at the hinged points on anchors,

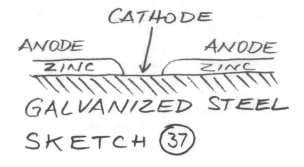

CATHODE

ANODE | ANODE

ZINC | ZINC

GALVANIZED STEEL

SKETCH 37

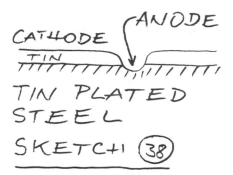

CATHODE | ANODE

TIN

TIN PLATED STEEL

SKETCH 38

are still protected. This is because small places of exposed steel, **Sketch 37**, are surrounded by large areas of zinc which become the anode to the small steel cathode which is being perfectly protected. The explanation, of course, is clear from the positions of zinc and steel in **Table 3**. In contrast, steel cans and kitchen utensils with tin coatings will rust at pin holes in the tin coating because here, the steel will be the anode, **Sketch 38**. Tin is used there because it is not toxic (tin = stannum, as in stannous fluoride in toothpastes) while zinc is modestly toxic.

The rate of zinc loss from anchors and chain in sea water and all brackish water is approximately 0.5 ounces per square foot per year which corresponds to about 1 mil per year or 0.001 inches per year, or the thickness of a thin piece of paper in two to three years. Since the ground tackle is not immersed all the time, the hot dipped zinc will last a long time. In addition, zinc on the chain will protect an anchor which has lost its zinc here and there. If you paint such anchor, less zinc from the chain will be used. Note that the very large zinc surface of an anchor chain will make for a very large anode if in electrical contact with your bronze hull fittings and propeller. Also consider that a cell develops between chain near the bottom (low oxygen, colder temperature, or greater salt content) and the chain near the surface. And, with a look at **Table 3**, it is clear that no metals other than galvanized or plain steel should be used anywhere on anchor or chain.

Stainless Steel

The alloys generally used for marine hardware are referred to as 18-8 which indicates the chromium and nickel contents. Separate designations are used for individual stainless steel alloys for wrought or cast applications, and many of the small stainless fittings which are made from sheet metal stampings or bent round rod probably are the type 304. Many if not most of these fittings are also nickel plated so that the outer surface looks and behaves like nickel. Stainless steel bolts, on the other hand, are clearly identified and the top grade there is called 316. This alloy contains molybdenum and is considered the most corrosion resistant stainless steel for use on the boat.

We have discussed the active and passive states of stainless steel, with the resulting two locations on the list in **Table 3**. The passive stainless steel and passive nickel have the behavior of noble metals which, however, depend on a passivating layer of oxides which can be destroyed relatively easily if oxygen becomes scarce at the stainless steel surface. With an electrolyte, present, corrosion starts where the stainless steel surface is covered and access of oxygen restricted. The kind of pitting corrosion occurs on other metals but is most noteworthy for stainless steel. Pitting, shown in **Sketch 39**, is by the dissimilar metal mechanism described earlier. An anode develops where access is blocked, and remains the bottom of such pit. Conditions favor this anode the deeper the pit. Protection with a zinc anode usually is not effective because pitting starts under a barnacle or other cover which renders the anode on the stainless steel inaccessible to protective current from a zinc. For this reason, stainless steel fittings no matter what the alloy, are far from perfect for use below the water line and may perform very poorly.

Salt Water—Fresh Water

We have used the terms salt water and sea water often, and keep talking about electrolytes and their electrical conductivity. But most of the electrolytic corrosion mechanisms are not limited to sea water but proceed in river or lake water as well, just possibly somewhat slower. In addition, there are causes for electrolytic corrosion in fresh water which we should not overlook. When moving from sea to fresh water, concentration of some film forming chemicals In the water around the boat may change from saturated to less than saturated, so that films involving calcium, lime, may dissolve in the fresh water, with some loss of protection. Polluted river water may contain sulfur, acids, ammonia, and corrode copper alloys more than sea water, as will softened fresh water high in bicarbonate. Finally, the dissolved salts in sea water lend stability to its "pH" value" which measures acid or base character. Sea water is normally at pH 8.1 to 8.3 and is relatively well "buffered" meaning that some acid added to it will not change the pH as much as the same amount of acid added to fresh water. The fresh water would change its pH more greatly, become more acidic and more corrosive.

Conductivity of Water

Water increases its conductivity for electric current as its content of ions increases, for example, from dissolved salts. As conductivity increases, resistivity decreases. When measuring resistance, our familiar Ohm unit is used except that we have to consider the distance through the water. Resistivity is expressed in Ohm X centimeter (Ohm cm), and conductivity, the opposite, in 1/ohm cm.

Table 8

Pure water	20,000,000	Ohm cm
distilled water	5,000,000	,,
rain water	20,000	,,
tap water, approx.	3,000	,,
river water, approx.	200	,,
sea water, coastal	30	,,
sea water, open sea	20	,,

Sea water resistivity of 20 Ohm cm corresponds to a conductivity of 1

$$\frac{1}{20}\frac{1}{\text{Ohm cm}} = 0.05\frac{1}{\text{Ohm cm}}$$

You can verify the electrical conductivity of the water around your boat with a volt ohm meter (VOM): switch to Ohm range, hold test wires into water which you scoop up in a bucket. Since the internal battery of the meter makes current flow between test wires, you will, after a while, begin to corrode the anode and affect the accuracy of the reading (which will gradually increase).

Stray Electric Current Corrosion

We discussed the sizes and required currents of zinc anodes. You may have thought about your boat and wondered how it ever survived with such small zincs, and so few of them. Or you may have guessed that there must be more to the story of the protecting zincs and, or course, there is. We have covered the mechanism of electrolytic corrosion, sorted the various metals and alloys into good and not so good ones, and you may have decided that all around, things are fine on your boat. In fact, you may have one of the relatively few boats which do not use any zinc ever, yet have the same propeller and shaft from ten years ago. That is quite possible because the alloys under water were chosen to be corrosion resistant in the first place, to be similar to each other, and your boat may be at a dock, mooring, or slip free from stray electricity.

Of all the zinc consumed on fiberglass boats with bronze propellers and hull fittings, probably more than half is eaten away by stray electricity and most of the other half is dissolved by the sea water as is inherent in the character of zinc, without much protection to anything. In other words, if you routinely fit zincs at hauling time and the old ones always are badly diminished, better keep up the routine and, next opportunity, measure stray electricity around your boat.

The effect of stray current on a piece of metal is shown in **Sketch 1**. The electric current here is generated by a battery and flows between anode and cathode. Conventional current flow is in the direction from the anode

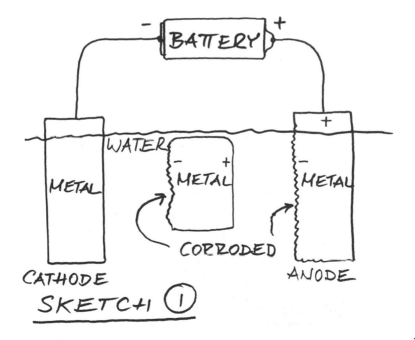

through the water to the cathode. Any metal object in the water would, because of its low conductivity, collect current on one side and discharge current on the other side. In this example, the anode would protect the cathode but the piece of metal would corrode on the side toward the cathode, as sketched.

If the voltage between two electrodes in water would be, for example, 0.8 Volt, then each fraction of the distance between them would show a proportional change in voltage which we could measure, **Sketch 2**, by dipping test wires in the water. This is much like a long resistor which along its length has voltages which correspond to the distances, **Sketch 3**. The point here is that along the path of a current in the water there is also voltage. If the distance were 12 inches and the battery 12 Volt, we would find one Volt difference at each inch, or measure the two, three, or seven Volts in the sketch.

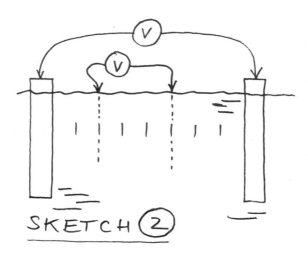

SKETCH ②

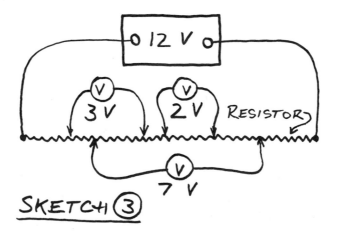

SKETCH ③

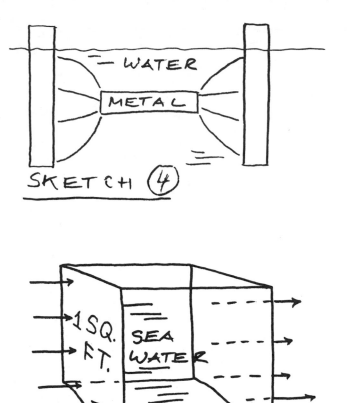

SKETCH ④

SKETCH ⑤

Metal in the water will pick up stray current because the resistance in the metal is nil compared to that in the water which is bound to be magnitudes greater. In the example, the longer the metal extends between anode and cathode, the bigger a voltage it will bridge and the more readily it will collect current. Flow will then be as in **Sketch 4** where the curved lines indicate current.

To give you an idea about the differences in conductivity, imagine the water being the most conductive sea water.

Its specific resistance of 20 Ohm centimeter, compare **Table 8**, makes a conductor of sea water with a cross section of one square foot have a resistance of 0.6 Ohm for each foot of length, see **Sketch 5**. Granted, that makes sea water quite conductive, but a copper conductor with the same resistance can have a cross section as thin as a hair. As you can see, the longer metal conductors are most likely to pick up stray current, especially when they are oriented toward anode and cathode.

HULL FITTING

BONDING WIRE

CURRENT

SKETCH ⑥

On many boats, one such long conductor is made when a hull fitting at the forward end of the boat is connected with a bonding wire to other hull fittings aft, to the propeller via engine ground and shaft, or to a ground plate aft. Should there be any current in the water flowing in a fore and aft direction, such bonding system is certain to pick up part of that current, **Sketch 6**. The bridged distance may be 20 feet or more, and the resistance in the bonding wire practically zero. Bonding wire connections between fittings on opposite sides of a boat would bridge a shorter distance but stray currents are perhaps more likely between boats in a marina and would run athwartship to your boat. Usually, if a boat is fitted with a bonding system, all metal fittings are included and such boat is then likely to collect, spider net fashion, any current, whatever its direction.

Direct current conducted through the bonding system would, as explained in the previous section, corrode the metal or fitting from which electrons are extracted while the fittings at the opposite end of the boat would enjoy protection unless the current significantly changes the water chemistry toward greater alkalinity, see earlier details.

Alternating current in the water is usually not considered detrimental because in lab experiments or in electroplating, no net transport of material occurs. At metal surfaces under water, the chemical processes at anode and cathode differ, and it is unlikely that alternating current at a metal surface under water will flow in either direction with the same ease. It is more likely that the metal hull fittings will have a rectifying effect by allowing electron flow with preference in one direction. This suggests that we search for alternating current as well, and consider it as detrimental as direct current. With so much alternating current in use on boats, and often less than perfect wiring, AC current leakage is likely almost anywhere in marinas and harbors.

How to Find Stray Current

If enough electric current is picked up by the boat's bonding system, you would be able to measure it at the bonding or grounding wires. A milliam-

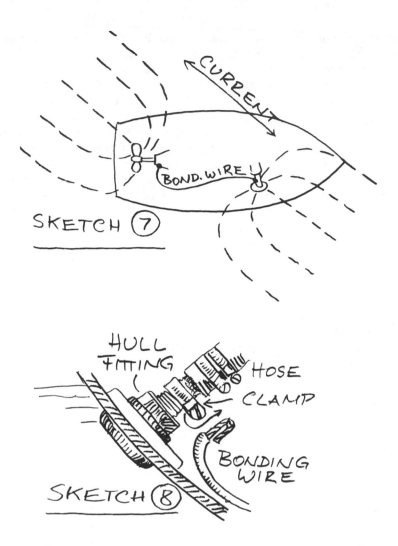

SKETCH ⑦

SKETCH ⑧

pere meter, or the mA range on a volt ohm meter, would serve, and measurements are carried out as shown in **Sketch 8**. Most significant will be the fittings farthest forward and aft. Take off the bonding or grounding wire from the fitting and contact the meter wires to fitting and the end of the bonding wire. If there are several fittings at the forward end of the boat, you can improve the measurement sensitivity by first disconnecting the bond wires from all those forward hull fittings, then taking the measurement at any one of them. This way, there will not be several conductors competing for current.

If through hull fittings are bonded to improve their corrosion behavior, that is bound to have little effect if a zinc is only fitted at one point, usually near the propeller. That zinc is far too distant to generate any protective current for a hull fitting near the forward end of the boat. As a collector of stray current the bonding system is certainly undesirable. But bonding systems probably reduce the danger should lightning strike the boat. Here, better access from the highly conductive mast to the less conductive sea water is offered the lightning discharge via the bonding wires to all of the hull fittings. Where 110 VAC shore electricity is used with a ground fault circuit interrupter, the bonding system offers a path which allows proper tripping of the interrupter in case of a leak. After tests, you should therefore reconnect all bonding wires until all possible effects have been considered.

Measurements of current in the bonding wires will give an approximate value since the meter resistance has been added during the measurement. To correlate magnitudes of current with amounts of corroded metals see the section on zinc and the following **Table 9**. While zinc and the more active metals will corrode by themselves, and will do so faster with a superimposed current in the "right" direction, more noble metals such as the copper alloys will have some other reactions compete with the corrosion of metal, their "corrosion efficiency," black humor, is less than 100%, and not all current is used to oxidize or corrode metal. The losses therefore are less than the table predicts.

Table 9
Metal corroded by direct current

A direct current of 1 mA = 0.001 A flowing between metal and water will corrode or dissolve the following amounts in one year. The more noble metals will corrode less than the predicted amounts while less noble metals will have near 100% "corrosion efficiency."

Metal	Corrosion in grams per 1 mA year:
Nickel	19.2
Copper	20.8
Tin	19.4
Lead	33.9
Iron	18.3
Zinc	21.4
Aluminum	8.8
Magnesium	8.0

To find stray current elsewhere in the water, without using the boat's bonded hull fittings, you need a meter with very long test wires, as in **Sketch 9**. Instead of measuring current, in milliampere for example, we have to look for voltage differences at different places in the water because current measurements would be strongly influenced by the sizes of the two metal electrodes. The meter should therefore be a millivolt meter with a range of 500 mV which is one half volt. The electrodes must be of the same metal to eliminate the voltage which dissimilar metals would generate. Measurements will be more sensitive with greater distance between the

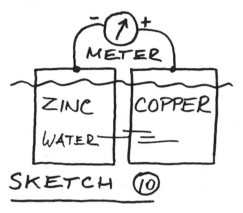

LONG WIRE 500mV

WATER — WATER

MUST BE SAME METAL

SKETCH ⑨

electrodes, and the distance, direction, and polarity should be noted with every voltage reading. A current will be flowing between places in the water which indicate a difference in voltage. You can verify the sensitivity and polarity of the meter by connecting a pair of dissimilar metals to the meter as in **Sketch 10**: pieces of zinc and copper with a few square inches of surface area each will develop about 800 mV in modestly conductive water, and enough power for a meter with average sensitivity. Polarity is shown in the sketch.

METER

ZINC   COPPER

WATER

SKETCH ⑩

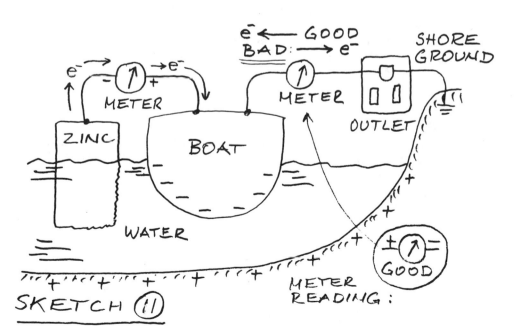

e⁻ ← GOOD
BAD: → e⁻

SHORE GROUND

e⁻ →   → e⁻
METER

ZINC

BOAT

OUTLET

WATER

SKETCH ⑪

METER READING:

± GOOD

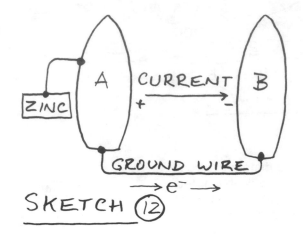

SKETCH 12

Another source of stray electric current is the ground wire which connects many boats to the shore ground of the electric outlet on the dock. Your boat may be affected even though you are not using shore power. **Sketch 11** gives a summary of conditions with boat and zinc anode, and shows the two directions for electron flow in a ground wire: if electrons flow from boat to shore, your zinc is being consumed by this current and, when it is used up, other metal parts of the boat will corrode, unless the current then stops. **Sketch 12** shows how boat A with zinc is protecting boat B which has no zinc. Even though the degree of protection for boat B may be marginal, its contribution to the use of zinc may be very substantial.

The 110 VAC shore electricity is beyond the subject of this book, but the possible effect of the shore cable ground wire is so overwhelming that we have to include some aspects of AC (alternating current) wiring.

WARNING: SHOCK HAZARD. Do not attempt any measurements at or near any of the dock power outlets or the outlets on board unless you are thoroughly familiar with all safety and wiring code aspects of AC wiring.

Shore Ground Wire

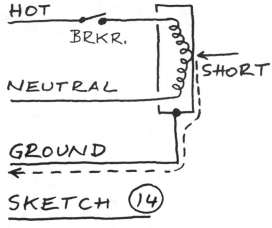

You cannot simply disconnect the shore ground wire to avoid corrosive current. The ground wire in **Sketch 14** carries enough current to trip and open the "BRKR" circuit breaker or fuse if the coil of any appliance should touch the housing, see box in the sketch, to create a short. Without the ground wire, the housing would become "hot" with 110 V and be a very *serious shock hazard,* the circuit breaker would not trip and the short would become a fire hazard. On some boats, the ground wires of on-board 110 V AC outlets and appliances are connected to boat's ground, **Sketch 15**, and no ground wire from the dock connected to boat's ground. This eliminates the ground wire corrosion current but may easily create leakage currents from electric equipment on board. Worse, in case of a short as in the sketch, the extra current, dotted line, has to flow through water which in most cases will not allow high enough currents to trip the circuit breaker. While the shock hazard is solved, both fire hazard and corrosion problem remain.

HOT

BRKR.

NEUTRAL

SHORT

GROUND

SKETCH ⑭

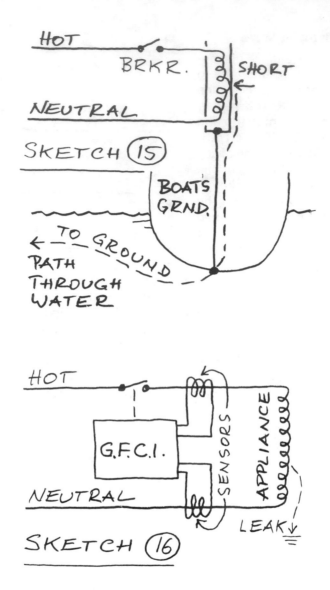

HOT

BRKR.   SHORT

NEUTRAL

SKETCH ⑮

BOAT'S GRND.

← TO GROUND
PATH THROUGH WATER

HOT

G.F.C.I.   SENSORS   APPLIANCE

NEUTRAL   LEAK

SKETCH ⑯

Only when a ground fault circuit interrupter is used as in **Sketch 16** can small leakage currents into boat's ground trip the circuit breaker. Such electronic devices are available in the shape of main panel circuit breakers, or combined with outlets to fit into wall outlet boxes. Ground fault interrupters sense the current both into and out of the appliance, **Sketch 16**, and trip the circuit breaker if a leak causes the current in one wire to be different from the other. Critical size of the leak is usually 15 milliampere which is considered the limit of tolerance for human touch shock hazard. Since the ground fault interrupters use electronic circuitry, your safety depends on proper performance, and frequent testing is recommended: GFCIs have a test button for that purpose.

A method which allows the boat's wiring to remain as in Sketch 14 but eliminates corrosive current in the ground wire is outlined in US Patents 3,769,926 and 3,636,409. Since the corrosion causing currents are usually in the millivolt ranges while currents from shorts, dotted line in Sketch 14, will be caused by much higher voltages up to 110 V line voltage, silicon diodes in the ground wire, Sketch 17, will block low voltages and corro-

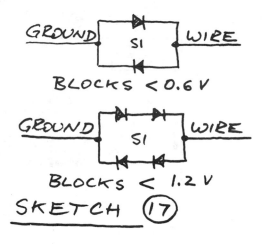

sive current but will become conductive enough in case of a short to cause a circuit breaker to trip. Threshold voltage for a silicon diode is about 0.6 V, diodes must be in both directions for AC use, and current ratings must equal or exceed circuit breaker tripping current. Again, safety depends on the reliable performance of the components.

Test the Zincs with Boat in the Water

You can use the meter of Sketch 9 to test whether the zincs on your boat are intact and working, whether the boats at the dock near yours have their zincs properly fitted or help consume yours, whether a bonded through hull fitting forward is too far away to get protection from a zinc aft, or you can simply walk up and down the docks of your marina and test all the boats, or most, by just touching a test wire to a stay or pulpit.

The job is easiest with a corrosion indicator meter which has a scale similar to Sketch 18 and a polarity reversing switch. With other millivolt meters, you have to watch the needle closely to see whether it wants to pull below the zero mark. You then have to change polarity: flip the switch, or exchange the test wires.

As a basic measurement, and to determine the direction of current through the meter, attach a piece of copper to one wire, a piece of zinc to the other, and hold in water so that only the copper and zinc "electrodes" are immersed, not the alligator clips or other metal attachments, Sketch 9, and Sketch 10. The meter will show a reading of 8, for 800 millivolt, in modestly conductive water.

To test whether a boat has zincs attached and working, all you have to do is touch a stay or pulpit as in Sketch 19 since usually mast and rigging is grounded and in direct contact with the bonded hull fittings and its zinc. You hold the copper electrode as shown, and touch the wire from the zinc to the boat instead. Now, instead of the zinc electrode, you will see the boat's zinc give a similar scale reading since that zinc impresses its stream

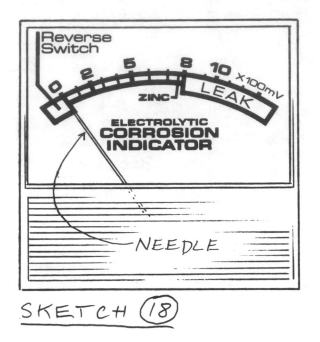

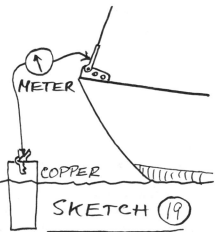

SKETCH 18

of electrons to all bonded fittings on the boat and the grounded rigging. Where there are no grounded fittings on deck (which you find easily by touch with the test wire in **Sketch 19**), the wire must be touched to a bonded hull fitting, the engine, or other metal part which is accessible below deck and is connected and protected by the zinc on the boat.

Low readings as in **Sketch 19** mean that the boat is at the level of the copper electrode and that there is no zinc on the boat, or the zinc is too small or too far away. In this case, you can verify that there is no zinc by using a zinc reference electrode on the meter. We have often used big galvanized nails for that purpose.

The meter will give no reading if: you have zinc on both test wires, a zinc reference versus a boat with zinc, or copper reference versus a boat of copper fittings but no zinc. In all these cases, the meter will give low readings, near or at zero.

The bronze fitting in **Sketch 20** will give a low reading, near zero with the boat's zinc intact and connected as shown. With a piece of copper as the meter electrode, the meter would show a reading near 8 and again show you that the boat's

SKETCH 19

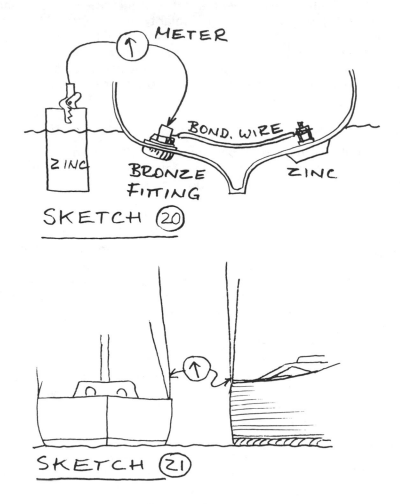

SKETCH 20

SKETCH 21

zinc is present and working. The same applies if you used the zinc electrode as in **Sketch 19**.

If the distance between boat's zinc and bronze fitting in **Sketch 20** were greater than shown here, the meter readings would increase with zinc attached to the meter wire, and decrease with copper on the meter wire: with less protection from the boat's zinc, the bronze fitting will be nearer the level of copper and increasingly different from the level of zinc. Compare this with the examples in the section on dissimilar metal electrolysis.

Before you measure between two boats as in **Sketch 21**, make sure that the two are not electrically interconnected, for example by the ground wires in dock power cords. Hold the meter wires to grounded shrouds or, if necessary, to boat's ground such as engine or propeller shaft or hull fittings bonding system. Meter readings will be similarly low if both boats have zincs working, or both have lost their zincs.

You can tell which is the case with a test as in **Sketch 19**. If the reading taken between the boats is high, note polarity or compare with the zinc-and-copper test which boat is "zinc" and which boat is "copper." If the two boats are electrically connected as by a shore power cord, the "copper" boat which has no zincs helps to consume the zinc of the "zinc" boat which apparently has working zincs which may then be insufficient and short lived.

Action?

If your propeller is in good shape after one or more seasons without zinc, then apparently no zinc is needed and you should keep an eye on any change of the boat's surroundings, dock or mooring, and the on-board electrical equipment. An occasional test for stray curents would be a good idea. If you routinely replace zincs on the hull during haulout, and the old zincs are normally quite corroded, you should probably run a zinc test as in **Sketch 19 or 20** during the second half of the zinc's expected life, to make certain that it did not lose electrical contact and become ineffective.

Stray current could easily help to consume a zinc much earlier than expected and stray current tests would give you peace of mind if nothing else. Boats in busy marinas will usually have the greatest problems, and stray current and electrical leaks which may change from day to day are likely. In all cases, new electrical equipment, changes in wiring or use of electricity should always be viewed as a possible new risk for electrolysis. With shore power on the boat, treatment of the ground wire deserves special attention, and inadvertent connections from electric water heaters through water lines to engine ground, from reverse polarity buzzers from neutral wire to boat's ground, from battery chargers to battery minus and boat's ground, from grounded housings of electrical appliances through conductive tubing of fastenings to boat's ground may all need inspection and help from a qualified electrician.

If you have measured an electrical current or the voltage or potential which would cause a current, you can usually take immediate steps to halt electrolytic corrosion. Any specific metal hull fitting can be protected with a piece of zinc fastened to a length of stainless steel wire and suspended over the side as in **Sketch 22**. The stainless wire, for example 1/16 inch stainless welding electrode wire, is soldered with plumbing solder and acid flux (because electric rosin core solder will not wet stainless steel) to a stranded copper wire, for example number 14

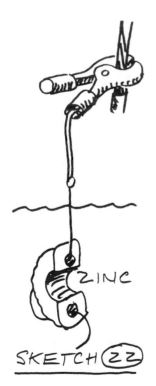

SKETCH 22

ZINC

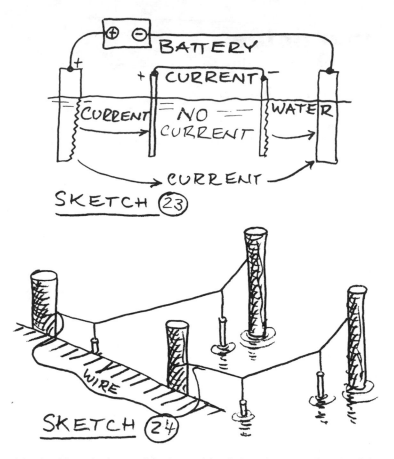

SKETCH 23

SKETCH 24

AWG with vinyl insulation, with the solder joint above water, and the copper wire electrically connected to that hull fitting. That may be as easy as clipping it to the nearest shroud or chain plate on deck as long as they are grounded (test with VOM Ohm meter).

With stray electric current, the damage is done to the zinc first, wherever it is located, and then to the fitting in the bonding system, or the end of the metal conductor corrodes and must be protected which becomes the minus end with conventional current flow, **Sketch 1** and **Sketch 23**. This again can be done with a zinc anode over the side near that fitting.

Alternately, in view of the possibly large amount of zinc consumed by such current, you can make a collector from pieces of steel rod, bar, pipe, or scrap which you position to collect stray current on one side of the boat and conduct to the other side. If things were as easy as in **Sketch 23**, all we had to do was short the battery with a wire directly. If your dock has steel pilings, you could ground more collecting rods to them. Otherwise, an arrangement as in **Sketch 24** might be best, rods or whatever metal is available suspended and interconnected with wire. Direct and alternating current could be collected except current between the bottom and the boat hull.

For your notes:

Lightning

Thunderstorms present us with extremes of voltage and current. Since on the boat we are unwillingly exposed to them, let us take a closer look and try to reduce the risks.

Books on meteorology can tell you how and when thunderstorm clouds will form, and how the energy in such cloud is used to generate separate poles of positive and negative electric charges as shown in **Sketch 1**. At any given time, an estimated 1000 to 2000 thunderstorms are in action, each lasts for about 15 to 30 minutes but in that time may grow to a height of six miles, over ten miles in the tropics.

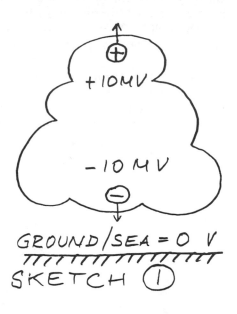

Rapid upward flow of air at speeds in excess of 100 knots is driven by differences in temperature and humidity, and is opposed by masses of precipitation, thousands of tons of water per thunderstorm cloud. Charges are separated when falling drops and ice crystals collect negative ions with preference. Positive and negative charge centers are formed with potentials in excess of ten million Volt. During its short life, a cloud may develop several such centers which lead to lightning strokes within the cloud.

If air were completely nonconductive, there possibly might be no lightning between cloud and ground. But the air contains ions which form from different molecules and have positive or negative charges. Such ions make air electrically conductive. Its resistance is high, about 4×10^{13} Ohm meters, but so are the voltages, and a thunderstorm is estimated to conduct a current of about one Ampere upward to the ionosphere which is kept at a high positive charge by thunderstorms.

Currents between thunderstorm cloud and ground or sea are also flowing when there is no lightning. Such current is carried by ions which are always present in any weather. With increasing field strength which is the voltage difference over a given distance, expressed for example in Volt per meter (V/m), more current is forced to flow which in turn creates new ions called corona ions. A more conductive path through the air is created which allows short bursts of very high current: lightning.

High Voltage

You may encounter relatively high electrostatic voltages quite regularly: in winter, walking across nylon carpeting, sparks from several thousand

Volt may jump from your hand to the next grounded door handle. Such charges can be demonstrated with two threads and a nail as in **Sketch 2**. Hold the nail by its plastic insulator and have someone else walk across such carpet, or rub any piece of plastic with a dry cloth, then touch to the tip of the nail. The threads will push away from each other because same charges, all plus or minus, repel each other and the loose ends of the two threads. Opposite charges, on the other hand, attract, and neutralize each other if allowed to travel in a conductor. The charges on two surfaces of a condenser, **Sketch 3**, hold each other in place unless the charge is so high, or the distance so low, that a spark jumps across.

In the thundercloud, **Sketch 4**, positive charges are at top, negative charges near the bottom except in the area of intense rain where the rain

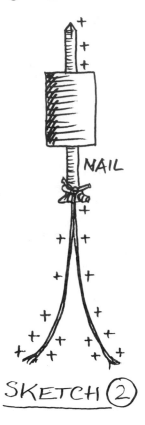

NAIL

SKETCH ②

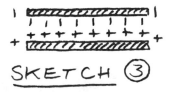

SKETCH ③

has created a downward flow of air. On the surface, the high potential at the bottom of the cloud accumulates charges of opposite sign as shown in the sketch, by attraction as in **Sketch 3**. With more than one positive and negative charge center in the cloud, and after lightning discharges between them within the cloud, both high negative and positive charges may face us under such cloud. The voltages of either polarity may reach 10,000 Volt per meter: this is the voltage between two points one meter or three feet above each other, a measure of "field strength."

Lightning

Under such conditions, lightning strokes between cloud and ground or sea are likely. From the relatively low currents which flow via the ever present ions in the air (3×10^{-13} Ampere per square foot), preferred paths are generated by discharges which proceed in steps, carry enough electricity to generate a more conductive path by greatly increasing the concentration of ions. These so-called leaders are normally not visible but may be heard. Though slow in comparison to subsequent strokes, leaders cover the distance between cloud and ground in a fraction of a second. Along this conductive, ionized path, several lightning strokes may follow in very rapid succession and in both directions, carrying either polarity. These main discharges are confined to an increasingly narrow path which, in spite of appearance, may only be a few inches wide.

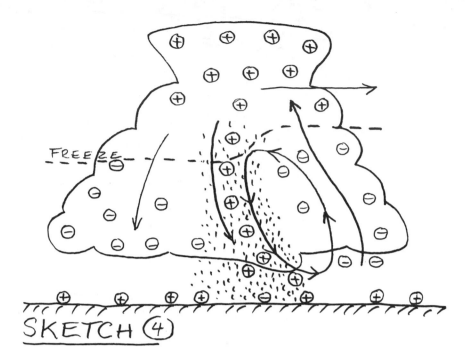

SKETCH (4)

And what appears to be a single stroke may actually be ten or more separate discharges. Currents may exceed 20,000 Ampere for very short fractions of a second. You know about the bright flashes and the sounds which take their time to reach you, since they may come from miles away, from the far end of the lightning stroke.

What To Do

First of all, try to get away. Reduce the likelihood of lightning striking your boat. At sea, you can make out individual clouds over distances of five to ten miles, while their life is limited to only about half an hour. Even if they drift at 30 knots which is probably rare, you can see some to windward which will have spent most of their power by the time they reach you, and you may be able to dodge some younger ones at least so that the center does not pass directly over your boat.

On inland waters, rivers, creeks, high shore lines will tend to attract lightning strikes, as will towers, bridges, large vessels, and boats with masts higher than yours. If you anchor in a creek near higher shore or trees as in **Sketch 5**, the extra height will make it easier for lightning to strike there by several hundred thousand Volts, not much considering the total voltage involved, but enough to change the probabilities. You will of course think about other aspects of safety and good seamanship, including the possibility of a tree being split and falling over.

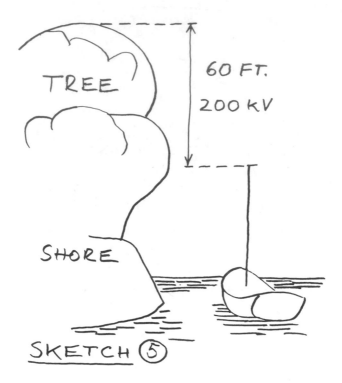

TREE

60 FT.
200 KV

SHORE

SKETCH ⑤

All trees and most solid objects will be better conductors than the air and will therefore be more likely struck than level ground, as will a person standing upright on level ground. Once hit, a tree, mast, or tower must distribute the electric current into ground which on land may make high currents flow horizontally at the surface when that is rain soaked and most conductive. In the water, this current will be greatest near the boat, **Sketch 6**, and in both cases extremely hazardous to a person flat on the ground or in the water.

On board the boat, make a survey of the major metal objects which are more than about a foot long, wide, or deep. Your mast and rigging will normally be grounded and may be tied to bonded through hull fittings: fine, more about that in a moment. But there are usually a number of large metal "conductors" on board which are not purposely connected to anything but which deserve attention.

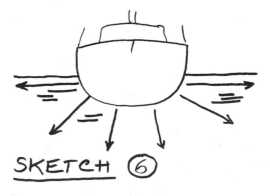

SKETCH ⑥

With a simple experiment you can demonstrate how a noncharged piece of material can become highly charged by being near another charge. If you rub a piece of plastic with a dry cloth, its end usually becomes charged with static electricity: very high voltage but no current. The charged end can attract or repel small bits of paper, dust, powders, and when you hold it near another piece of material "B" in **Sketch 7**, that piece develops the opposite charge on the nearby end, and the same charge at its far end as shown. In this case, piece "A" with plus charges attracts minus charges to the near of piece "B" so that there will be an excess of plus charges at the far end of "B." Thus in turn will affect another nearby piece "C." If the original charge or voltage of "A" was high enough, we can cause a spark between "B" and "C" without "A" touching "B" and without any spark between "A" and "B."

Now look around the boat, especially below deck, for conductive equivalents of A, B, and C. There are two reasons for this exercise: First, we want to know where in the boat there might be likely places for secondary sparks in the event of a lightning strike to the mast, or where there might be a buildup of voltage only, at places you should not touch while waiting out a thunderstorm below deck.

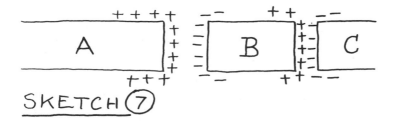

SKETCH 7

Then, some of these metal parts such as genoa tracks, metal cap rail moldings, copper tubing below the floor boards, could be incorporated into the already existing bonding system and grounded rigging to become something resembling a Faraday cage, **Sketch 8**, which in its most effective form is a sphere or round tube of metal which, when struck by lightning, conducts the charged voltage evenly around the surface. Since all surfaces are then charged alike, plus or minus whichever might be the case, there will be no field at the inside, and sparks cannot strike toward the inside since such charges repel each other.

Metal parts below deck might include genoa and toe rail tracks, other sheet travellers and tracks, spinnaker and reaching struts, whisker pole, pulpits, metal rub rails, life lines, boom gallows, jib boom, ground tackle, longer metal window frames, curtain tracks, heating stove and stove pipe, dodger frame, binnacle, pedestal, steering cables and mechanism, anchor windlass and supply cable, head and metal pipes, shower, sink, drain pipes, water system tubing, metal tanks and lines, autopilot motors, pumps, hydraulic lines, centerboard cable and winch, galley stove and fuel lines, pots and

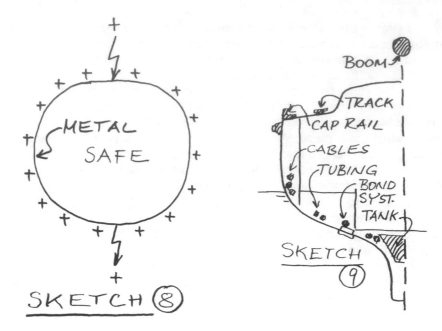

SKETCH ⑧

SKETCH ⑨

pans locker, refrigeration machine and tubing, spare anchor, tool boxes, water heater and tubing, engine room equipment and accessories.

Effort Versus Risk

Decide on a priority based on the weather in your area and the use of your boat and its risk of exposure to thunderstorms. Your actions may then range from doing nothing, to having a few cables with clips as in **Sketch 10** on hand for temporary interconnections when needed, to permanent connections between the best suited long metal parts on the boat.

Permanent connections can be made with battery cables or welding cables, copper tubing, or strips of sheet copper. Tubing makes a better conductor for this purpose than solid or stranded wire of the same area of copper cross section, **Sketch 11**, and copper sheet has the advantage of needing very little space when installed flat against the hull or deck.

The goal is to interconnect existing metal tracks, molding, tubing, at forward and aft ends and in between if practical, to create as complete a grid of conductors around a safe space, and to at least approach the protection afforded occupants in airplanes and cars by their metal enclosure. Large openings in the grid can sometimes be covered with a flat strip of sheet copper or a temporary cable with clips.

Ground

An adequate path to ground is absolutely necessary and is not related to the conductor grid of **Sketch 9** or the Faraday cage of **Sketch 8**. There

124

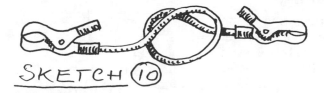

SKETCH (10)

must be a substantial conductor between the aluminum mast foot and the propeller. Such conductor will usually run below the cabin sole and in practice will connect mast foot or mast support pipe with engine block, **Sketch 12**. Such conductor is essential to avoid discharges jumping in unpredictable fashion through the cabin between the big lightning rod; the mast, and the biggest conductor in the water: the propeller. A heavy battery cable, large copper tube or sheet metal strip should easily find room under the floor. Similar connections are made to the through hull fittings which are all part of the grid in **Sketch 9**. Because of the substantial offset between mast foot and engine, additional grounding of the mast is highly desirable, by lengths of chain which can be stored very compactly in canvas bags and suspended over the side with a few feet in the water and one end hooked over a cleat on the mast or wrapped around fore stay, shrouds, and back stay. The better you provide such paths into the water, the less likely will lightning have to search for complicated, hazardous, and destructive paths to or from ground, and the better your peace of mind during a storm. Since the resistance of water including sea water is magnitudes greater than the mast and other metal conductors, there is bound to be a bottleneck in this path where current is first distributed into the nearest layers of water, compare **Sketch 6**.

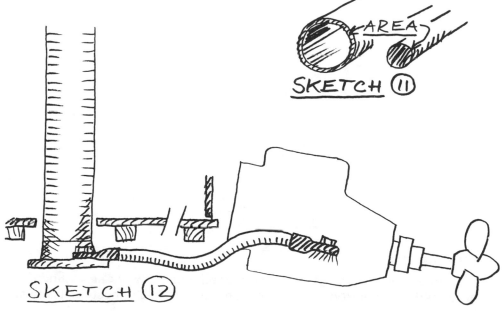

SKETCH (11)

SKETCH (12)

Electric Wiring

The electric wiring of the boat can become a part of the grid in **Sketch 9** even though 12 Volt or 110 V wires cannot be directly grounded. But during a lightning strike, these wires will assume the same momentary high voltage if there is a spark gap wide enough to prevent flow of the boat's working electricity but small enough to be easily jumped by the vastly higher voltages associated

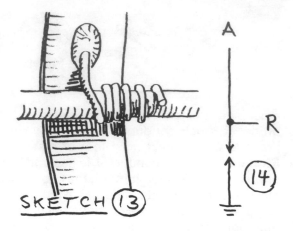

with lightning. Where 12 or 110 V wires cross copper bonding strips or grid connectors, attach a short solid copper wire of 10 or 12 gauge size and wrap it around the wire and its insulation as in **Sketch 13**. The insulation will then make the spark gap. Fittings are commercially available which accept antenna cables with PL-259 plugs, connect to radios and to ground via spark gap. Inside, **Sketch 14**, antenna A connects to radio at R, and to ground only with high voltage. A capacitor may be part of the R leg.

The 60° Cone

A cone of protection is often mentioned which covers areas under a grounded lightning rod such as an aluminum mast. On most boats, mast and rigging will easily cover people on deck under such imaginary cone whether measured from the horizontal or vertical. It is likely that mast and rigging will collect and ground any lightning before it can enter such cone. However, what about induced voltages as in **Sketch 7**? A helmsman, or anyone on deck **Sketch 15**, should not rely on protection from mast and rigging and should avoid contact with metal objects especially if they are not solidly grounded as discussed.

Damage to Electrical Equipment

Direct lightning strikes into the mast top will usually cause damage to electrical and electronic equipment even though the mast was perfectly grounded. Induced voltages will occur in all wires and other metal components on board, their magnitude will mainly depend on the length of wire and its orientation in the electrical field. Disconnecting antennas from receivers will eliminate one source of a voltage peak. For more complete protection, all wires probably must be disconnected, so that the unit only extends its one foot width or depth in any momentary electrostatic field.

For your notes:

Meters

The two most important electrical meters are ammeter and voltmeter, one measures current or rate of flow, the other potential or pressure. The two are designed similarly, usually have a coil which moves a needle, but have two very significant differences: voltmeters must have high internal resistance or a coil of very thin wire with many turns, **Sketch 1**, while ammeters must have low internal resistance, made with heavy conductors. There is a simple reason. To measure voltage, the voltmeter must be connected between plus and minus terminals of the battery or the circuit as shown in **Sketch 2**, and any current through the voltmeter is a drain on the battery.

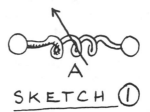

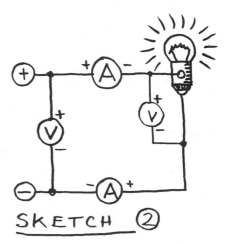

SKETCH ①

Voltmeters on the boat will have resistances ranging from a few hundred Ohm of relatively crude meters, to many thousand Ohm for better ones. All of them are designed to move their indicating needle with a minimum of current.

Ammeters on the other hand are installed directly in the current carrying wire, see **Sketch 2**: the current to the lamp must flow through the ammeter which will respond with a needle indication. In order to offer least resistance to the current, ammeters are designed to have the lowest possible resistance, to use just enough power in their coils to be able to move the indicating needles. Ammeters with a range to 10 A typically will have an internal resistance of a few thousandth of an Ohm, larger ranges will have even less resistance while ammeters with 1 A range or milliampere meters will have resistances near one Ohm.

SKETCH ②

If you connected a voltmeter in the place of the ammeter, in series with the "load," very little current could flow and the lamp in **Sketch 2** would remain dark. If you connected an ammeter in the place of the voltmeter, parallel to the load, massive current would flow through the ammeter, overheat it or blow a fuse.

Second Ammeter

To connect a second ammeter, choose any place in the wire to or from the load: current will be the same at all places except for the slight current through voltmeters. The new meter must have approximately the same range as the maximum current expected to flow. It may have a different Ampere range than the existing ammeter if that range is too high and that meter too insensitive to low currents. In practice, proceed as shown in **Sketch 3**. Ammeters have terminals with plus and minus notation: minus is the "downstream" terminal which will be at the same positive 12 Volt as the other terminal. Installing an ammeter in reverse will do no harm except that the needle will pull against the zero stop and give no reading.

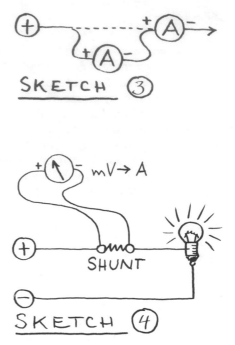

To measure relatively higher currents where the meter must be located some distance from the heavy wiring, a shunt type ammeter is used. The shunt, **Sketch 4**, is a carefully built resistor with a stable low Ohm value. When current flows, there will be a slight voltage drop at the resistor, compare examples in the Basic Electricity section. The two terminals of the shunt will have slightly different voltages, the difference is measured by the meter, a millivolt meter with its scale calibrated in Ampere, matched to the shunt. For example, if the shunt had a resistance of 1 Ohm, a current of 1 Ampere would cause a 1 Volt difference at the shunt which the meter would then measure.

Ammeter Improvements

Many Ampere meters (ammeters) have a range which covers a maximum current which only rarely occurs. They are then bound to be insensitive to low currents which you may wish to measure much more often. Ammeters on electric main panels often have 50 A ranges and are near useless when trying to measure current to an anchor light or cabin light. Such measurements can be improved if a second ammeter with lower range is installed, **Sketch 5**, and one or the other chosen with a SPST switch (single pole—single throw, see switches). To protect the new meter from higher currents when the switch is in the wrong position, connect a diode with, for example, 25 A rating parallel to the meter as in **Sketch 6**.

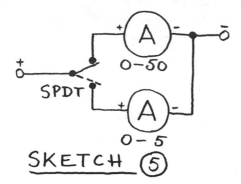

SKETCH 5

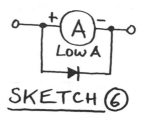

SKETCH 6

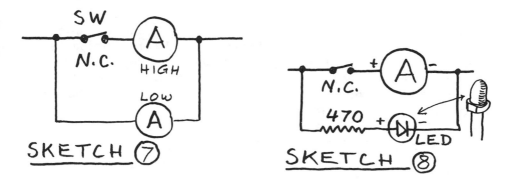

SKETCH 7

SKETCH 8

Another way to connect a low range ammeter or milliampere meter is shown in **Sketch 7** which uses a normally closed momentary switch. The old ammeter is always connected unless you want to check whether the anchor light is still on, or make sure all cabin lights have been switched off. To do that, you would push the button and get a reading on the low range meter.

All sketches show the connections in the style of wiring diagrams. Any connections of lines (wires) by dots (joints) would normally be made directly at the terminals of the switches and meters.

If you have an ammeter with relatively high range and want to be able only to check that no current flows when the meter needle is near zero, use the circuit in **Sketch 8**. Instead of an additional meter, you install a light emitting diode in a small hole next to the meter, connect it with a 470 Ohm, ½ Watt resistor as shown, and install the momentary push switch. The LED has its minus lead marked with a small flat area, observe its polarity, see details in the Lamp List. The LED will light if there is any current flowing.

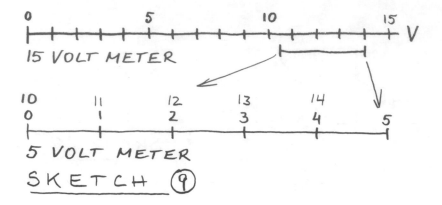

15 VOLT METER

5 VOLT METER

SKETCH ⑨

Voltmeters

Most voltmeters used on 12 Volt systems have scales similar to that in **Sketch 9**, with a range of 0-15 V. Voltages under 10 V are of no interest to us at all: if the battery is under 10 V, it is dead and we need not measure how dead. On the other hand, the voltage range between 11.5 and 14.0 is highly important, here are the measurements which tell us how the batteries are charged, how the alternator or battery charger is working, and how much electricity is left in the batteries. This range, unfortunately, is tiny on good meters with fine needles and scale markings, and obscure on most other meters. The expanded scale voltmeters on engine panels usually range from 8 to 16 V and use a spring to hold the needle back at low voltages. With their colored ranges, they pretend to give accurate information. Usually you can do better by watching the brightness of a cabin light.

Expanded Scale Voltmeter

You can expand the voltage range to a scale as in the lower part of **Sketch 9** by blocking a constant 10 Volt with electronic components, and measuring the excess above 10 Volt with a voltmeter with 0-5 V range. That meter would point to 1 V at 11V, 2 V at 12 V and so on. To make such meter, use the parts in **Sketch 10**. The voltmeter is connected in series with one zener diode which becomes conductive at its voltage rating V_z, for example 10 V. Additional silicon diodes in the forward direction as shown

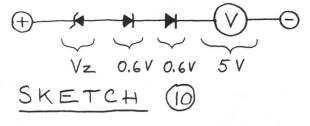

V_z 0.6 V   0.6 V   5 V

SKETCH ⑩

can be used to further increase the voltage blocked from the meter. Each silicon diode, for example type 1N4001, adds approximately 0.6 Volt. In this

132

way, meters with 0-3 V DC to 0-5 V DC range can be converted into meters which give the important voltage range from about 11.5 to 13.5 or somewhat wider with great resolution.

You could mark the voltage of your fully charged batteries on the meter, mark the voltage when batteries are full while the alternator is still charging, and decide on a low voltage for the empty point of the batteries.

Battery Charge Meter

Since the battery voltage gives an indication of the state of charge of each battery, a further improvement is a meter with a percent scale, to give direct readings of electricity in the batteries in % of full charge. Such meter must be calibrated to take the nonlinear discharge curves of lead acid batteries into account*. This and all other voltmeters are best installed with selector switches which connect the meter to individual batteries. The switches can be small since very little current is

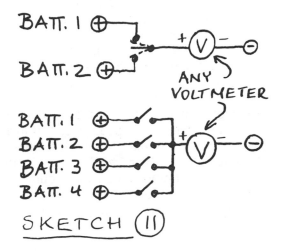

switched. For two batteries, a SPDT switch with center-off position will work. Normally open momentary push button switches or rotary switches can be used for greater numbers of batteries, **Sketch 11**.

To verify a single voltage, for example the half way mark when draining a battery, the fully charged voltage when using a manual alternator control, or to test the presence of other voltages as in batteries of portable equipment, connect a light emitting diode in series with a zener diode as in **Sketch 12**. Red and green LEDs use slightly different voltages, the following examples are for a green LED. A red LED will have all voltages lower by 0.2 V.

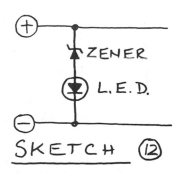

*Available from Weems & Plath, 222 Severn Ave., Annapolis MD 21403

With a zener diode 1N5237B of 8.2 V, the LED will light up above 10.4 V, with 1N5239B of 9.1 V above 11.3 V, with 1N5240B of 10 V at 12.7 V, with 1N4242B of 12 V at 13.2 V and so on. All zener diodes are rated 400mW, and both zener diode and LED must be connected with proper polarity.

Disadvantage of the circuit in **Sketch 12** is that voltages much higher than the turn-on voltage may cause excess current and eventually burn out the LED. A better circuit is that in **Sketch 13** which uses a small NPN transistor to turn on the LED. The 470 Ohm resistor limits LED current for use on 10 to 16 V. The other two resistors may be anywhere from 1.5 K to 5 k Ohm, their size and the zener voltage rating determine the voltage above which the LED will be on.

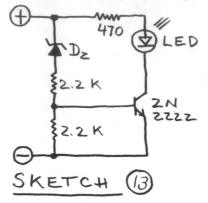

If a pilot or warning light is needed which goes on when voltage falls below a certain value, use the circuit in **Sketch 14**. At high voltages, the zener diode is conducting and the lower transistor will be on, connecting the base of the other transistor to ground so that it is off. When voltage falls, the zener diode stops conducting and the first transistor is turned off. Now, current through a 2.2 k resistor turns on the transistor on the right which allows current through the LED: it becomes bright.

Low Battery Alarm

To switch on greater loads or more power, for example a buzzer or bell, a transistor with greater wattage rating is needed, for example to make a

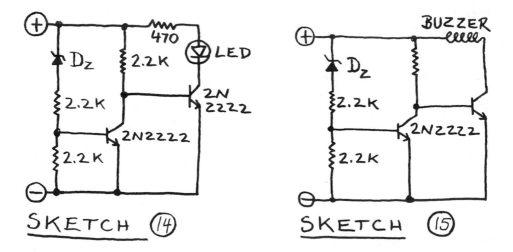

low battery alarm* as in **Sketch 15**. The circuit consists of the same zener diode and voltage divider, coupled to a small transistor such as the 2N2222 shown, or any of the many other small signal NPN types available. The other transistor must be able to handle the current of the buzzer or bell or horn which might be a few Ampere, the transistor then needs a rating of about 30 to 50 Watts. Since its base current may also have to be greater, the unspecified resistor in the sketch will be lower than before, between 1.5 k and 2.2 k Ohm. The buzzer will sound an alarm if, for example, the house battery is being deep cycled or discharged by the cabin lights while nobody pays any attention.

Low Battery Cutoff

SKETCH 16

One step further in this direction is a low battery cutoff in the form of a circuit breaker with a low voltage sensing trip mechanism, **Sketch 16**. This relatively drastic measure to prevent deep cycled batteries is more intended for charter boats where there is little time for instructions on battery management and less motivation to extend the life of the batteries. A pilot LED light is connected across the circuit breaker contacts as in **Sketch 8** which lights up to tell that the battery is now empty and the cutoff has been triggered.

An integrated circuit, Intersil ICM7201, **Sketch 17**, is offered as low battery voltage indicator. In addition to the LED light, it requires three external parts and offers some advantage over the other low voltage circuits described here. Other integrated circuits are available for interesting and very useful metering applications:

The next step above "analog" meters with scale and mechanical pointers are the bar graph meters which consist of a chain of LED lights. One integrated circuit of interest to serious experimenters is type LM3914 called bar graph driver. It is made as type NSM3914 on a small printed circuit board with ten small LEDs, **Sketch 18**, and with a few external parts can be made to display battery voltage. Its LEDs are very small, a version NSM39146 with yellow LEDs is somewhat more visible.

A battery charge meter with full sized red and green LEDs and calibrated directly in percent of battery charge is also being made, **Sketch 19**, next page.

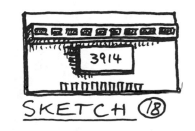

3914

SKETCH 18

---

*Available from Weems & Plath, 222 Severn Ave., Annapolis MD 21403

Digital Meters

Their great advantage is high resolution together with wide range. Other meters offer one or the other, never both. Digital meters can display differences of 1/10 Volt (or 1/100 Volt, not necessary) and cover a range much wider than the needed 0-15 Volt. There are several makes of so called digital panel meters on the market, as well as kits with parts and printed circuit board. The displays include the popular LED or light emitting diode displays which are usually red, fluorescent displays with blue-green digits as in some marine wind and speed instruments, and liquid crystal displays which appear to be gaining ground.

Digital panel meters are most often made for a 5 VDC supply voltage. Most of these meters have tabs on the edge

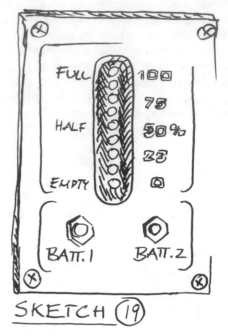

SKETCH (19)

of a printed circuit board, intended for edge connectors. For our applications, solder a type 7805 integrated circuit voltage regulator directly to the tab and to the boat's 12 V system. Noise from the alternator must be filtered, it will otherwise cause random numbers. You may connect the meter's input terminal to normally open push button switches or a rotary switch to measure the voltage of all batteries. **Sketch 20** shows a digital panel meter (DPM) with 3½ digits: The left digit can only be "1" or nothing. There are very few digital panel meters available with fewer than 3½ digits. Since application details vary between makes, all other installation details should be taken from the manufacturers instructions.

SKETCH 20

Engine Instruments and Alarms

There are mechanical oil pressure and temperature gauges: they are becoming rare. You can recognize them by the absence of electrical terminals at the back of the meter (except for electrical illumination), and by a stiff, wire-like tube connecting the gauge to a place on the engine.

Sketch 1 shows four types of sensors which are mounted directly on the engine, or on components near the engine. Note that "A" has two electrical terminals while the others have only one. All have pipe thread connections at base: normally ⅛ NPT for oil pressure switches A and B, and oil pressure gauge sensor or sender D. And ¼ NPT or bigger for temperature sensors as the one at C.

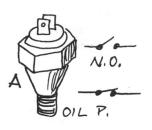

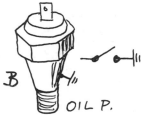

A: **Oil pressure switch,** is either the N.O. or normally open type (which closes contacts only with applied pressure), or the N.C., normally closed type (which opens contacts with applied pressure). Trouble shooting, measure with VOM low ohm range: with wires taken off, both terminals have high ohm (100 K or better) to ground, regardless whether N.O. or N.C. type.

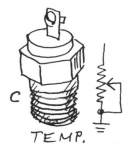

B: **Has only one terminal at top**. The switch housing is the other terminal. This switch also may be N.O. or N.C. type, but most frequent is the N.C. type which opens contact when pressure is applied.

Pressure ratings: switches are used in lube oil and fuel system, and the pressure, in PSI, at which the switch reacts, may range from 2 to 6 PSI for fuel pressure switches, to 10 to over 50 PSI for oil pressure switches.

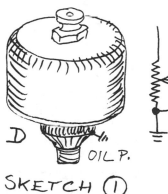

SKETCH ①

Trouble shooting for type B: with VOM at low ohm setting, no intermediate ohm readings between terminal and ground: meter to read either less than one ohm (difficult to distinguish on some meters) or more than 10 K (10 kilo Ohm = 10,000 Ohm). Readings of 100 to 1000 Ohm probably indicate a faulty switch.

C: **Temperature sensor:** a variable resistor or "thermistor" reacts to change in temperature by changing resistance. Shape may vary. Wire connects directly to temperature gauge, see wiring example. Trouble shooting: with wire off and engine cool, VOM meter will show 100 to 5000 Ohm, but never less than 50, or more than 10K Ohm.

D: **Pressure sensor:** often with relatively large body, with plastic or rubber boot. Single contact, with wire directly to oil pressure gauge. Internal variable resistor reacts to change in pressure. Trouble shooting, in operation, should have about 12 V between terminal and ground. With wire off, engine off, should have neither zero nor infinite Ohms, but some value between 50 and 10K Ohm. See example about further testing.

Oil Pressure Alarms: If your system has an engine key switch, or a switch on the main panel for ENGINE, then this switch will very likely activate the engine oil pressure alarm. It will probably also switch power to the engine instruments and to the alternator (field and reg-

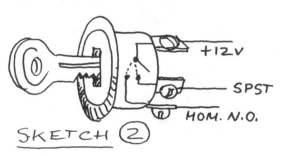

ulator). If you do not have such a switch, and can start the engine as long as the battery main switch is on for starting power, then a type A pressure switch, with two terminals, probably in the fuel system, powers the alarm. Or you may have both, as in **Sketch 3**:

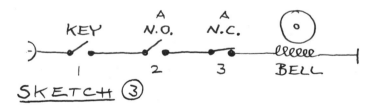

Switch (1) is closed with the key. Switch (2) closes with the first few turns of the engine and connects to switch (3) which is in the oil system and still closed, so that the bell rings. Then, as oil pressure builds up, switch (3) is opened and disconnects the bell. Lack of fuel pressure would stop the engine, lack of oil pressure would ring the alarm. To test, turn key on, measure 12 V at one terminal of switch (2) but not on the other. Bridge the terminals to make the bell ring. If it does not, bring a wire with 12V to +Bell to make it ring (Bell is ok, switch (3) is not).

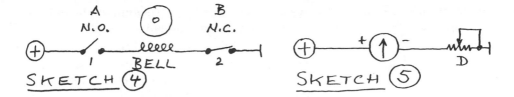

SKETCH 4

SKETCH 5

The alarm circuit in **Sketch 4** is slightly different: switch (1) could be a type A fuel pressure switch or a key switch. With the engine running, power reaches +BELL, the bell rings until oil pressure builds up and opens the N.C. oil pressure switch (2) which interrupts the bell ground wire. To test this circuit, the VOM meter, on low range Ohm, will show high Ohm to ground at both sides of the bell. With engine off, but switch (1) closed by key or by bridging the switch terminals, bell should ring. If it does not, but +12V, measured against engine ground, show at both + and − terminals of the bell: switch (2) is faulty. Bridge its terminal to ground, to ring the bell and to prove the point.

Electric Oil Pressure Gauge: The most common arrangement is shown in **Sketch 5**. Power is switched to the + side of the gauge by instruments switch. A wire connects from the other gauge terminal to the sensor at the engine. With oil pressure, the sensor will vary its internal resistance and allow current to flow to ground. The meter, responding to current, will point to the corresponding PSI values on its scale. In troubleshooting, you want to find out first whether gauge or sender are at fault.

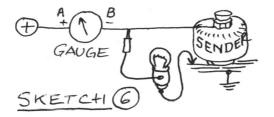

GAUGE

SENDER

SKETCH 6

Test the gauge: With VOM or trouble shooting light (shown **Sketch 6**) make sure that you have +12 V at A at the gauge, otherwise fault is elsewhere upstream in the wiring. At B, the other terminal, you should also have 12 V since the meter is basically a milliampere meter, with low internal resistance. If you touch the trouble shooting light to B, the meter needle should change reading: probably it will show full scale, indicating the current which flows through the test light to ground: touch only very briefly, and don't connect point B to ground directly since that will ruin the gauge. Also, the test light probably will not light up between point B and ground. But if the meter needle moves, the gauge should be all right.

The sensor: disconnect the wire, with instrument power off, and measure Ohms between sensor (sender) terminal and ground, VOM meter at low Ohm range. The reading should be greater than about 100 Ohm, but not infinitely high, to indicate a functioning sensor. If practical, leave the

VOM securely connected and measure resistance, in Ohm, while starting the engine. A distinct decrease in Ohm, measured with wire off, between sensor terminal and ground, indicates that sensor is all right.

Electric Temperature Gauge: Wiring schematic as in **Sketch 5**, except the sensor looks like C, page 137, with bigger threaded base than the oil pressure sensor D. Sensor C will be mounted somewhere on the engine cylinder head or upper (hot) part of the block, where water cooling passages are nearby inside. With test light or Volt-Ohm Meter (VOM) you can search for trouble as with the oil pressure gauge. With the test light, **Sketch 6**, enough current will flow from point B through the light to ground to make the gauge change its reading, although not enough current to actually make the test light shine. When you use the VOM meter, set to read DC Volt, you should measure 12V between point B and ground. But since the VOM has high internal resistance, much higher than the test light, not enough current flows through the VOM to make the gauge register any change.

To test the temperature gauge sensor, disconnect the wire from it (do not let it touch ground) and measure, with the VOM set to low range Ohm, from sensor terminal to engine ground or sensor body. You can do this first with engine cold, and again, with engine hot but shut down. Working sensor should show significant difference in Ohm, hot versus cold.

Water Temperature and Oil Pressure Alarm: To warn you about high water temperature, a normally open (N.O.) water temperature switch closes contacts when temperature gets too high. The oil pressure alarm switch is a normally closed (N.C.) switch which is opened by the oil pressure but closes contacts when oil pressure drops. In **Sketch 7**, two such switches are shown, connected at right to a 12V bell (plus 12V coming from the switches, a connection to GROUND is shown at the right side of the bell: compare wiring diagram symbols, elsewhere in this text).

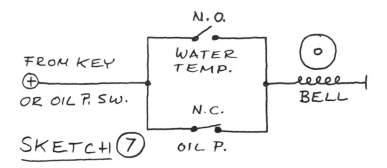

Since the alarm has to be switched *off* when the engine is off (otherwise the bell would ring since oil pressure is down), but has to be switched on reliably every time the engine is *on,* the safest two methods are key- or fuel pressure switches, as shown. With gas engines, the ignition key or ignition switch is a good source of power for the alarm. Some diesel engines also have an "ignition" key which has to be switched on for instruments and alternator. This, too, would be a reliable source of 12V power for the alarm.

Some diesel engines only require the battery main switch to be on (for starter motor electricity) which may remain on after the engine has been stopped. Here, a pressure switch in the fuel system, with N.O. contacts, sketch A, is used: Fuel pressure closes the contacts and supplies power to the alarm circuit, and the bell may ring until oil pressure has built up to open the oil pressure alarm switch.

To identify your alarm system, you may see the fuel- and oil pressure switches in the engine wiring diagram, or you may be able to distinguish by the performance: power from fuel pressure switch will make the alarm bell ring just when the engine is first being turned over. Complication: if your engine has an electric fuel pump, fuel pressure would build up before the starter turns the engine over.

To make an engine alarm, first search for (or ask engine man for location of) oil pressure connections or the oil pressure gauge sender (looks like D on page 137), and a plug on the cylinder head which can be replaced by a temperature switch. Oil pressure connections are most often ⅛ inch pipe thread (⅛ NPT), you may need a short nipple, a T fitting, and the new oil pressure switch, to connect to the engine where the oil pressure sender was, see **Sketch 8**. Then use a bell, a beeper or other sound or light device, or both.

Also see the bilge alarm, which can be added to the engine alarm.

For your notes:

Low Ohm Meter

You have probably noticed that the usual volt ohm meter (VOM) can not measure low resistances even on its lowest Ohm range: values under ten Ohm all look alike. It is useful though to be able to measure low resistances such as the alternator field coil, regulator resistances, terminal connections, switch contact resistance, wire continuity et cetera. The circuit in **Sketch 1** is a low ohm meter which you can make from a DC voltmeter and some small parts.

You can choose the scale range which will have its values distributed as in **Sketch 2** which has a mid scale value of 3 Ohm. Some examples for meters with different internal resistances and for several mid scale values are given further down.

Most voltmeters have an internal resistance of 50 or 100 Ohm, one sold by an electronics chain store is identified as 85 Ohm.* You can measure the meter resistance with a VOM. Then decide on the desired scale and select the shunt resistor R which in most cases will have to be made up from two parallel standard resistors. The switch is essential because the meter uses considerable battery power while it is on. One of the 100 Ohm resistors is variable as zero adjustment.

Table 1 gives some examples for meters with 50, 85, or 100 Ohm, mid scale values of 3, 6, and 10 Ohm, and the necessary values for "R" which you make up from the standard resistors shown there, all ½ Watt.

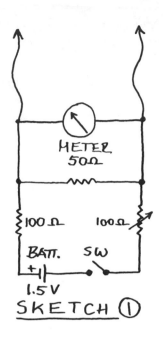

SKETCH ①

SKETCH ②

---

*Radio Shack Panel Meter No. 270-1754

Table 1
Values for Shunt Resistor in Low Ohm Meter

Meter internal resistance, Ohm	Mid Scale Value, Ohm	Shunt Resistor, Ohm	Make from: Ohm
50	3	3.19	3.9 and 18
50	6	6.8	6.8 (standard)
50	10	12.5	18 and 39
85	3	3.11	4.7 and 10
85	6	6.46	6.8 and 120
85	10	11.33	18 and 33
100	3	3.09	6.8 and 5.6
100	6	6.38	6.8 and 100
100	10	11.11	18 and 27

Calibrating resistance of 3 Ohm: connect in parallel as in **Sketch 3** one standard resistor each of 3.9, 18, and 47 Ohm. Other calibrations: use measured lengths of wire and calculate its resistance from these values:

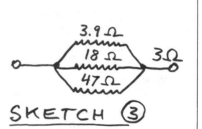

SKETCH 3

Iron: steel

Size, AWG	16	18	20	22
Ohm per foot	0.0233	0.0370	0.0589	0.0936

Brass

Size, AWG	18	20	22	24	26
Ohm per foot	0.0259	0.0412	0.0655	0.104	0.166

Copper

Size, AWG	18	20	22	24	26
Ohm per ft.	0.0064	0.0101	0.0161	0.0257	0.0408

Battery Capacity Meter, Ampere Hour Meter

Our only knowledge of battery capacity normally is the manufacturer's specification in Ampere hours (Ah) for the new battery, or "Cold Cranking Amps" which can be converted to Ah, see section on batteries. But battery capacity measurements give different results if carried out at different rates and to different voltage end points, and the battery capacity decreases with age of the battery. It is therefore desireable to measure the Ampere hours which a battery can supply, and to repeat the same measurement after a season or more to determine how battery capacity has been lost, to predict the probable life of a battery.

Battery capacity meters are routinely used by battery manufacturers but have not been available in simple versions for use on board. The capacity meter in **Sketch 1** is connected to a fully charged battery, is then switched on, consuming current from the battery and measuring time with an hour meter. The internal circuit is shown in **Sketch 2**: it holds the contact of a relay closed until the battery voltage has fallen to a predetermined value, the end point. At that time, the relay opens, current flow stops as does the hour meter. The battery capacity is the hour meter reading multiplied by the current in Ampere, to give Ampere hours (Ah).

You could make a similar measurement with a resistor, by watching voltmeter and time, and switching the test off at the voltage end point. This usually is impractical, a waste of manpower, and the end point unreliable. The meter will perform the test automatically, and the reading can be taken

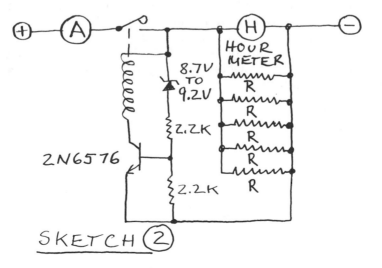

SKETCH 2

the next day or weekend whenever convenient. The meter is designed not to deep cycle or deep discharge the battery during the test.

The circuit senses the battery voltage with a zener diode. At the end point it switches off the transistor so that the relay contacts open. The transistor is a Darlington NPN power transistor. In its place, many other NPN power transistors with a small signal NPN transistor in Darlington circuit will work as well, **Sketch 3**. The power resistors "R" should draw ten, twenty, or thirty Ampere and must have a sufficient wattage rating to avoid excess heat. For example, a 3 Ohm power resistor would draw about 4 A and generate 48 Watts of heat, it should have a 50 W minimum rating. Five of them in parallel would draw 20 A.

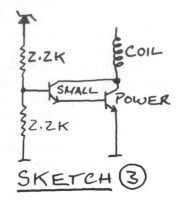

The 8.7 V zener diode will result in an end point voltage of 10.5 V, a zener diode of 9.2 V will increase the endpoint to 11.8 V. With high test currents (20 A or more), the end point may be chosen lower because the battery voltage will recover once the meter has switched off. With low test currents, the end point voltage should be higher (11.8 V) to avoid deep cycling and the associated damage to the battery.

Once you have assembled the meter, it will perform the same test with constant end point and rate, and will give you comparable results of battery capacity and change of capacity over the years. All you have to remember is to take hour meter reading before and after each test, and to keep a record.

Refinements can be made by installing a switch between two groups of power resistors to have a high and low test current range, or a "start" push switch parallel to the transistor, to first close the relay. The transistor should be protected against reverse voltage peaks by a diode parallel to the transistor and with its anode at the minus terminal. Copper battery clips are handy to connect the test wires to the battery posts.

Before each test, the battery must be fully charged, for example by battery charger which is left connected over night, or until all cells are gently fizzing with gas bubbles.

Alternators

A very simple alternator is shown in **Sketch 1**. If you held a voltmeter to the ends of the coil of wire and pulled the permanent magnet away, the meter needle would move. If you brought the magnet back, the needle would move again, but in the opposite direction. To make a working alternator out of it, we could fasten the magnet to a shaft and rotate it, or rotate the coil. Both methods are used in practice, and the only important detail is that the magnet poles at the ends of the coil must change. With any change, for example from North to South at the upper

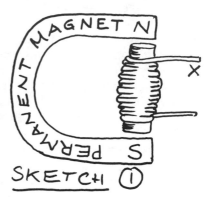

end in the sketch, a pulse of electricity is generated during the change. The design can be improved by bigger and stronger magnets and coils. More turns of wire will generate higher voltages, thicker wire greater current. The gap between the rotating part called the rotor, and the stationary part called the stator can be made very small and the parts rounded as in **Sketch 2**, and the speed made as high as practical so that there will be many changes of poles at the coil and many pulses of voltage and current. Coils are wound on soft iron which is able to collect the magnet's field. Usually thin sheets of iron are used, to reduce currents in the iron which would generate heat.

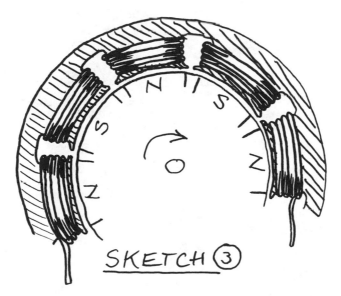

Another improvement is used in bicycle dynamos which have a permanent magnet with four poles instead of two, so four impulses are generated with each turn of the coil. A disadvantage is that moving contacts, wipers, or brushes are needed to make contact with the wires of the rotating coil. In larger alternators, this is avoided by rotating the magnet, and keeping the coil stationary which can then be made to consist of many individual coils as in **Sketch 3**. And the rotor in the alternator on your engine probably has at least eight, probably ten, twelve, or fourteen magnet poles: half of them North poles, the other half South poles. **Sketch 4**.

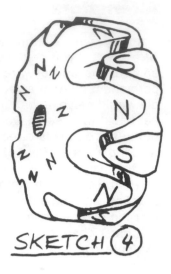

SKETCH 4

A complication arises from the need to reduce the alternator output when batteries are fully charged, no more electricity needed, but the engine still running. Instead of permanent magnets, our alternators use an electromagnet. Rotors are made from two soft iron pieces with star like shapes which form the North and South poles of the rotor. A coil between the two makes them more or less magnetic when direct current flows through this "field coil," **Sketch 5**. To get the "field current" to the coil, most alternators use two carbon brushes and two slip rings, made from copper and connected with the ends of the field coil wire.

Another complication has to do with the alternating current which alternators normally generate. Since we need direct current to charge batteries, the alternating pulses from the coils must be rectified. Silicon rectifying diodes are used, mounted in the alternator housing, and only the plus and

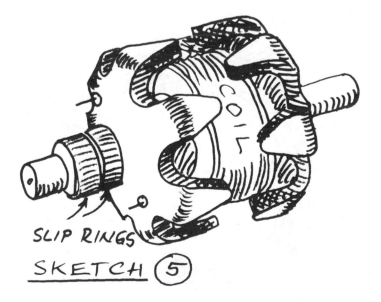

SLIP RINGS

SKETCH 5

STATOR CORE

COIL

POLE PIECES

SKETCH 6

minus terminals of the rectified current are brought to the outside. Most alternators have the minus pole connected to the aluminum housing, and have an insulated terminal as plus pole.

The stator is made from laminated layers of sheet iron, riveted together and partly visible like an equatoror between the aluminum housing halves of the alternator.

The space for the stator windings is limited: the coils must be close to the rotor's North and South poles, must have enough turns of wire to generate high enough voltge, and heavy enough wire to allow high current. Alternators therefore use several coils in series, each with only a few turns, but the total great enough for the needed voltage. Then there is enough space for more wire, on the iron pole pieces as in **Sketch 6**. There are three groups of coils, each acting like one separate coil, the turns always made around three pole pieces. Each group is offset from the next by one pole piece and the output pulses will come one after another, as North and South poles pass by.

With three groups of generating coils at the stator, the alternator is generating three separate "phases" which must be rectified separately. If you took each group off and layed it out flat, the pattern would be as in **Sketch 7**, each offset from the next by one pole piece, and within a group, each coil three pieces from the next. Note that the wire turns change direction: as one individual coil faces a North pole, the next will face a South pole, the generated pulses have opposite polarity. To have all individual coils in a group push in the same direction at the same time, turns must change left, right, left as shown. In some alternators this problem is solved by skipping pole pieces as in **Sketch 8** and winding more turns, all in the same direction.

149

SKETCH ⑦

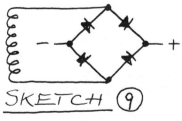

SKETCH ⑨

You can usually see the windings of the stator, made with magnet wire of copper with lacquer insulation. The individual coils in **Sketch 7** have about seven turns of wire each.

To rectify the pulses of each of the coils with a bridge rectifier, **Sketch 9**, would require a total of twelve diodes. Instead, the three stator coils are interconnected as in **Sketch 10**, one arrangement being called "Y" or "wye", the other "Delta" for obvious reasons. Each of three terminals are connected to positive and negative terminal by silicon diodes. As you can see, three diodes have their anodes connected to the minus terminal and three their cathode to the plus terminal. The two kinds of diodes used in alternators are shown in **Sketch 11**: the one on the left is called "cathode base," the other "anode base," and there are three of each, press fitted into an aluminum bar which is part of the positive output terminal, and directly into the alternator housing which then serves as negative terminal.

In order to make the rotor magnetic, some field current must flow through the field coil which is part of the rotor. Field coils normally have resistances ranging from two to five Ohm, and full 12 Volt would make more field current flow than is necessary. To regulate alternator output current, a so-called voltage regulator is used which, in spite of its name, regulates output current, a function of voltage and resistance. Before we look at different makes and models of alternators, we should distinguish between certain groups:

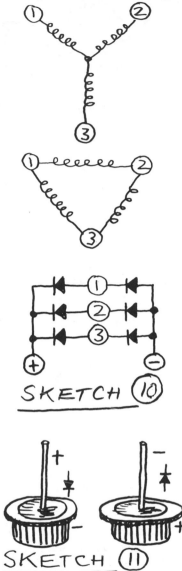

SKETCH ⑩

SKETCH ⑪

There are alternators which have a regulator built into, or fastened directly on to the alternator itself, while other alternators have a remote regulator, connected by wires, **Sketch 12**. The voltage regulator is connected to the alternator field coil: it supplies the field current. The arrangement of voltage regulator and field coil can be in two different ways, **Sketch 13**, with the regulator either between plus 12 Volt and field coil, or between field coil and ground. Whether the voltage regulator is mechanical, with one or more relays, or transistorized or solid state is of minor importance. Internal regulators are the solid state type. Some alternators are designated "Marine

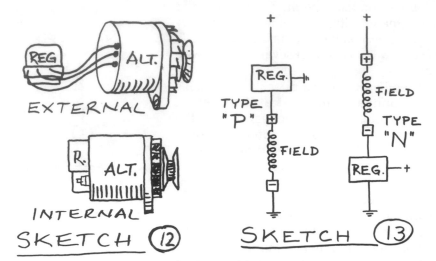

EXTERNAL

INTERNAL

SKETCH ⑫

TYPE "P"

REG.

FIELD

TYPE "N"

FIELD

REG.

SKETCH ⑬

Alternators'' and have the slip ring and brushes of the outside of the rear bearing, within a metal housing, and are thus less likely to ignite gasoline fumes. On boats with gas engines or other fire risks, such alternators should be retained or replaced with similar designs. **Table 1** shows some of the

Table 1
Groups of Alternators with Different Voltage Regulators and Field Coil Arrangements, and Methods of Regulator or Field Coil Supply.*

	From + 12 Volt to Voltage Regulator to Field Coil to Ground (Type P)	From + 12 Volt to Field Coil to Voltage Regulator to Ground (Type N)
External Regulator	A Most common	C Very rare
Attached Regulator	B Motorola, becoming less common	D Motorola and others, becoming common
Internal Regulators	Probably nonexistent	Almost standard
Regulator supplied from 12 V System by switch (key switch)	was standard in older designs	Probably nonexistent
Regulator supplied directly from plus rectifiers, with isolating diode(s)	Motorola, to about 55 A max., becoming rare	Probably nonexistent
Regulator or Field supplied from extra set of rect. diodes called ''diode trio''	Rare	Almost standard

*For details see ''The 12 Volt Doctor's Alternator Book''

combinations and serves as a reference to help describe any given alternator.

Most of the early alternators were of type A, still the most popular on automobiles, least expensive, easiest to repair, easiest to connect to a manual regulator. Type B and D with internal regulators are quite common on marine engines, probably because of ease of installation by the engine manufacturer. Many Motorola alternators are type B although there are also many Motorola type A and few type D alternators, and Delcotron and most Hitachi alternators are examples of type D.

Main function of the voltage regulators is to adjust the field current in response to the voltage of battery and electric system. All regulators must have a plus and ground terminal as in **Sketch 14**, and a field terminal F: this either supplies positive field current or "sinks" negative field coil terminal to ground, the two alternatives in **Sketch 13**. Voltage regulators typically reduce field current when a particular voltage is reached, usually near 14 Volt. Directly after starting the engine, the battery voltage will be relatively low and the voltage regulator therefore will supply greater field current to the alternator which in turn will generate higher output current. As this current is charged to the batteries, their voltage rises rapidly: current can only flow into a battery if a voltage greater than that of the battery is applied. You will therefore see that ammeter readings will be high right after starting the engine, but will drop considerably soon afterwards. This creates a problem where batteries must be charged within limited lengths of engine running time. Solutions are offered in this section.

The voltage regulator performs another function with elegance: while engine and alternator are running, any change in current being consumed causes an immediate response by the regulator which changes alternator output current accordingly. In a car, for example, you may switch the headlights on, draw an extra ten or more Ampere without any strain on the battery: the voltage regulator responds to the slight change in voltage, and the alternator is made to take on the extra load and generate extra current. On the boat, this of course only applies while the engine is running.

The voltage which the regulator is designed to maintain, usually slightly above 14 Volt, can be adjusted. How that can be done with mechanical and solid state regulators will follow. Since the setting will affect battery charging and may overcharge during long engine runs, the setting should not be increased to accelerate battery charging: there are better ways to accomplish that. The regulator setting should cause the alternator output current, the ammeter reading, to fall to near zero when batteries are fully charged during long engine running, where batteries barely begin to develop gas bubbles. Compare details in the section on batteries.

Voltage regulators may have more than the terminals shown in **Sketch 14**. There may be an additional terminal connected to 12 Volt for the power supplied as field current, or a terminal for an "idiot light" or alternator pilot light or charging indicator light.

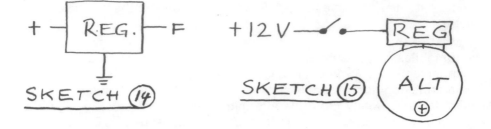

SKETCH ⑭

SKETCH ⑮

All alternators fall into one of three groups depending on the method of electric supply to the regulator and field as indicated in **Table 1**. One group takes the electricity from a key switch, oil or fuel pressure switch or other switch in the 12 Volt system, **Sketch 15**. The switch is necessary to switch off alternator field current when the engine is not running, to prevent waste of electricity.

Alternators with a set of auxiliary diodes as in **Sketch 16** use extra rectifiers, connected to the same points "1," "2," and "3" of the stator coils as the main rectifying diodes. When engine and alternator have been stopped, no more power is generated and the auxiliary terminal will no longer supply current to the regulator. Therefore, no switch is needed.

The arrangement in **Sketch 17** also does not need a switch. Here, power for the regulator is taken from the main positive rectifying diodes, at a point "X" which is separated from the main plus output terminal by another diode called isolating diode. Although the main plus terminal will be at 12 Volt even when the engine is not running, power will not reach point "X" because the isolating diode will not conduct in that direction. Alternators with internal regulators often use auxiliary diodes as in **Sketch 16** (Delco, Bosch, Hitachi) or isolating diodes as in **Sketch 17** (Motorola).

Many alternators have a terminal which supplies alternating current impulses to a tachometer. The terminal is usually identified as AC tap and is connected to one of the stator coil terminals. Since the AC frequency or

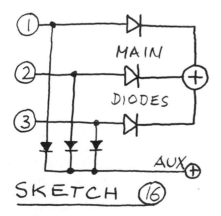

SKETCH ⑯

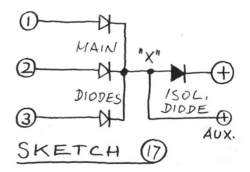

SKETCH ⑰

number of pulses per second is directly proportional to the speed of the alternator, electronic tachometers can convert this frequency to engine RPM. Once calibrated, the pulley ratio and the much faster alternator RPM is taken into account. If you see your tachometer needle show unusual changes in speed, a slipping alternator belt likely is the cause.

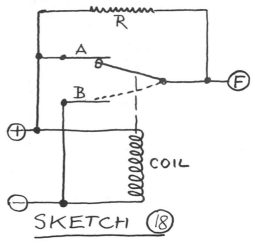

SKETCH (18)

A mechanical voltage regulator schematic is shown in **Sketch 18**. It consists of a single pole—double throw (see section on switches) relay and a fixed resistor R of a few Ohm, high wattage. The relay normally makes contact at "A" and is held there by spring tension. With increasing voltage, the coil becomes more magnetic and pulls, to make contact at "B." While at "A," full positive voltage is applied to field terminal "F." When at "B," the field terminal is grounded, alternator output falls, relay coil releases, opens contact "B," and field current is applied again. This sequence repeats itself rapidly, and in practice the relay contact vibrates between "A" and "B." Since only part of the field current flows through the contacts (some is supplied through the resistor), such regulators will operate for many thousand operating hours, are rugged, easily diagnosed and repaired. Contacts can be cleaned with number 600 silicon carbide wet sand paper, pulled between contacts with light pressure on contacts. Voltage setting is adjusted by spring tension: higher spring tension tends to keep contact "A" closed longer which increases voltage setting. Function may be tested by gentle force on the contact arm while the alternator is running. The ammeter will respond with large changes in output current. Fusible wires are often used to make connections within the regulator. If one of these has melted, you will see the leftovers. In an emergency, replace it with a strand of copper wire of similar thickness. Cause of wire melting may be large battery capacity at low charge, connected to alternator running at high speed and producing unusually high charging current.

Sketch 19 shows a solid state regulator of a Delco type D (Table 1) alternator, the type with regulator between field coil and ground. Terminal "2" senses voltage and the zener diode D_z becomes conductive at the critical voltage setting, makes the base of the NPN transistor Q_1 more positive so that this transistor begins to conduct: it allows all current from terminal "1" through resistor R_3 to flow to ground. This keeps base current from power transistor Q_2 which becomes nonconductive: it stops field current. As the alternator output drops and voltage at terminal "2" decreases, base current to transistor Q_1 stops, this transistor ceases to conduct, and

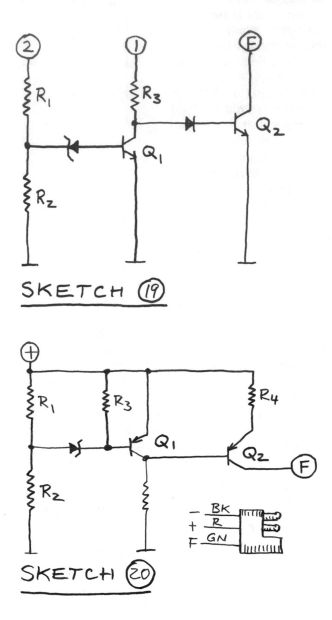

SKETCH ⑲

SKETCH ⑳

current through resistor R_3 again reaches the base of power transistor Q_2 and makes it conductive: field current flows again. Regulators like this are molded of plastic and mounted in the rear alternator housing. Terminals "1" and "2" are metal tabs which extend through the alternator housing. If less than full voltage reaches terminal "2," the regulator will react with increased field current flow and higher output current as the normal function of the regulator is defeated. Internal regulators in other type D alternators use very similar circuits.

A solid state voltage regulator for type A and B alternators (**Table 1**) is shown in schematic **Sketch 20**. Field current flows from the plus terminal through resistor R_4, PNP type power transistor Q_2 to terminal "F," alternator field coil to ground. When voltage increases, the zener diode becomes conductive the base of transistor Q_1 becomes more negative and the transistor is turned on: it conducts between positive terminal and the base of power transistor Q_2 which is thus turned off and interrupts field current. As with all regulators, the subsequent slight voltage drop at the plus terminal causes field current to be turned on again and the process repeats itself in rapid succession.

Solid state voltage regulators sometimes incorporate a variable resistor in parallel to, or in place of resistors R_1 or R_2 in **Sketch 19** and **20** which allow an adjustment of the voltage setting. Also, a thermistor is incorporated in the circuit which compensates for changes in the operating temperature. (A thermistor is a resistor which changes its resistance with temperature.) All solid state regulators must be protected with a diode as in **Sketch 21** which protects the transistors from inductive reverse voltage when field current is switched off. Also see the comments on page 178.

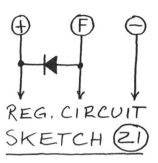

REG. CIRCUIT
SKETCH (21)

How Well Is Your Alternator Doing?

We have seen how the voltage regulators control the output current of the alternator by sensing voltage. In order to charge a battery, the alternator must apply greater voltage than that of the battery. Only then will there be current from the alternator into the battery. Even if your boat has a fifty, sixty, or even eighty amp alternator, its voltage regulator will prevent even modestly high charging rates except during the first few minutes after starting the engine. Even though alternator and regulator respond beautifully to any current drawn while the alternator is running, charging the batteries *now,* for currents to be drawn *later* is a problem.

Sketch 22 shows a plot of ammeter readings taken for an hour after starting the engine. If your boat has an ammeter, even the hard-to-read 60-0-60 A type where the needle is five amps wide and never at zero, watch it immediately after starting, during the first few minutes, then take a look every ten minutes or so, and plot the readings on quadrilled paper.

The daily current consumption on your boat, away from the dock, may be as little as 20 Ampere hours, or as high as 80 Ampere hours. Regardless of the size or capacity of your batteries, these daily Ampere hours (Ah) will

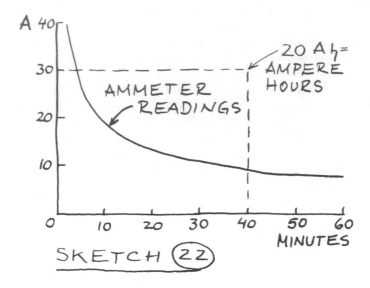

SKETCH 22

have to be regenerated and recharged to the batteries. The area under the curve in your sketch equals Ampere hours: in **Sketch 22**, the rectangle represents 20 Ah: 30 Ampere times ⅔ hours = 20 Ah.

The example in the sketch was a 55 Amp alternator, engine at 1400 RPM, charging two batteries of 110 Ah capacity each, both more than half empty. So you should not be too surprised to find that during the first hour, you are charging only a fraction of the daily Ah demand, and during subsequent hours, alternator output current will have fallen so low that you almost never catch up.

Unfortunately, the problem is common on almost all sailboats where the auxiliary engine runs only limited hours each day. Unfortunately also that some owners not diagnose the problem, or try to combat it with battery charging from shore power, larger batteries, bigger alternators, or longer engine running time under way, all bound to be rather ineffective, expensive, a nuisance, or all of these.

Fortunately, the problem can be solved relatively easily by temporarily overriding the control of the voltage regulator. During the early experiments with manual alternator controls about ten years ago, some skeptics argued that we would ruin alternators and "cook" batteries, or probably both. Some simple precautions can protect the alternators, and batteries are rather being ruined by repeated deep discharging, probably most common electrical problem on boats. Maximum continuous output current of alternators is ⅔ of their Ampere rating at best. Such current, for example 40 A from a 60 A alternator, charged into batteries of a few hundred Ampere hours of capacity, will still be a modest charging rate for each battery. We have to keep in mind that alternators as well as regulators are automotive equipment, no matter what the labels say. And what would overcharge a small car battery is only an average rate to the bigger battery capacity on board.

Alternator Controls

As you can easily test on your boat, battery charging with the alternator and voltage regulator can be frustratingly slow, leave the batteries at a low state of charge most of the time, and reduce battery capacity and life through frequent deep discharging. The basic method to improve battery charging with the alternator is to temporarily increase the alternator output current, by increasing the alternator field current.

In all cases, a resistor parallel to the voltage regulator is necessary. For alternators of type A and B in **Table 1**, that will mean a resistor between a source of plus 12 Volt and the field terminal F on the alternator. For alternators of the types C and D in **Table 1**, the resistor will be between the negative field coil terminal or the negative brush and ground, compare **Sketch 13**. The resistance of most alternator field coils is in the range from 2.5 to about 4 Ohm, usually about 3 Ohm, and field current ranges from less than 0.5 A to about 2 A. The simplest manual alternator controls consist of two, three, or four fixed power resistors and two, three, or four SPST switches, to select ranges of charge current in steps. Or a rotary switch with three, four or more positions may be used instead of toggle switches. Such controls, shown in **Sketch 23**, have the advantage of being very compact so that they can be incorporated in existing electric panels. Resistor ranges must be selected so that about two third of the Ampere rating of the alternator can be reached at low cruising speed of the engine. Power resistors with adequate wattage ratings must be used to avoid excessive heat. The examples in **Sketch 23** show all necessary values, rotary switches may be the shorting (make before break) or non-shorting type, the controls may be switched at any time, switched on and off without harm while the engine is running, and regulators do not have to be disconnected or switched while such control is being used. An ammeter should be within view, and currents in excess of ⅔ of alternator rating avoided, as well as high charge currents into nearly fully charged batteries. See details in the section on batteries.

Sketch 23 shows a control in two steps, with two resistors and two switches. One switch turns on and off, a second switch bypasses one resistor in the "HIGH" mode. Arrangement of switches on panel is shown in lower part of the sketch, as are Ohm and Watt ratings.

Sketch 24: alternator control with three steps, arrange switches in a vertical row, switch on LOW first, then MEDIUM, then HIGH for the three ranges.

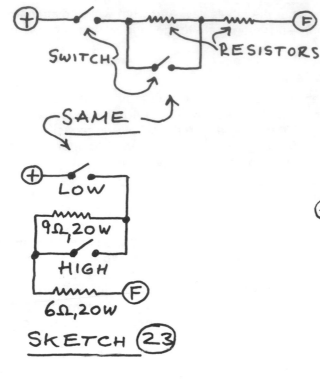

SWITCH

RESISTORS

SAME

LOW

9Ω,20W

HIGH

6Ω,20W

SKETCH 23

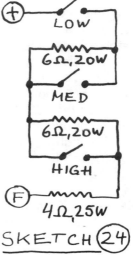

LOW

6Ω,20W

MED

6Ω,20W

HIGH

4Ω,25W

SKETCH 24

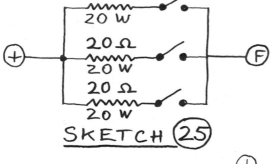

20 Ω
20 W

20 Ω
20 W

20 Ω
20 W

SKETCH 25

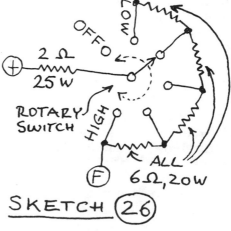

OFF

LOW

2 Ω
25 W

ROTARY
SWITCH

HIGH

ALL
6Ω,20W

SKETCH 26

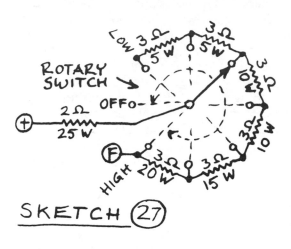

ROTARY SWITCH →

LOW 3Ω 5W   3Ω 5W

10Ω

2Ω 25W   OFFo

10W

HIGH 2Ω   3Ω   3Ω   15W

SKETCH ㉗

Sketch 25: here resistors are used in parallel, note higher resistance values. More resistors and switches may be added for additional steps.

Sketch 26: uses a rotary switch with six or more positions or poles. Farthest counterclockwise pole is left open: OFF position.

Sketch 27: uses a rotary switch with eight or more poles, one pole left open as OFF position. Resistors near low range end may have lower wattage ratings as shown since less current flows there.

Sketches 23 to 27 show PLUS and F terminals for use on type A and B alternators, **Table 1**. To use with type C or D alternators, connect between field coil minus terminal and ground, in parallel to the voltage regulator.

A Manual Alternator Control with Rheostat

This is the design published in the first edition of The 12 Volt Doctor's Practical Handbook, now in use on large numbers of boats with auxiliary engines. The prototype is now well over ten years old and working well. The installation instructions have become simpler since it was unnecessary to switch between voltage regulator and manual alternator control as originally recommended. Since the various alternator controls feed some additional field current to the alternator, the alternator output voltage always increases at least somewhat, so that the already hesitant voltage regulator senses what it interprets as a full battery and turns itself off. The alternator controls are simply connected in parallel to the voltage regulators.

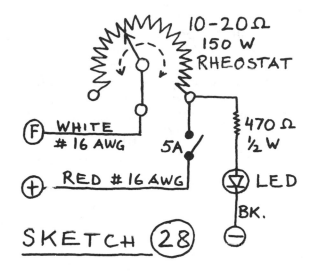

10-20Ω 150 W RHEOSTAT

(F) WHITE #16 AWG   5A

(+) RED #16 AWG

470Ω ½W

LED

BK.

SKETCH ㉘

A rheostat or variable power resistor is needed as shown in **Sketch 28**, connected in series with an ON-OFF switch which can be omitted if the rheostat has an OFF position. If you connect a pilot light, you will be able to monitor the alternator field at all times. With the switch off, the pilot light will still be connected to the field terminal and, with alternators type A and B in **Table 1**, will light as long as the voltage regulator is in action. The rheostat setting does not affect brightness of the LED (light emitting diode) pilot light because rheostat resistance is insignificantly small compared to the series resistor of about 500 Ohm in series with the LED.

For alternators of type C and D, **Table 1**, the pilot light of the manual alternator control ("MAC") must be wired differently, details are in **Sketch 29**. Here, the pilot light will be on while the alternator and voltage regulator are in operation. It will go off when the manual alternator control is switches on.

The optional resistor of one to two Ohm prevents extremely high field current and allows rheostat wattage ratings to be lower. In all cases, an ammeter should be in view close by, to show the alternator response to changes in rheostat settings and to avoid currents which would overheat the alternator. A 0 - 50 A ammeter will cover the output range of all alternators up to 80 Ampere. A manual alternator control (MAC) panel with ammeter, rheostat, LED pilot light, switch, and wires is available.* If you think that any alternator control may inadvertently be left on during long engine runs, add a time

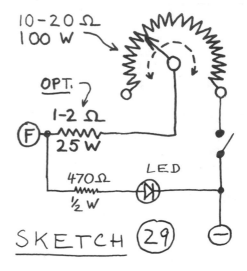

switch, **Sketch 30**. The switch of the timer then takes the place of the "LOW" or the ON-OFF switch of the control. Spring operated timers with one hour range are well suited for the purpose.

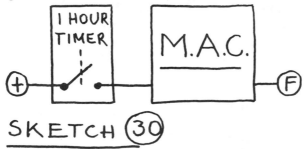

(See page 233 for description of the new improved AUTOMAC).

*Available from Weems & Plath, 222 Severn Ave., Annapolis MD 21403

All controls should be labelled or ammeters marked with the approximate maximum continuous alternator current. You can determine this upper limit by operating the alternator for about one hour with gradually increased output current while at the same time feeling the alternator housing temperature. Alternators will get hot to the touch. Too hot is the alternator which you can touch no longer than about five seconds. Include instructions on the label to readjust the control when the engine speed is being changed. Higher engine speed will increase the alternator output current with any given magnitude of field current.

With mechanical voltage regulators, a diode must be installed between voltage regulator and alternator. Use a type 1N5400 and connect in the wire between regulator F terminal and alternator F terminal, cathode toward the alternator.

Changing Alternators, Adding Alternators

Your engine may be fitted with a small alternator (35 Amp) with high replacement value. If it is a type B or D, **Table 1** which might need internal connection of a field wire for a M.A.C., you should instead determine if one of the type A alternators might physically fit in the same space, and if so, if it can be fastened so that pulleys will line up. Bracket adapters are made by some

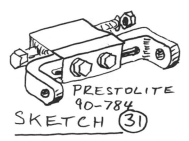

PRESTOLITE
90-784
SKETCH 31

alternator manufacturers, one such "mounting kit" by Prestolite is shown in **Sketch 31**. It allows fore-and-aft shifts of the alternator to align pulleys.

Several suitable type A alternators for external regulators are available as automotive replacement parts and, if "rebuilt," are quite inexpensive. You may decide to add a voltage regulator, or operate from a manual alternator control only.

Sometimes it may be desirable to have a second alternator driven by the engine. Rarely will there be mounting space on the engine, but such alternator can be fastened to bulkheads, engine bed, or other solid surroundings. You might, for example, use a GM - Delco 63 Amp alternator for external regulator, and mount it with two NICRO number NF-23 fittings and a ⅜ inch bolt as in **Sketch 32**. Or use two stainless steel tangs or dinghy chain plate fittings with fiberglass as in **Sketch 33**. Since the drive belt is bound to be relatively long, there are no problems with engines on elastic mounts.

SKETCH 32

SKETCH 33

Alternator Makes and Models

When we asked a wholesaler of alternator parts to name the twenty most popular alternators, he laughed and said he might name the top two hundred, and then some. Apparently it is hopeless to make a complete listing here. The following sketches show some alternators which we have run into. All show the type description of **Table 1**, and the field F terminal necessary for a M.A.C. connection. B + or + is the output terminal, AUX is the auxiliary terminal which supplies power to the regulator, GND is ground or minus. R, BK, GN, Y are wire colors red, black, green, and yellow. All alternators are shown the same size although there are differences, and there are many more not sketched here.*

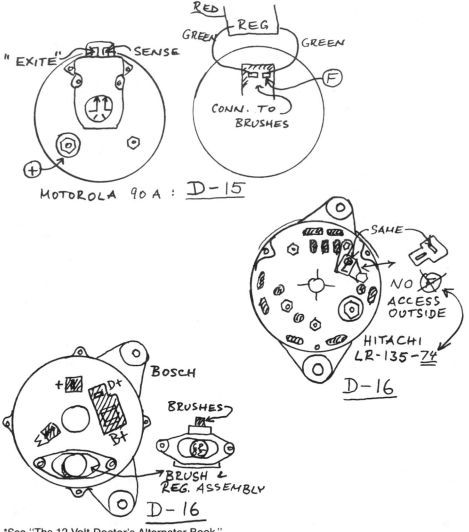

*See "The 12 Volt Doctor's Alternator Book."

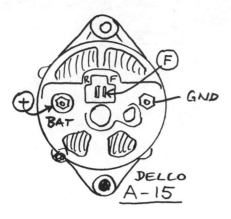

DELCO
A-15

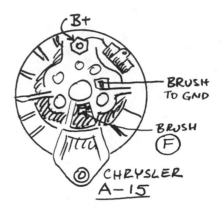

B+

BRUSH
TO GND

BRUSH
Ⓕ

CHRYSLER
A-15

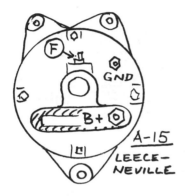

Ⓕ

GND

B+

A-15
LEECE-
NEVILLE

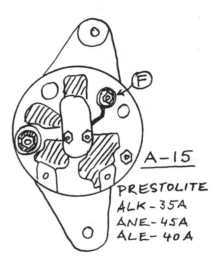

Ⓕ

A-15

PRESTOLITE
ALK-35A
ANE-45A
ALE-40A

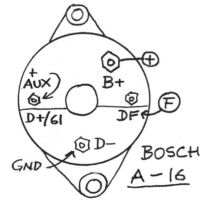

+
AUX

B+

Ⓕ

D+/61   DF

GND   D-

BOSCH
A-16

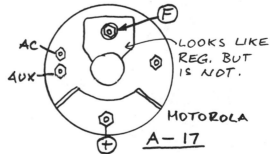

Ⓕ

AC

AUX

LOOKS LIKE
REG. BUT
IS NOT.

MOTOROLA
A-17

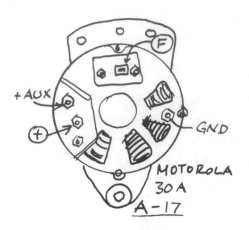

+ AUX

+

GND

MOTOROLA
30 A

A-17

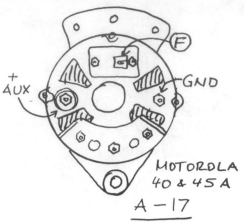

+ AUX

GND

F

MOTOROLA
40 & 45 A

A-17

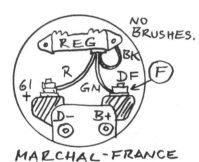

NO
BRUSHES.

REG

BK

R

GN

DF

F

61
+

D-

B+

MARCHAL-FRANCE
B-16

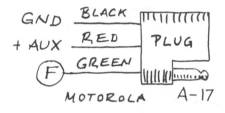

GND — BLACK

+ AUX — RED

F — GREEN

PLUG

MOTOROLA   A-17

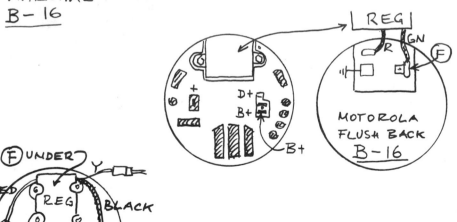

REG

R

GN

F

D+

B+

B+

MOTOROLA
FLUSH BACK
B-16

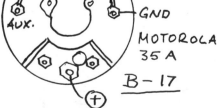

F UNDER

Y

RED

REG

BLACK

AUX.

GND

MOTOROLA
35 A

B-17

+

*See "The 12 Volt Doctor's Alternator Book."

166

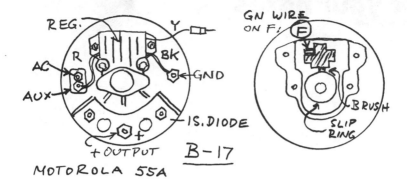

REG.   Y

R   Bk

AC   GND

AUX

+ OUTPUT   IS. DIODE

B-17

MOTOROLA 55A

GN WIRE ON F.

F

BRUSH

SLIP RING

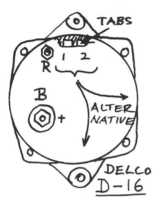

TABS

R   1   2

B +

ALTER NATIVE

DELCO

D-16

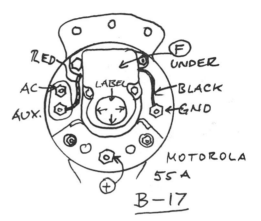

RED   F   UNDER

AC   LABEL   BLACK

AUX.   GND

MOTOROLA 55A

B-17

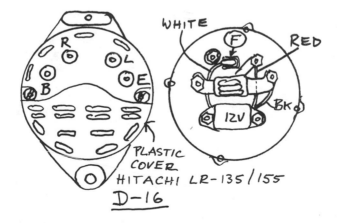

R

L

B   E

PLASTIC COVER

WHITE   F   RED

12V   Bk

HITACHI LR-135/155

D-16

For your notes:

Tiny Alternator: Bicycle Dynamo

This compact little machine **Sketch 1** is a great object for experiments. It consists of a permanent magnet with two or four poles, and a rotor with coil: the other way around from larger alternators. It generates alternating current when the knurled friction wheel is held against the bicycle tire. The wheel is driven at high speed because of its small diameter. But even if you twisted it between your fingers you could make a bicycle headlight begin to glow.

High shaft speeds are more easily reached with water driven propellers towed behind the boat than with wind propellers, but either are worth an experiment. A water propeller can be made from a round disc of sheet aluminum as in **Sketch 2**. Diameter about 4 to 6 inches, a hole in the center for a long shaft of at least 12 inches, with an eye for the tow line. Cut slots and bend the resulting blades very slightly, to only have minimal pitch which will help to reach high RPM when towed at only a few knots. Sheet metal thickness of 12 gauge will do for smaller propellers, 10 gauge or more for greater diameters or faster speeds through the water. **Sketch 1** shows the bearing. Before assembling the towing bracket, make sure that the bearing has enough lubrication. Attach a bale with hose clamps

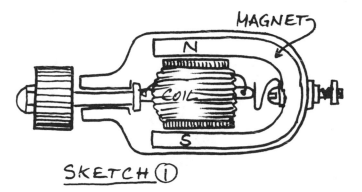

MAGNET

N

COIL

S

SKETCH (1)

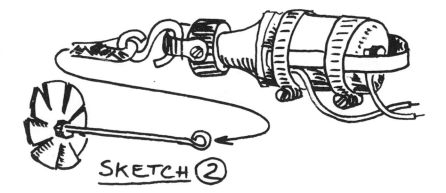

SKETCH (2)

and connect one wire to the housing under one of the hose clamps. Connect the other wire to the terminal. Use braided line and be prepared for the propeller to jump out of the water: a longer shaft or a lead weight around the line may help there. Alternating current from the dynamo must be rectified if it is to be used for battery charging. Use a single 1N4001 diode, or four of them in bridge rectifier arrangement.

Alternator with Permanent Magnet

As nice and powerful as alternators are in the engine room, they are of little use as wind driven generators unless some changes are made first. But since that is possible, you may want to try an alternator in such application.

Alternators need field current, to make the rotor magnetic. Rotors with permanent magnet could not be regulated. To make a permanent magnet rotor, and avoid the need for field current, the alternator must be taken apart and the rotor removed. Use any alternator which allows you to take off its pulley. The example is for a Delco or GM alternator. Four thin screws hold the two aluminum housing shells together which have the stator with windings clamped in

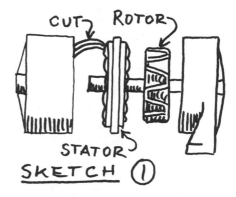

SKETCH 1

between, **Sketch 1**. Cut the stator wires to separate stator from back housing. The rotor must be taken to someone with a press, to separate the star shaped pole pieces from the shaft. Hammer blows are quite ineffective and will only ruin the shaft. Between

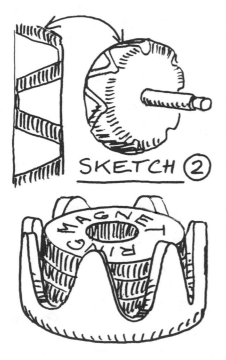

SKETCH 2

the two star shaped pole pieces is the field coil, all three press fitted on the knurled shaft. Discard the coil and replace it with three or four ring magnets as used in loudspeakers. Such ceramic magnets have their North and South poles at the round faces. Stack them so that they cling together, and locate them inside one of the star shaped pole pieces, then try the other half before permanent assembly. The hole in the pole pieces must be enlarged to fit the shaft more easily: since they are made of soft iron, drill or round file will do that. Now measure where the rotor must be located to be directly in or under the stator again, then assemble rotor parts and ring magnets on the shaft, use silicone rubber or other resin adhesives, and see that the star shaped poles are evenly spaced as they were originally, **Sketch 2**.

171

Remove all wire from the stator: it had too few turns of wire to generate enough voltage at lower shaft speeds. Rewind with thinner magnet wire so that you will have enough space for additional turns. Leave the small fiber insulators on the stator poles. They avoid shorts between wire and stator core.

There will be three times as many stator pole pieces, **Sketch 3**, as there are rotor poles, namely 42 on Delco and many other alternators. Make your windings, with magnet wire of 22 gauge AWG, for example, around three stator poles at a time, **Sketch 4**, and make as many turns as space allows. To avoid the crowding between adjacent coils, you may make turns around only two stator poles, **Sketch 5**, but must still space the coils to be three pole pieces apart. Note that turning direction must alternate, right turn for one coil, left turn for the next. That is because there will be a rotor North pole at one coil while a South pole is at the next, but all coils must generate their voltage pulse in the same direction. Instead of the three separate coil windings in the original alternator, where each coil only had six or seven turns, we can make one coil, consisting of 14 individual coils, all in series. You could number the 42 stator pole pieces, then make a wiring sketch around the numbers. Secure the two ends of the new stator winding, slip pieces of plastic spaghetti insulation over them, then reassemble the stator, rotor, and housings. Fish the wires out through any of the smaller holes at the back and seal them in, or fasten with a cable tie against strain.

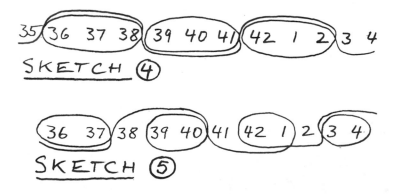

Spin the rotor and hold the wire ends together: the shorted winding should create increased rotor friction through the shorted current. The output from the new windings is alternating current, seven full cycles per turn. To make direct current out of it, use four silicon diodes, type 1N4001

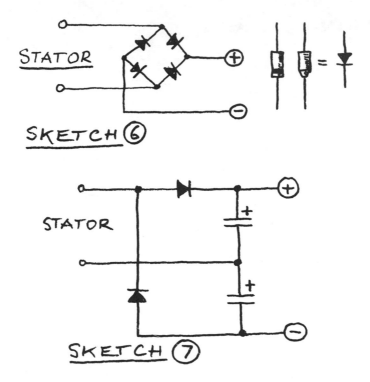

STATOR

SKETCH ⑥

STATOR

SKETCH ⑦

or 1N5400 (bigger) and connect as a "bridge" rectifier, **Sketch 6**. Or make the circuit in **Sketch 7** which increases voltage at the direct current terminals by directing pulses from capacitors. Try capacitors with ratings between 10 and 50 MF, and 25 Volt.

For your notes:

Charging Diodes

A diode is a semiconductor which is highly conductive in one direction and not conductive in the other. It acts like a check valve, allows current flow in one direction, for example into a battery, but not back out of the battery. Charging diodes are also called isolating diodes, splitters, and other names. They are installed with the purpose of charging all batteries at all times when the alternator is running, regardless of the position of the battery main switch. You ordinarily switch to ALL before you start the engine, so that all batteries are being charged when the alternator runs, then switch back to a selected single battery after the engine has been stopped. All that is simpler with charging diodes. You may switch between batteries even while the engine is running, even to OFF without harm to the alternator. The diodes charge the greatest current to the lowest battery and, once charged, do not let any current flow back out. Current can only be used through the main switch, when you select any particular battery. The batteries remain isolated instead of becoming one big battery when the battery main switch is in the ALL position.

To make charging diodes for your boat, you need silicon diodes as in **Sketch 1**, available in two different arrangements: either base being cathode (left) or base being anode (right). Either is useful but you must install them correctly. To test a diode, connect a 12 Volt lamp in series with the diode and to a battery as in **Sketch 2**. Note the diode symbol: it points from plus to minus, from anode to cathode, in this direction the lamp will light up brightly. In the opposite direction, only extremely small leakage current may flow: the lamp remains dark. You may test diodes with a VOM (volt ohm meter) by comparing with a diode of known polarity. Diode ratings should be about 50 Ampere and 50 PIV: the diode capable of conducting 50 A in

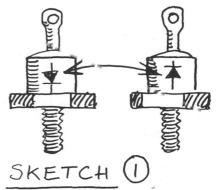

SKETCH ①

SKETCH ②

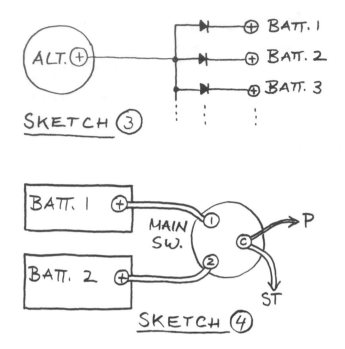

SKETCH ③

SKETCH ④

the forward direction, and blocking up to 50 Peak Invert Volts in the reverse direction without breaking down. Diodes in that range are made with a case called DO-5, as in **Sketch 1**, with ¼ × 28 threaded mounting studs, which is ¼ inch fine thread or ¼ inch SAE thread.

We need a conductive path from the alternator through a diode to each battery, **Sketch 3**: we need one charging diode per battery regardless of the battery size. In the case of two batteries with battery main switch, **Sketch 4**, the charging diodes can be conveniently connected to the main switch terminals: the alternator output terminal is always connected to the "C" or common terminal which is shown here with wires to ST starter and P ship's electrical panel. The battery terminals are already connected to the switch terminals with heavy wires, so all that remains is one diode from "C" to terminal "1" and another from "C" to terminal "2" as in **Sketch 5**.

In order to become conductive in the forward direction, the diodes need a slight push, much like a check valve in which a spring holds the mechanism shut. About 0.6 Volt are necessary for all silicon diodes regardless of size. Since high charging currents will develop some heat at the diode, it should be mounted on a heat sink as in **Sketch 6**, or a piece of aluminum "L" as in **Sketch 7**. The amount of heat in Watt is easy to calculate: Watt is Volt times Ampere, in this case the threshold Volts of 0.6 V and the current flow

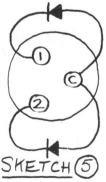

SKETCH ⑤

176

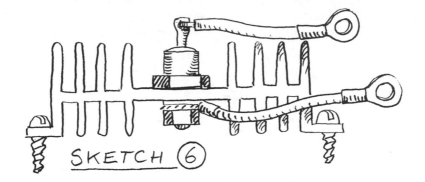

SKETCH (6)

in Ampere. If 20 Ampere are flowing through one diode, $0.6 \times 20 = 12$ Watt of heat are generated, easy to dissipate with a heat sink of about 2×4 inches or an "L" section of about 8 inches.

If you are using "cathode base" diodes, mount each on its own heat sink as in **Sketch 8** and connect as shown there. If the diodes are the "anode base" variety, you may mount both (or all) on a common heat sink which you make slightly larger, then connect as in **Sketch 9**. Use number 10 AWG stranded wire and solder to the tip of the diodes, with a large and hot solder iron so that the soldering takes place quickly.

SKETCH (7)

Do that BEFORE you mount the diodes on the heat sinks. Use a wire with ring terminal lug and a lock washer to fasten to the diode bases. Use ring terminals with 5/16 inch hole or larger, to fit the terminals of the battery main switch. Mount the diodes to the bulkhead next to the main switch, and be aware that the aluminum itself is at plus 12 Volt, just like the main switch terminals. Do not short them to ground which would generate sparks and heat.

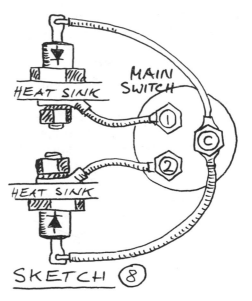

SKETCH (8)

Trouble Shooting

The only problem you might have is a diode connected in reverse. No harm, but the corresponding battery would not be charged. Instead, current could flow from that battery even though the main switch was off. After installing the diodes, test by switching the battery main or selector switch off, then test cabin lights or other lights: if they still work, a diode is reversed.

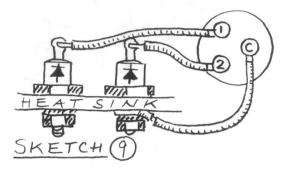

Other Sources of Charging Current

Most automatic battery chargers or converters are equipped with usually three diodes, to charge three separate batteries which are kept isolated. To charge a fourth isolated battery, another charging diode as that in **Sketch 6** can be added but must be connected parallel to the existing diodes, usually outside because the housing will not offer enough space.

If two alternators are used to charge batteries, their plus output terminals may be interconnected since their internal rectifying diodes prevent reverse current. However, two voltage regulators, those used with alternators and in automatic battery chargers, tend to interfere with each other: one will see the voltage increase generated by the other and turn its units off, as normally only happens when batteries reach full charge.

Voltage Regulators

The threshold step of about 0.6 Volt at diodes causes the voltage at the alternator during charging to be about 0.6 Volt higher than the voltage directly at the battery terminals. If you are not using a manual alternator control, make certain that the voltage regulator positive wire is connected to the normally lowest battery on board, or the voltage regulator adjusted to a 0.6 V higher voltage setting. If instead it takes its voltage reading at the alternator output terminal, it will cause battery charging to remain incomplete and to be extremely slow. Only with a manual alternator control you can afford to ignore this problem.

How much Current?

1 A (Ampere, Amp) = 1000 mA (milliamp)

Component	Current, A	.01	.1	1	5	10	20
Voltmeter							
Ammeter—none							
Oil pressure gauge							
Water temperature gauge							
Tachometer							
Sea water thermometer gauge							
Engine hour meter							
Rudder angle indicator							
Sonalert beeper							
Knotmeter							
Log with knotmeter							
Wind speed indicator							
Wind direction indicator							
Depth sounder							
Depth recorder							
AM-FM broadcast receiver							
VHF receiver							
Loran receiver							
CB receiver							
Omega receiver							
SSB receiver							
Small electric bell							
Bell, 6 inch and larger							
Oil pressure alarm, on							
Engine temperature alarm, on							
Horn							
Strobe light							
Tape deck							
Stereo							
Bilge blower							
Cabin fan							
Instrument lights, engine							
Ignition, 4-cylinder gas engine							
Electric fuel pump							
Lights: *see lamp list*							
Anchor light							
Spreader lights							
Running lights, tri-color							
Running lights, red, green, stern							
Cabin light, small							
Cabin light, 40 Watt lamp							
Water pressure system pump							
Bilge pump							
VHF transmitter							
SSB transmitter							
Autopilot, Averaged							
Spotlight 100 Watt							
Anchor windlass							

For your notes:

Noise and Filters

Although we are dealing with direct current, some alternating current is usually blended in which sometimes creates problems. This "noise" can have a distinct frequency or consist of random peaks of voltage superimposed on the 12 Volt direct current. Alternators generate pulses of direct current, 21 of them per revolution with a rotor of seven North and South poles, or 700 Hz (Hertz, cycles per second) with the engine at 1000 RPM and a 2:1 pulley ratio. Other frequencies are generated by resonance, and random noise is primarily generated by sparks at switch contacts, electric motor brushes, and ignition points. Spark generated noise unfortunately contains a fraction which is radiated in the form of electromagnetic waves, and collected again in all wires which then act as antennas. Noise is amplified with other desirable signals in electronic equipment.

Fortunately, direct current can be filtered to remove essentially all noise. More difficult is the battle against radiated noise from sparks, especially those not on your boat. Filters are made from coils and capacitors and make use of the fact that alternating current faces "inductive resistance" in inductive coils while direct current does not, and alternating current can flow through capacitors while direct current can not. Filters therefore are

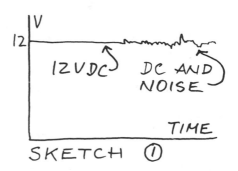

SKETCH ①

arranged as in **Sketch 1**: direct current flows through the coil while alternating current is held back and instead flows through the capacitors to ground. This scheme works increasingly better with higher frequencies. Inductive coils become more resistive and capacitors more conductive to the alternating current.

In practice, the normal pulses of the alternator output current are completely absorbed by the batteries which act like giant capacitors. Noise of higher frequency can be shorted to ground by a capacitor connected directly to the alternator housing as in **Sketch 2**. Noise from the brushes in the

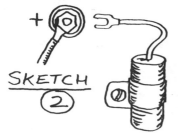

SKETCH ②

alternator will be of two kinds: radiated noise which cannot reach the outside of the alternator because it is being collected by the grounded metal housing, a "shield," and noise transmitted by wire. This may be shorted to ground with a similar capacitor connected to auxiliary and field terminals, see the section on alternators. In all cases, the bracket of such capacitors makes the minus connection to ground via the fastening screw.

181

SKETCH 3

4

To put an inductive coil into the alternator output wire is highly impractical because the high direct current would require a heavy wire which would make an enormous coil with only limited inductive resistance. It is easier to install such inductive coil in the supply wire of any electronic equipment. A coil as in **Sketch 3** can be made from magnet wire (solid copper wire with lacquer insulation) and wound on a nail. For currents of a few Ampere, five to ten feet of number 18 AWG wire would not present a significant resistance to the DC current. Its inductive resistance also would be low and mostly block high frequency noise. A coil as in **Sketch 4** is made from much thinner wire and has more direct current resistance. Since there are many more turns, its inductive resistance is much higher. Such coil is suitable for small electronic instruments which only draw fractions of an Ampere. A choke, **Sketch 5**, is built like a transformer but has only one coil or winding. Chokes are rated in Ampere to show how much DC current can flow, and in µH (micro Henry), units of inductivity. A choke would block audible frequency noise from a stereo system. Instead of a choke, a transformer may often do

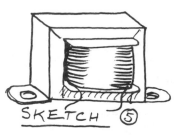

SKETCH 5

a similar job if it has a winding which allows sufficient current. Short other windings and be cautious: transformers can generate high voltages from direct current pulses.

SCETCH 6

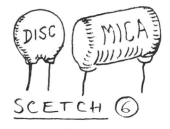

SKETCH 7

Capacitors are used to conduct alternating current noise to ground. For very high frequencies, only small capacitance is needed and capacitors as in **Sketch 6** are used. Their capacity ranges from a few pF to several hundred pF (pico Farad, 100,000 pF = 1 µF, micro Farad). For larger capacitance, electrolytic capacitors, **Sketch 7** are used. Theses are made in sizes to many thousand µF. Note the polarity signs: electrolytic capacitors must be connected with plus wire to plus voltage, otherwise they will fail and may explode.

To make a filter, start with an electrolytic capacitor, **Sketch 7**, connected between plus terminal and ground or minus, at the unit (radio, depth sounder, receivers, stereo), then test the results. Capacitor size may range from 50 to several hundred µF (micro Farad), rated for 25

Volt, better 50 Volt. Observe polarity. If necessary, add an inductor as shown in **Sketch 8**: it must be made from heavy enough wire or have an Ampere rating to about match the current needed by the unit. You may test its DC resistance with a VOM (Volt Ohm Meter). As a rough guideline, the coil should have no more than 10 Ohm if the unit draws 100 mA, 2 Ohm if the unit draws about 0.5 A, 1 Ohm if the unit draws about 1 A, 0.5 Ohm for 2 A et cetera. For accurate Ohm measurements you will need the low ohm meter described elsewhere in the book.

Before you start searching for a choke, make a wire-on-nail coil as in **Sketch 3** from a few feet of magnet wire and try it. Add a mica or disc capacitor parallel to the electrolytic capacitor for better shorting of high frequencies. A size in the range from 30 to 300 pF should do. Voltage ratings are always high enough for this kind of capacitor, and polarity does not matter.

A more elaborate filter may need a coil in the minus wire as well, installed at the same location as the inductive coil in the positive wire. Then connect one electrolytic and one mica capacitor across the battery side of both coils and the unit side of both coils, similar to **Sketch 8**.

Wires can be guarded against radiated noise by shielding, and shielded wires may contain one or more individual wires within a shield which may be braided copper or aluminum foil. Shielded antenna cable is an example, **Sketch 9**. Metal housings of electronic instruments, battery chargers, generators and alternators also act as shields. To conduct "clean" direct current or the downlead from an antenna or the signal from a transducer, the shield, which is the antenna to pick up noise before it can reach the inner wires, must be complete, tightly braided, and connected to ground as shown in **Sketch 10**. It usually is connected to the housings and, on longer runs, may be grounded again at places along the way. Read about "ground loops" in books on electronics or consult your local electronics expert if you have problems which you cannot solve.

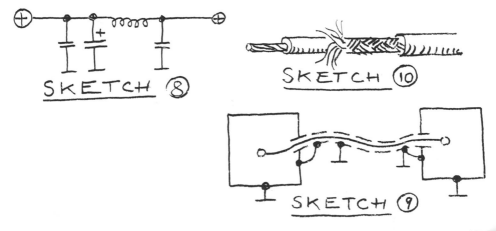

SKETCH 8

SKETCH 10

SKETCH 9

For your notes:

Power for the Calculator: Voltage Regulator ICs.

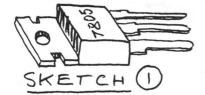

SKETCH 1

Any equipment which uses internal batteries may instead be powered directly from the boat's 12 Volt system. There are a number of inexpensive and highly reliable electronic voltage regulators, available as small integrated circuits, not at all like the voltage regulator in the car which comes to mind.

An integrated circuit (IC) voltage regulator is shown in **Sketch 1**. Although there are many different types, regulating positive or negative voltage, and made in many different "packages," we will concentrate on this one, its package is called a TO-220, and it has three terminals: unregulated plus input, regulated plus output, and ground.

This regulator IC is available for output voltages of 5, 6, 8, 9, and 12 Volt and if that does not happen to match the voltage which your calculator or radio needs, we will see how to manipulate it. Even then, the new circuit will cost little more than one set of calculator batteries.

First, find out what the actual operating voltage is: count the number of individual AA, C, or D cells which are usually connected in series, each supplying 1.5 Volt to the total. Or there may be a single 9 V battery. The operating voltage may also be listed on the label or inside the battery compartment. Some examples are shown in **Sketch 2**: note that the battery size (AA, C, or D) does not affect the operating voltage.

Next, find a way to connect the calculator (or other piece of equipment) to outside power. Many calculators and radios have a socket for that purpose, intended for a power supply on 110 V AC. If there is a socket, get a plug, or wire with plug, from your local electronics store. Most sockets are for ultra-miniature, miniature, or standard phone plugs, shown in **Sketch 3**. If there is no socket, you could solder a small washer to the ends of two wires and wedge them to the plus and minus terminals in the battery compartment. To apply pressure, cut strips from stiff foam, slightly longer than the batteries, see

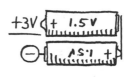

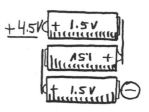

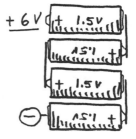

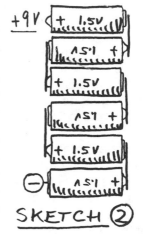

SKETCH 2

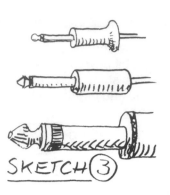

SKETCH ③

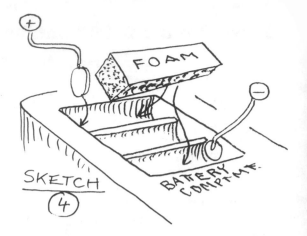

SKETCH ④

7805

+12
TO +30V

+5V

SKETCH ⑤

Sketch 4. Or you might solder directly to the metal contacts in the battery compartment if you do not intend to return to using internal batteries.

The ends of the two wires are connected to regulated positive terminal and to ground, **Sketch 5**. You could mount the regulator IC in a small plastic box or, in some cases, directly in the battery compartment. The unregulated 12 V input does not have to be switched off since only minute amounts of current are flowing when the calculator or radio are turned off by their built-in switches.

For regulated output of 4.5 V connect a silicon diode such as 1N4001 at the output terminal as in **Sketch 6**. The diode will cause the usual threshold of 0.6 V. The cathode of the diode is marked with a band. An additional diode in series would drop the output to about to 3.8 V, three diodes in series between regulator and calculator to about 3 V, to replace two internal batteries.

To increase the regulated output voltage of the integrated circuit regulator, a diode in the ground connection as in **Sketch 7** will lift the output by 0.6 V, two such diodes in series to about 6 V to replace four internal batteries. Additional increases or decreases of the nominal regulator voltage are possible in steps of about 0.6 V with silicon diodes, or in steps of 0.2 V with germanium diodes.

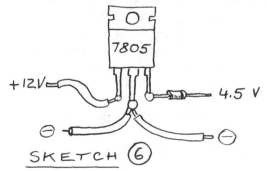

7805

+12V

4.5 V

SKETCH ⑥

186

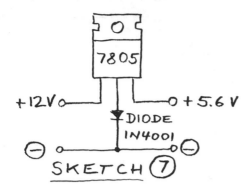

SKETCH ⑦

+12V ——o ——o +5.6 V

DIODE
1N4001

TO-3 CASE
SKETCH ⑧

Voltage regulator ICs are made for several fixed output voltages, the TO-220 case shown in the sketches above, in metal case called TO-3 shown in **Sketch 8**.

There are also regulator ICs with variable or adjustable output voltage. All of them have in common the tolerance for high input voltages up to 30 V DC from which an output voltage is made which is constant regardless of current. A minimum current of a few mA must flow to allow the regulating circuit to work, all are protected against excess current or heat. For electronics with internal batteries, currents of much less than one Ampere will usually suffice, but regulators are also useful to charge batteries in rechargeable equipment such as cordless hand tools, photo strobe lights, portable tape recorders, hand held transmitters or the like which might require higher currents.

The following **Table** gives some type numbers with current ratings and case or package.

As you can see, the output voltage is always somehow included in the type numbers.

The integrated regulator circuit must be protected from reverse voltage. If a filter capacitor is used as in **Sketch 9**, a diode "D" must be connected as sketched, to discharge the capacitor when the input voltage drops, or is switched off while no current is drawn at the output.

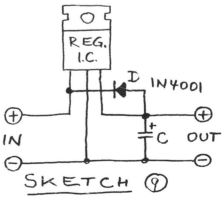

SKETCH ⑨

Table:
Integrated Circuit Voltage Regulators with Positive Output

Letters Mean: C,T: TO-220, K: TO-3 package

Fixed Output Voltage:	Type Number	Current
5 V ± 0.2	7805, LM7805T, MC7805, LM309K, LM340K-5	1.5 A
	LM323K-5	3 A
6 V ± 0.3	MC7806	1.5 A
8 V ± 0.4	LM7808T, LM7808CK	1.5 A
12 V* ±0.6	MC7812CT, LM340K-12	15.A

Adjustable Output Voltage:

	LM317K, T	1.5 A
	LM350K	3 A

*Input voltage must be about 2 Volt higher than regulated output. This regulator therefore of limited use with 12 Volt systems.

An example with the adjustable regulator type LM317 is shown in **Sketch 10**. Note that the input and output terminals of the TO-220 case are different from the fixed voltage types. Input may be as high as 30 V and must always be a few Volt above the output voltage. Minimum output current must be 4 mA. Output voltage depends on values for "R":

Resistance R Ohm	Output Voltage Volt
1800	3
3300	4.5
4700	6
7500	9

Note that the metal tab is electrically connected to the output terminal.

Greater current can be drawn if the LM317K type in TO-3 metal housing is used, mounted on a heat sink. **Sketch 11** shows the TO-3 case viewed from the bottom. Note that the two pins are located slightly off center, to be identified. Output voltage is selected by the value of resistor "R":

resistance "R" Ohm	Output, Volt
330	3.1 V
470	3.9
510	4.1
560	4.4
620	4.8
820	6
1200	8
1800	11.5

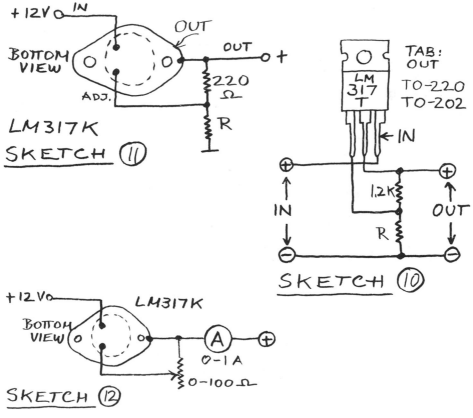

+ 12V IN

OUT

BOTTOM VIEW

OUT +

220 Ω

ADJ.

R

LM317K

SKETCH ⑪

TAB: OUT

LM 317 T

TO-220
TO-202

IN

IN

1.2K

OUT

R

SKETCH ⑩

+ 12V

LM317K

BOTTOM VIEW

Ⓐ ⊕

0-1 A

0-100 Ω

SKETCH ⑫

189

Current Regulator

Instead of regulating voltage, the regulator ICs can also be used to regulate current. In the example of **Sketch 12**, the type LM317K, viewed from the bottom has the adjustment terminal connected to a variable resistor of 100 Ohm which is not (!) connected to ground. changes in current affect the adjustment terminal which limits current. This circuit is useful where constant charging current to nickel cadmium (NiCad) batteries is needed. Adjust the resistor to the desired current, shown by the ammeter. Current will remain constant in spite of changing battery voltage as long as the input voltage is a few Volts above output voltage.

R adjusted to:	Current limited to:
1 Ohm	1 A
2	0.5 A
10	0.1 A
100	0.01 A

Lamp Dimmer

Finally, several regulators can be controlled in parallel, shown in the example in **Sketch 13** which uses them as lamp dimmers. The resistors are selected to change the lamp voltage from two Volt below input to 8.5 V when the variable resistor is at its low resistance. A switch between input and output would be needed for full brightness, and a protective diode might be a good idea.

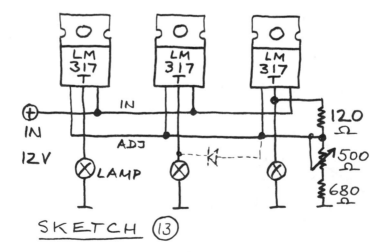

SKETCH 13

190

Safety Standards for Small Craft

Under this title, the American Boat and Yacht Council, P.O. Box 806, Amityville, N.Y. 11701, publishes a binder with very extensive technical information and recommended practices which probably most, if not all, builders follow. Among the Divisions which deal with hulls, machinery, equipment, and engineering standards is an Electrical Division which you should consult with questions concerning bonding and grounding of both direct current and alternating current systems on board, safety and electricity, corrosion and electrolysis, and lightning protection.

Pages E-9-13 and E-9-14 (4-7-75) contain tables which show required wire sizes (in AWG number code) for 6 Volt, 12 Volt, 24 Volt, and 32 Volt, for currents from 5 to 25 Ampere in 5 A increments, and for lengths of the conductor from Source to Most Distant Fixture up to 85 feet. The tables are based on voltage losses of 3% and 10%.

For your notes:

Electric Power from the Sun

Silicon solar cells are used to convert light energy from the sun directly into electric power. The basic solar cell is a thin silicon semiconductor wafer which produces a voltage of .45 V in ideal direct sunlight. The output current is proportional to the cell surface area, typically about .16 A or 160 milliampere per square inch. The basic cells are available in round and rectangular shapes, and as sections of round cells.

In order to charge electricity into a 12 V battery, a solar cell panel will have to produce a voltage higher than that of the 12 V battery, in order to make electricity flow into the battery. A fully charged 12 V battery has 13.8 Volt, and solar cell panels intended to charge such a battery will have to develop 14 V or better. To do that, it is necessary to connect several individual solar cells in series: the first one will generate .45 V, the next one will bring that from .45 to .90 Volt, then to 1.35 V, and so on, each cell adding its voltage to the series. It takes a minimum of 32 cells in series, in practice usually 36, to make a panel for charging of 12 V batteries. The nominal output is 14 V, in practice it may range from 12 to 18 V for a 36-cell panel.

How about output current? When connected in series, each of the cells in the panel adds its voltage to the total, to reach the output voltage of the panel, for example 14 Volt. But the current which flows through each cell is the same, and is the current which one individual cell can generate, so that panels of 36 3"-cells will have a current output of about 1 A. Panels made from round cell fractions, such as half rounds, quarter round sections, or ⅙ sections will produce ½, ¼, or ⅙ of the current of the corresponding full round cell.

Efficiency: Radiated sun energy in full brightness is equivalent to about 100 mW (milli Watt = ¹⁄₁₀₀₀ Watt) per square centimeter. Actual electric output under ideal conditions is cell voltage X current: Volt X Amp equals Watt. Silicon solar cells range from 10% to about 15% in conversion efficiency. A practical aspect with solar cell panels on board is the mounting position. Unless the panel were continuously tilted to follow the sun and keep the panel perpendicular to the incoming light, rated output will only be achieved with sun directly overhead for horizontal mounting. At other angles, sunlight reaching the front surface of the panel will be reduced to:

Angle:	90°	80°	70°	60°	50°	40°	30°
% of ideal:	100%	98%	94%	87%	77%	65%	50%

As a material for the top surface, glass is often used in solar panels. It has the advantage of retaining its transparency even with intense ultraviolet light which would cause degradation and yellowing in most plastics. Unavoidable is the loss of efficiency from light which is reflected by the glass, with the incoming light other than perpendicular.

Panels made with other clear cover materials apparently tend to suffer from gradual loss of light transmittance.

Solar Panels: Installation

Many solar cell panels are supplied with a length of cable. Best is to lead this cable below decks and make the first connection in a reasonably protected, dry place. Soldering is highly recommended. Wire size will depend on current load: most single panels will have 2 A or less output, and any light wire will do.

If you are going to charge more than one battery, connect diodes of same type and rating, as shown in **Sketch 1**, between positive panel lead and battery main switch terminals of batteries 1, 2, etc.

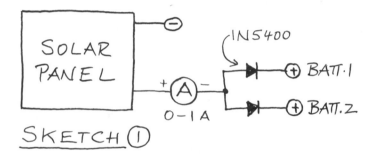

Do not install a voltmeter permanently in the circuit since its value is not justified by its electricity loss. However, a small Ampere meter, sensitive enough to show fractions of one A, can be useful, does not cause loss, and can be installed as in **Sketch 1**.

Where more than one solar electric panel is being installed, connect two or more 14 Volt panels in parallel. Total current will be the sum of each panel's output current.

Should you have access to 6 Volt panels, you may connect three in series to serve your 12 Volt system. And you may connect two such banks of three in parallel.

Output: Generated power in Ah (Ampere hours) will be average current in A (for example 1.6 A) times number of hours with current output (for example 6h) or 1.6 A × 6 h = 9.6 Ah. Voltage regulators: with normal panel ratings of less than 3 A, and typical battery capacities of 100 Ah or more, no regulating will be needed.

Solar Electric Panels: How to compare the specs

Capacity of a panel will be given for full sunlight, and will be in WATT. If Ampere rating is given, you can multiply it by 14 Volt, to get absolute maximum Watt rating. 1000 mA (milli Ampere) = 1 A, and 1000 mW (milli Watt) = 1 W.

In practice, Volt and Ampere values depend on the "load." The panel's maximum Amp rating occurs when the panel is short circuited and Volts = 0, and maximum Volts are measured when no current flows.

Example: a panel is charging into a relatively "low" battery at 12.0 V, at a current of .65 A. Panel output here is 12.0 Volt × .65 A = 7.8 Watt. As the battery is charged, its voltage climbs to 13.5 V and current now is down to .58 A of charging current, but wattage is still .58 A × 13.5 V = 7.8 W.

What can you expect? Make two estimates, in two different ways:

First, calculate the amount of electricity which the panel will generate under the very best conditions. Take the panel's Amp rating and multiply by 7, (for seven hours of full output current: more than you can realistically hope for). The result: Ampere hours generated, per day, maximum.

Now divide this value by the Ampere rating for the equipment which you want to operate. Ampere hours generated, divided by Ampere rating of the equipment, gives hours of operation. If these hours of operation are too few, discard the idea.

Example: A solar panel with 2 Ampere rating will generate 2 × 7 = 14 Ah maximum per day. A cabin light (2 A rating) will operate 14/2 = 7 hours, an anchor light (1 Ampere) will operate 14/1 = 14 hours, both may be practical, see the second estimate. An electric motor (6 Ampere, such as refrigeration) will operate 14/6 = 2.3 hours: impractical, here you can safely discard the idea, without the second estimate.

Second estimate: calculate the very least which the panel will generate. Multiply the panel's Amp rating by 3: you will almost always be able to collect the equivalent of 3 hours of full sunlight. Then, again, divide the generated Ampere hours by the Ampere rating of the equipment which you want to operate with the generated power, again based on one day.

Example: A panel has 1 A rating, will therefore generate a minimum of 1 × 3 = 3 Ampere hours per day. You plan to operate the bilge pump with the solar electricity: the bilge pump draws 6 A when running or has a 6 A rating. 3 Ah of generated power /6 A bilge pump rating = ½ hour. Your bilge pump may run three times per day, each time for less than 5 minutes, which would be a total of .25 hours: this application would be quite sound. Even with the minimal output estimate, there is reserve power which would remain in the batteries.

Bilge Pump Supply Circuit

Automatic bilge pumps must remain switched on when boats are left unattended. For that purpose, the main switch is left in the "1" or "2" position or, for added power, in the ALL position which parallels or interconnects the batteries. This also leaves power connected to the main electric panel.

Instead, the bilge pump can be powered through the circuit in **Sketch 1** which consists of one diode for each available battery, connected between battery plus terminal and float switch so that the pump may draw from the best charged battery first, from all other batteries if there should be unusual demand for extra power. The diodes do not allow one battery to discharge into another but keep the batteries perfectly isolated. The battery main switch may or should be turned off. Diode ratings should be 10 to 12 A each, with 25 V reverse rating, anode base type, mounted on a commmon heat sink.

The same circuit can also be used to supply power to receivers and other electronic equipment while autopilots or other high power equipment may cause power surges at any given battery. The circuit avoids drops in voltage for example to a Loran set, by drawing from the highest charged battery on board automatically.

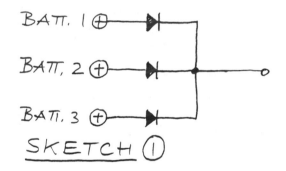

196

Alarms: How About Your Bilge?

Small amounts of water can be taken care of by the electric bilge pump. The pump probably draws between 3 and 6 Ampere and might run 10 minutes per day. A normal battery with 80 Ah of available power would last 80 days (6 Ah every 6 days, or 80 × 6 / 6 = 80). But when layed up or unattended in a marina, a larger leak, from a broken hose for example, would draw electricity for the pump at a much higher rate. For an outside observer, the leak would remain invisible if the pump kept up with it, until battery power would run out. A useful bilge alarm should warn about the impending trouble ahead of time. Here is one possibility for a bilge alarm:

Present bilge pump arrangement: most boats have a pump with float switch, and a MANUAL-AUTOMATIC selector switch. On MANUAL, the float switch is bypassed and the pump runs continuously. On AUTOMATIC, the pump only runs when bilge water rises and closes the float switch contacts. In **Sketch 1**, a wire is connected to the existing switch on the MANUAL side, at point A. When the switch is in its AUTOMATIC position, as it would be on boats tied in a marina, this point A will have + 12 Volt whenever the float switch closes, to make the pump run.

We connect from A to the heater element of a thermal delay switch with N.O. contact, which in turn connects to a normal 12 V relay with N.O. contact. The relay is wired to stay on even after the delay switch or bilge float switch opens again, to keep the bell ringing, or the strobe light flashing. Hopefully, someone will react to that.

The time delay relay is selected to have a delay time much longer than the normal single running cycle of the bilge pump when it operates by float switch.

Suitable delay relays are Amperite No. 12NO060 (1 minute), 12NO120 (2 minutes), and 12NO180 (3 minute delay time before contacts close).

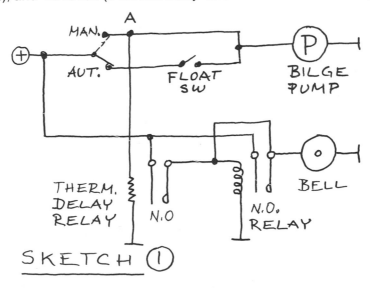

SKETCH ①

For your notes:

Batteries

There are two groups of batteries: primary batteries such as the zinc carbon or alkaline flashlight batteries, and secondary batteries which are rechargeable and include the lead-acid and nickel-cadmium types. Almost all rechargeable batteries on boats are lead-acid batteries and we will concentrate on these. Nickel batteries are used in some portable equipment but never as the boat's main batteries, as explained in a paragraph on these batteries.

Lead Acid Batteries

Their main function is to store electrical energy, ordinarily expressed in Watt hours or kWh (kilowatt hours). As a simplification, we normally measure electricity on board in Ampere hours. This is practical because we are always dealing with approximately 12 Volt. We measure battery capacity in Ah: a battery with 100 Ah theoretically can supply 1 A for 100 hours, or 100 A for one hour, or any numbers which multiply to 100 Ah. In doing so, we ignore the fact that more Watts have to be charged into a battery than will come out: it may take 100 Ah to charge and, if we are very careful, we may get 100 Ah back out. But to charge, we have to apply at least 14 V, while current from the battery will be supplied at perhaps 12.5 V or less. Charged wattage would be 100 Ah × 14 V = 1400 Watt hours (A X V = W), but in return we get only about 100 Ah × 12 V = 1200 Wh = 1.2 kWh. In addition, some current is always lost when gas bubbles are formed: the current is used to decompose water into oxygen and hydrogen gas, as discussed in greater detail later. We could talk about a battery's power efficiency and compare wattages. Instead we usually only look at current efficiencies: current in, compared to current out.

Why are batteries such frustrating subject on the boat? Probably because no other piece of equipment on board is so short lived, its life expectancy so difficult to predict, its degree of usefulness, the capacity, as difficult to measure and compare. Batteries are shrouded in a cloud of descriptive language big on qualitative terms but almost completely missing quantitative information. We buy batteries with the manufacturers stated capacity which, after a few years, diminishes to nothing when the battery has spent its useful life. Is the loss of capacity gradual, or does it come suddenly near the end? Most of us will never know. But knowing what goes on in the battery, how to treat it to extend its life, what not to do to avoid harm, will help at least a little, and may counteract the trend to make us believe that batteries could ever be maintenance free.

How it works

To store electricity, the battery uses chemistry. The simplest lead-acid battery could consist of two sheets of lead in sulfuric acid. With a charging current, one plate would form a film of lead peroxide. The other plate would generate hydrogen bubbles. The charged battery could then give back an electric current while chemical reactions take place at the plates.

The chemicals on the plates, lead oxide, lead sulfate, and lead metal all are insoluble in the electrolyte which is dilute sulfuric acid so that the charged electricity is stored with relatively little loss from internal discharge.

But things get complicated because more battery capacity is needed, and the plates must be made to both carry more chemistry and have more surface area. Batteries are made from positive and negative plates which are alternately stacked, close to each other, and loaded with "active material" which is placed in spaces of a lead grid. Negative plates are made with sponge lead so that there is an enormous surface area of lead metal in contact with the electrolyte. Positive plates consist of a lead metal grid filled with lead peroxide, the active material. To work, each grain of lead oxide must be in electrical contact with the metal grid which catties the current, and must also in contact with the electrolyte which carries current and supplies the chemical, sulfate ion or sulfuric acid, needed to supply electric current. To increase battery capacity, positive plates could be made thicker to contain more active material but then the inner regions in a plate would have poor access to the electrolyte. The plate could be made more porous so that the acid could reach in, as into a sponge. But then small parts are likely to break off and loose electrical contact with the grid. And the plates would not allow high current as needed for starting. To allow high current, plates are made thin, and more of them are stacked together, porous separaters keeping them from touching each other, close enough for shortest distance through the electrolyte, and with enough surface area to allow high surges of current. But thin plates are more likely to warp, since the lead oxide is converted to lead sulfate every time the battery is discharged, and back to lead oxide when it is recharged. The changes create mechanical stress. A compromise is needed between all properties: high storage capacity, tolerance for high current, tolerance for deep discharges, and long life, all in the smallest space.

Table 1 shows how sulfate ions from the electrolyte are used both at positive and negative plates when current is drawn from the battery. Note that lead sulfate is formed in the process, and decomposed again by charging current.

When the plates are charged, the voltage between them is about 2 V no matter what their size. To make a 12 V battery, six so-called cells are connected in series, each adding about 2 Volt to the total. The current through each cell is the same, and the capacity of each cell is the same as the capacity (Ah) of the whole 12 Volt battery.

Performance

As you know, the voltage of the battery during charge and discharge is not constant, mainly because the active material, especially at positive plates, is not all working under the same conditions. **Sketch 1** shows a

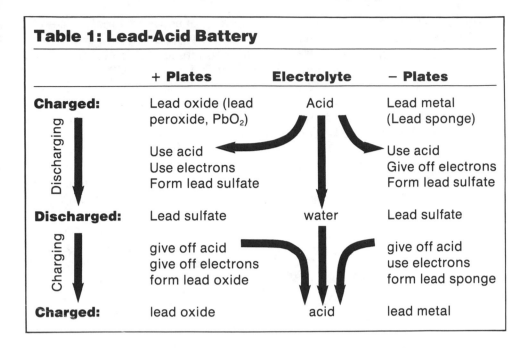

Table 1: Lead-Acid Battery

	+ Plates	Electrolyte	− Plates
Charged:	Lead oxide (lead peroxide, PbO_2)	Acid	Lead metal (Lead sponge)
Discharging	Use acid Use electrons Form lead sulfate		Use acid Give off electrons Form lead sulfate
Discharged:	Lead sulfate	water	Lead sulfate
Charging	give off acid give off electrons form lead oxide		give off acid use electrons form lead sponge
Charged:	lead oxide	acid	lead metal

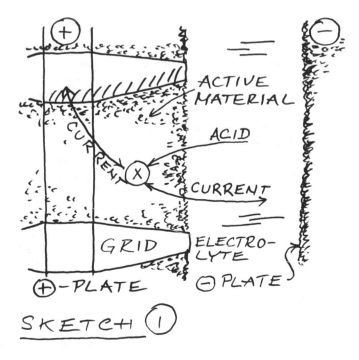

SKETCH ①

small part of a positive plate with one granule of active material marked X. The electrolyte is shown, as is the surface of the next negative plate. Non-conductive separators keep the plates from touching each other, not shown here. The active granule must have electrical contact with the nearest branch of the metal grid and with the electrolyte, to complete the electric circuit for charge or discharge current. Acid must be able to reach it when current is drawn, and acid must be able to reach the bulk of the electrolyte again when the granule is recharged and sulfate ions released. All of these processes which take place at each increment of the active material determine the performance characteristics of the battery. More active material may mean that there are fewer pores for electrolyte access, or that some of the material is greater distances away from the nearest branch of the metal grid.

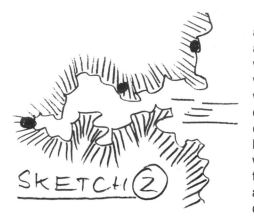

SKETCH 2

In all batteries, there will be some active material with excellent access to the electrolyte, some with excellent electrical contact with the grid of its plate, and much with intermediate positions, the dots in **Sketch 2**. When the first current is drawn from the charged battery, the best placed material with most direct electrolyte contact will be used to supply current at the highest voltage. As more current is drawn, the most accessible active material will become depleated and, with modest to high currents, the electrolyte in and near the positive plate will become locally depleted of sulfate ions, used up by the active material. With continued current, the battery voltage will fall. But if the current is interrupted, electrolyte will have time to diffuse into the deeper regions of the plate and make sulfate ions available there again. At the same time, some of the inner active material will regenerate the depleated outer material for a more even distribution. All of this has the effect that the battery voltage will recover, and the battery be able to supply another surge of higher current after the recovery period.

The curves in **Sketch 3** show the response of a fully charged battery to smaller and greater discharge currents. A battery will have a faster drop in voltage with higher current. With the load of 1 A, all active material will be used evenly and slowly and, when the battery voltage takes its more sudden drop near the end, the battery will be completely exhausted and will not recover at all. With greater loads though, voltage will fall faster but, when the load is disconnected, the battery will recover: its voltage will increase, not to the original value, but the closer to it the greater the discharge current. If you measure current and hours until the load was switched off,

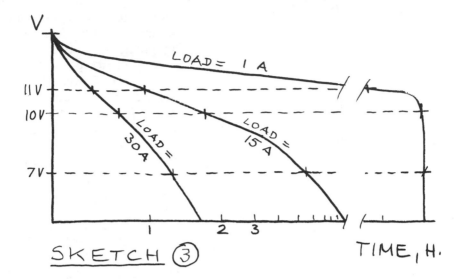

V

LOAD = 1 A

11 V

10 V

LOAD = 30 A

LOAD = 15 A

7 V

1   2   3

SKETCH ③

TIME, H.

the resulting Ah will be highest for the smallest load current, and much lower for greater currents. This is important when you compare batteries: the capacity measurement is only meaningful if it includes the current load, length in hours, and the end point in Volt where the load was disconnected.

The batteries on board the boat will normally be starting batteries, designed to supply the high current needed to start the engine. Its plates are comparatively thin, with much surface area, relatively vulnerable to the stress of deep discharging. Other batteries are made with plates more resistant to physical stress but will not be able to supply high starting currents. Although such batteries for deep discharging can be chosen in large enough sizes, or two or more of them used in parallel to supply engine starting current, this takes some of the flexibility away from two-battery systems where each battery can start the engine by itself.

Starting Power

How many Ampere hours does it take to start your engine? Very few: assume that the starter motor is rated somewhere between 4 and 8 HP and draws, for example, 400 Ampere. Most engines will start after a few seconds of cranking. If it started after 3.6 seconds, the starter will have drawn 400 A times 0.001 hours (3.6 seconds = one thousandth of an hour) = 0.4 Ah. That is less than half the Ah of what an anchor light draws in an hour.

How Batteries Fail

As you can see in **Table 1**, lead sulfate is formed on the plates when current is drawn. With charging current, this is converted back to lead oxide (peroxide) or sponge lead respectively. But if the lead sulfate is

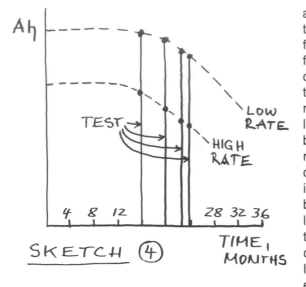

SKETCH ④

allowed to remain, it has the tendency to turn from very fine material into a dense form and to grow larger crystals. The inside of these then become inaccessible to recharge and some of the lead sulfate is not converted back upon recharging. The result is a loss of storage capacity. In addition, the internal resistance of the battery which is in the milliohm range increases and then insufficient starting current flows. A battery may lose its ability to start the engine due to increased internal resistance and may still make a useful lighting battery, or storage capacity may have been lost at the same time. To test for internal resistance changes, start the engine with each fully charged battery by itself. To test battery capacity, use the battery capacity meter or Ah meter described in the section on meters. Ampere hour values measured for the same battery over a period of years can be plotted as in **Sketch 4** as long as tests are with the same load current and end point voltage.

Deep Cycling

This term is often used to help sell batteries with rope handles. It means the same as deep discharging, the process where much or most of a battery's stored charge is drained. The term as such is quite meaningless without the current used in deep cycling, and the voltage end point at which discharge current was stopped.

As we have seen, the battery voltage decreases slightly as the charge of the battery is being used up. In addition, the voltage drops while a current is drawn from the battery: more so with higher currents. In fact, the voltage at the terminals of a starter battery, fully charged, may fall below 10 V while the starter draws its enormous current. Since very few Ampere hours are used for starting, the battery will still be nearly fully charged after this starting current. Under different circumstances, with low currents, a battery with 10 V would be quite empty. This may show you that the kind of deep cycling is important, and we will see that one example of deep cycling may mean absolutely nothing to the battery, while in another it may be certain ruin.

First Example: Golf cart batteries are being deep cycled. Assume that a golf cart is being driven until it absolutely does not want to move any more. The 12 V battery may then offer no more than 7 V and is switched off. The golf cart motor easily draws 30 A, more when it is being stalled. At such high current, the battery voltage will tend to drop quite considerably and when the load is disconnected at 7 V, will be able to recover its voltage by a substantial amount. Golf cart batteries are supposedly built with thick and stable plates which can endure deep cycling. Such plates will have much active material deeper within the plates and will be able to use that portion to recover appreciably. If we now took this battery and connected a small light to it, for example an anchor light, the battery may be able to keep that light bright for hours if not days. If we measured voltage, the battery would eventually fall below 10 V a second time and then would be completely exhausted. In other words, the high golf cart motor load made the battery voltage fall relatively rapidly, reach its end point voltage soon, and be switched off after only a fraction of its capacity had been discharged.

Second Example: The same battery, or any battery, fully charged, is connected to a small light. The light remains bright for a long time because it needs only a small current. The battery voltage falls more slowly but finally falls toward 10 V and the light dims. The voltage falls further, more rapidly now, and reaches 7 V very soon. At this point, the battery has been as deeply discharged as is possible. This case, which is common on board with anchor and cabin lights, deep cycles a battery more completely and severely than any golf cart motor, electric trolling motor, or other use often cited with deep cycle batteries.

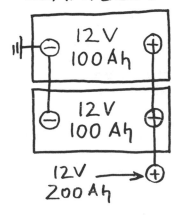

EXAMPLES :

Battery Capacity

Several tests are used to measure storage capacity. All involve a discharge current and measure time as well as voltage end point. **Ampere hours:** Ah. The basic unit of battery capacity is not significant without magnitude of the discharge current and the end point voltage. A battery with 100 Ah theoretically can supply 100 A for 1 h, or 50 A for 2 h, or 1 A for 100 h. Ampere hours are calculated by multiplying current in A by duration in h.

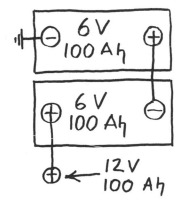

Cold Cranking Amps (CCA) or Cold Cranking Power (CCP) is used to gauge starting batteries. It is the maximum current in A which the battery can supply for 30 seconds to an end point at 7.2 Volt, the test carried out at 0°F. A battery with 500 CCA is reportedly able to supply 500 A for 30 seconds with the battery voltage not falling below 7.2 V during the test. Such battery has 500 A × 0.5 minutes = 250 Ampere minutes or 250/60 = 4.2 Ah capacity for this extremely high current test.

Reserve Capacity: A capacity test carried out at 25 A and measures the minutes until the battery voltage reaches an end point at 10.5 V. This test is carried out at 80°F. A battery with 150 minutes of reserve capacity has 25 A × 150 minutes = 3750 Ampere minutes, divided by 60 = 62.5 Ah. This is a very realistic test for batteries to be used with electrical equipment on board.

Hour Rate: 20 hour rate: Ampere hour capacity is measured at a current which drains the battery's nominal capacity in a 20 hour period. The test could be carried out with 10 hour, 3 hour, or any other rate. Load current is capacity in Ah divided by hour rate. Example: battery capacity is 60 Ah (20 h). Test current was 60/20 = 3 A. Also used to specify charge rate.

Wherever battery capacity is listed, you can convert to Ampere hours but should be aware of the vastly differing results caused by the conditions of the test. As discussed earlier, high currents will exhaust the more available charged plate material more quickly and cause battery voltage to fall fast, with the voltage end point reached quickly: the resulting Ah value will be low.

To convert: CCA or CCP into Ah, divide by 120. End point 7.2 V. Note that different current loads are applied to different batteries.

Reserve Capacity, minutes: into Ah, divide by 2.4. End point 0.5 Volt.

Example: deep cycle batteries with nominal capacity of:		
Capacity at discharge current of:	*80 Ah*	*105 Ah*
5 A	67.5 Ah	79 Ah
15 A	52.5 Ah	63 Ah
25 A	45 Ah	60 Ah

Battery Case Sizes

	Inches approximately: Length × Width × Height				
No. 24	10.5	×	7	×	9
27	12	×	7	×	9
3	19	×	4	×	9
4	21	×	9	×	10
8	21	×	11	×	10

Weight of batteries is sometimes given dry (without electrolyte) and wet (ready to use, actual weight). To calculate whether a larger battery or several smaller sizes in parallel are of advantage, compare battery data. The ratio of CCA divided by battery weight usually is between 10 and 12 for starter batteries. The ratio of Reserve Capacity ratings in minutes divided by battery weight is about 2. To compare different battery sizes made by the same manufacturer, (where test methods are bound to be uniform) calculate ratios for comparison. Think of your back before buying large batteries.

Battery Voltage

We have seen how the battery voltage is affected by current drawn from the battery. In addition, the stand-by voltage of the battery is dependent on the state of charge of the battery. Directly after charging, the full battery will show close to 14 V which will drop quickly as the charge from the most accessible plate material is used. After the first 15% of the battery's capacity has been used, the voltage falls proportionally to the remaining percent of charge, until below 20%, a more rapid voltage drop occurs, see **Sketch 5**. Battery voltage therefore can be directly interpreted as the percent of

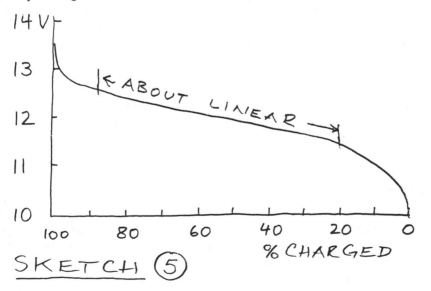

SKETCH ⑤

remaining battery charge. Many expanded scale voltmeters are available with such scale markings, and a meter with 0-100% scale is made by Spa Creek Instruments Co.

The Electrolyte

As you can see in **Table 1**, both positive and negative plates react with the sulfate ions in the electrolyte when current is drawn. The electrolyte consists of dilute sulfuric acid. The acid concentration can be measured with a hydrometer which indicates the density in grams per cubic centimeter. Fully charged batteries use electrolyte densities between 1.25 and 1.30 grams/cc (or g/milliliter). As current is drawn, sulfuric acid which is much denser than water is used and the density of the remaining electrolyte decreases and eventually may fall to 1.000 which is the density of plain water.

The acid in the electrolyte has another function: it makes the electrical conductivity. Because higher acid content means greater conductivity, here is another reason why high currents can be drawn better from highly charged batteries: they are more conductive, have lower internal resistance. If a battery is completely discharged (by accident), it may first run out of charged active material on the plates, or it may first run out of sulfate ions in the electrolyte which would leave plain water. Because of the much lower conductivity of water, such battery will then resist recharging current.

If you are accustomed to using a hydrometer regularly, note that on recharging, the sulfate ions released at the plates generate locally more concentrated sulfuric acid with higher density which will tend to sink and collect at the bottom of each cell. This has the effect that during the first half of the recharging, or sometimes longer, you may see no change in hydrometer readings. Don't let that lead you to any false conclusions about the battery's health but wait instead until gas bubbles begin to form. That happens with low charging currents only after about 70% has been recharged. The gas bubbles will stir the electrolyte and cause a sudden increase in hydrometer readings.

While electrolyte density is a linear function of charge, the upper and lower limits of readings will depend on the ratio of the storage capacity of the plates to the volume of electrolyte. Batteries with larger extra spaces below or around the plates will show slightly higher densities when the battery is discharged, compared to batteries which have the cells more completely filled with closely packed plates.

Distilled Water

The kind of water used to fill up battery cells is sold in drug stores and groceries right next to mineral water: don't confuse the similar packages. Distilled water is needed because it is lowest in unwanted minerals. It is also sold for steam irons, and if you cannot find any at all, collect the clean condensate which drips out of window air conditioners.

Battery Maintenance

The usual tasks of inspecting battery cells for electrolyte level, and occasionally measuring the electrolyte density with a hydrometer are so widely familiar that no further comments are needed. Beware of the wrong conclusions from low hydrometer readings, described under the "Electrolyte" heading.

It appears more important to point out how to test the starting batteries: even though you may normally start the engine with all batteries in parallel, if for no other reason than to subsequently charge all with the alternator, occasionally start the engine with each battery by itself. This will give you an early warning when a battery begins to develop increased internal resistance, not detectable with two batteries in parallel.

And again, you should be aware of the plate chemistry: whenever the batteries are less than fully charged, there will be lead sulfate on the plates. With time, this material will become more dense and less likely to be reconverted with charging current, thus reducing the battery capacity. More of this material is formed with deeper discharging which can then cause stress especially at the positive plates.

Manufacturers of industrial batteries, used for example on electric fork lift trucks, recommend so-called equalizing charges, described as the application of charging current after the battery has reached full charge and has started liberal gassing. At least one manufacturer of marine batteries has also recommended this practice. The idea is to convert all active material including that which during less complete charging has resisted conversion. For a 100 Ah battery, an equalizing charge would consist of 2 to 5 A of charging current applied for several hours after the battery had reached full charge. Distilled water may have to be added to the cells.

The most important measure, with the greatest effect on the battery's performance and life, is preventing deep discharging or deep cycling. Even if you are using so-called deep cycle batteries, these will suffer from deep cycling, though hopefully not as much as other batteries or you would have spent the premium in vain. On the other hand, preventing deep discharges will extend battery life which has the same end effect as greater battery standby capacity because you are reducing capacity loss.

There are many ways which help you there: you may make it a practice to measure battery charge frequently, for example with an expanded scale voltmeter or battery charge meter. To alert you and your crew when nobody is watching, there are low battery warning lights which begin to blink before batteries are deep cycled. There also is an audible alarm which needs no panel space or installation other than wire connections. It begins to sound its alarm when the battery then in use approaches deep cycling. The alarm switches itself off when the battery is switched off: this is because the battery recovers at least slightly. Then there is a battery cutoff, made like a circuit breaker which trips in response to the battery voltage when the battery nears exhaustion. A more drastic measure, but useful for non-essential equipment on board.

Finally, the capacity of the batteries, new and through the seasons, can be measured with a battery capacity meter or amp hour meter, described in a separate section in this book.

Battery Charging

We have to distinguish between two kinds of battery charging equipment: with and without regulators. The automatic battery chargers, also called converters which draw their power from 110 VAC shore electricity have built in voltage regulators, as do the alternators which charge batteries while the engine is running.

Battery chargers without regulators include most smaller portable chargers and trickle chargers. Even though their charging current diminishes during charging, this is only due to the increasing voltage of the battery which counteracts the chargers.

Voltage regulators both on shore power converters and alternators are designed to maintain or limit the charging voltage, usually to values between 13.8 and 14.2 V. As the battery then approaches more complete recharge, its voltage increases as shown in **Sketch 5**. The charging current which is caused by the difference between battery voltage and regulator voltage then diminishes as does the difference. The battery charging process with voltage regulators proceeds rapidly at first, with high charging currents while the battery is low, but charging currents are reduced, and approach zero as the battery voltage approaches voltage regulator setting.

High currents into the relatively empty batteries are fine: at that point, the more accessible plate material is converted and all charging current is efficiently used. As the battery voltage climbs and the battery reaches recharge levels better than about 70%, some of the charging current is used to decompose water at the outer surfaces of the plates, rather than reach and charge the less accessible material in the pores of the plates. While the gas bubbles indicate a less efficient use of charging current, this state is often preferable to incomplete recharging whenn the source of charging current, the alternator, is not continuously available. With automatic battery chargers or converters, the regulator setting which is always adjustable must be high enough to have the batteries reach near complete charge, even though that may take several days, and must be low enough to switch charging current completely off after the batteries have been fully charged. An easy indication of too high a setting is a continuous charging current where no current is drained from the batteries, and the continuous appearance of even small bubbles in the cells.

With alternators, the same limits apply even though a high voltage regulator setting may only become apparent after extended motoring. The regulator setting should never be increased to accelerate battery charging because of problems during subsequent long engine running times. Rather, the alternator controls described elsewhere in this book should be used and applied to temporarily override the alternator regulators, to accelerate battery charging from low states of charge to approximately 70% of charge. Higher charge currents are easily tolerated where battery capacity is high.

Charging diodes provide a method to distribute charging current, both from alternators and battery chargers of all kinds, and battery charge meters allow to estimate the charging current and time needed. For example, if measurements before starting the recharge indicate that two batteries are at 50% and 40%, each of 100 Ah, then an estimated 50 Ah and 60 Ah must be generated to fully recharge. This total of 110 Ah would be generated with a current of 36 A in about 3 hours.

Battery chargers without regulators usually have an output voltage substantially higher than 14 V when their battery cables are disconnected. Their design current is charged into the near empty battery, limited only by their capacity. Charging current decreases as the battery reaches full charge but continues at a lesser rate while decomposing water in the battery. Such chargers must be disconnected from the battery in time. The so-called trickle chargers do not avoid this problem but, due to their low capacity, decompose water at a lower rate when left connected. Continuous charge currents into fully charged batteries are not desirable. Rather, see the various applications of zener diodes and voltage regulator integrated circuits in this book which offer help.

To give you an idea how battery water consumption and electric current are related, consider that 20 Ah flowing through the battery without charging the plates will decompose about 1 ounce of water. Since the same current will flow through each of the six cells in a 12 V battery, that means 6 ounces of water must be replaced after 20 Ampere hours of overcharging. Batteries also produce some gas when high current is drawn from the battery.

Adding a Battery

If you make an estimate of the average amount of current needed each day for all 12 V equipment on board, you may find that one attractive method to avoid deep discharging of a single house battery, or using a substantial portion of the available stored power, is adding another battery. In addition to the extra supply of current, added battery capacity also means that you can charge higher currents with the alternator when you use a manual alternator control. The charging current will be distributed into more batteries, more battery capacity, and the higher charging current will be absorbed by the batteries with greater efficiency while the batteries are at a more complete state of charge. This simply because less current will go to any one battery.

You may add a battery by installing it with another battery main switch, charging diode, switch position or push switch at the voltmeter or battery charge meter, or you may connect another battery in parallel to an existing one: this you do by connecting the plus terminals together, and the minus terminals together, with the heavy battery cable material described elsewhere in the book. You are creating a single battery with greater capacity. Even if you connect a new battery to an older one, there are no serious problems. If you connect a fully charged battery parallel to a lesser charged one, current will flow from one to the other but this current is not being lost, it is merely redistributed and will be available from the new "bank" when current is drawn. Since batteries hardly ever fail by becoming shorted or conductive between plus and minus poles, the older battery will not drain the full battery beyond some current to recharge itself. Only when the battery bank is fully charged the new battery may be able to reach a higher voltage: as it is still charging, the older battery is gassing instead. Then no further charging of the bank is possible.

Nickel Cadmium Batteries

Small nickel cadmium rechargeable cells are available for use in flashlights and other portable equipment and are used in cordless electric drills. Their energy density is high: lots of power from a small package. But they are expensive. If you have any in use, and want to recharge them on board where no 110 V is available, build a current limiting charger with the details under "Power for the Calculator." The recharge rate is often expressed in hours: such batteries must be recharged slowly, over a 10 to 14 hour period, charge current then is the Ah capacity divided by 10 or 14 hours. Capacity is also expressed in mAh (1000 milli Ampere hours = 1 Ah). Nickel cadmium batteries can supply high currents but must be recharged slowly, especially when more than half full. They can tolerate small trickle charge currents even after they are fully charged.

Large nickel cadmium batteries are also made as wet cell packages comparable to our common 12 V lead acid batteries. Each nickel cadmium cell supplies 1.2 V so that 10 cells are needed in series to supply 12 V. One important difference is that potassium hydroxide solution is used as the electrolyte, a strong alkali which reacts violently with acids, such as lead acid battery electrolyte.

There are two reasons which prevent their exclusive use on the boat: they must be recharged more slowly than lead acid batteries and therefore are a poor match to alternators, and they are more expensive by a factor of 8 to 16 compared to lead acid batteries. On their positive side is an outstanding durability. Their application is justified only under very unusual conditions.

For your notes:

The Lamp List

The tables and sketches include most of the lamps ("light bulbs") found on board, exclusive of those for 110 VAC. Incandescent lamps produce light with a glowing tungsten filament within the gas filled glass bulb. This filament has a limited life, and there is a relationship between average life, voltage, current, and light output. This relationship can be used to advantage where several lamps are available for a given light fixture. For a masthead light, long life is important since it is difficult to replace the lamp. For a cabin or reading light, high light output is more important than life of the lamp since it can be readily replaced.

Listed in the tables are the design Volts, design Watt, light output in candlepower (C.P.), design Ampere, and the average rated life in hours. Note that the average life expectancy ranges from fewer than a hundred, to many thousand hours, determined by the manufacturers under lab conditions, with alternating current. When operated with direct current, the same lamp can be expected to last *only* one half to one tenth of the hours listed in the tables. If a lamp is operated at a higher than design voltage, its light output increases but its life is reduced: operating a lamp at a voltage only 5% above its design voltage will increase the light output by about 20% but reduce the lamp's life to only 50% of its rated life. On the other hand, operating a lamp at a voltage 5% below its design voltage will reduce light output by only 20% but will double the lamp's life.

Of course, you cannot change the voltage of your 12 Volt system, but you can often select lamps with higher or lower design voltage for a given application.

To test a lamp, use the VOM which will indicate near zero Ohm with all lamps: the tungsten filament cold resistance is only a fraction of the lamp's working resistance when bright.

Lamp Bases

 Midg Scr: Midget Screw Base

 MFl: Miniature Flange

 MScr: Miniature Screw

 MBay: Miniature Bayonet

 SC Bay: Single Contact Bayonet

 DC Bay: Double Contact Bayonet

 Caps: End Caps
Loops: Wire Loops

 Wedge: Wedge Base

 Bi-pin: Fluorescent tube bi-pins

 pinless: Fluorescent tube, pinless ends

Candelabra Screw Base

Lamp List

Lamp No.	Sketch No.*	Base	Volt	A	Brightness	Life, hours
1232	8	DCBay	13.5	.59	4	5000
1178	8	DCBay	13.5	.69	4	5000
1144	13	DCBay	12.5	1.98	32	400
1196	13	DCBay	12.5	3.0	50	300
94	16	DCBay	12.8	1.04	15	700
1004	3	DCBay	12.8	.94	15	200
90	8	DCBay	13.0	.58	6	750
68	8	DCBay	13.5	.59	4	5000
1142	16	DCBay	12.8	1.44	21	1000
1076	16	DCBay	12.8	1.8	32	200
904-2	30	DCBay	12.0	2.1	—	—
904-5	30	DCBay	12.0	0.83	—	—
2088	27	DCBay	14.0	3.6	95	150
1171	3	DCBay	12.8	1.35	21	500
1152	16	DCBay	12.8	1.34	21	500
97	8	SCBay	13.5	.69	4	5000
631	8	SCBay	14.0	.63	6	1000
1019	11	SCBay	12.8	4.75	100	100
1143	13	SCBay	12.5	1.98	32	400
1161	16	SCBay	12.8	1.35	22	500
1195	13	SCBay	12.5	3.0	50	300
1293	13	SCBay	12.5	3.0	50	300
1295	16	SCBay	12.5	3.0	50	300
93	16	SCBay	12.8	1.04	15	700
1141	16	SCBay	12.8	1.44	21	1000
1003	3	SCBay	12.8	.94	15	200
105	3	SCBay	12.8	1.0	12	500
89	8	SCBay	13.0	.58	6	750
67	8	SCBay	13.5	.59	4	5000
1155	8	SCBay	13.5	.59	4	5000
1777	16	SCBay	12.8	1.25	26	400
1073	16	SCBay	12.8	1.80	32	200
1156	16	SCBay	12.8	2.10	32	200
1095	16	SCBay	14.0	.51	4	5000
199	16	SCBay	12.8	2.25	32	1200
795	27	SCBay	12.8	3.9	100	200
796	27	SCBay	12.8	2.7	60	320
1383	—	SCBay	13.0	1.54		300
1940	30	SCBay	14.0	3.57	75	300
53	5	MBay	14.4	.12	1	1000

*Approximate appearance, note different bases. See page 220 and 221.

Lamp No.	Sketch No.*	Base	Volt	A	Brightness	Life, hours
1445	5	MBay	14.4	.135	.7	2000
57	10	MBay	14.0	.24	2	500
1895	10	MBay	14.0	.27	2	2000
293	10	MBay	14.0	.33	2	7500
1488	19	MBay	14.0	.15	1.5	200
1815	19	MBay	14.0	.20	1.4	3000
1826	19	MBay	18.0	.15	1.8	250
1816	19	MBay	13.0	.33	3	1000
756	19	MBay	14.0	.08	.3	15000
1891	19	MBay	14.0	.24	2	500
1889	19	MBay	14.0	.27	2	2500
1893	19	MBay	14.0	.33	2	7500
1813	19	MBay	14.4	.10	.8	1000
1892	19	MBay	14.4	.12	.7	1000
12RB	26	MBay	12.0	.17	—	12000
363	5	MBay	14.0	.2	2	250
431	5	MBay	14.0	.25	2.7	250
1826	19	MBay	18.0	.15	1.8	250
3509	25	Wedge	12.0	.17	.8	4000
3511	25	Wedge	12.0		1	2500
3504	25	Wedge	12.0	.25	1.1	4000
3501	25	Wedge	12.0	.42	2.6	1000
658	25	Wedge	14.0	.08	.3	15000
161	25	Wedge	14.0	.19	1	4000
158	25	Wedge	14.0	.24	2	500
194	25	Wedge	14.0	.27	2	2500
168	25	Wedge	14.0	.35	3	1500
1990	28	Wedge	12.0	1.6	20	200
1991	28	Wedge	14.0	2.9	40	200
1992	28	Wedge	14.0	2.5	64	200
1994	28	Wedge	14.0	3.6	95	200
2080	28	Wedge	12.0	1.0	24	30
2091	28	Wedge	14.0	4.6	115	150
163	4	MScr	14.0	.07	.07	3000
1446	4	MScr	12.0	.2	1.7	250
1449	4	MScr	14.0	.2	.7	250
52	4	MScr	14.4	.1	.75	1000
428	4	MScr	12.5	.25	2.3	250
1474	18	MScr	14.0	.17	1.7	250
1487	18	MScr	14.0	.2	1.4	3000
8362	—	MidgScr	14.0	.08	.3	50000
386	—	MidgGrv	14.0	.08	.3	50000

*Approximate appearance, note different bases. See page 220 and 221.

Lamp No.	Sketch No.*	Base	Volt	A	Brightness	Life, hours
7382	—	MidgPin	14.0	.08	.3	50000
211-2	23	Caps	12.8	.97	12	1000
212-2	23	Caps	13.5	.74	6	5000
214-2	23	Caps	13.5	.52	4	2000
561	24	Loops	12.8	.97	12	
562	24	Loops	13.5	.74	6	5000
563	24	Loops	13.5	.52	4	2000
564	24	Loops	14.0	.44	2	2000
566	24	Loops	14.0	.36	1	2000
2081	29	Pins	12.0	1.0	20	150
2082	29	Pins	12.0	1.0	20	150
2089	28	Pins	14.0	4.2	95	150
802	29	Pins	12.8	4.7	118	200
801	29	Pins	12.8	2.7	61	320
797	29	Pins	12.8	3.9	105	200
805	29	Pins	12.8	5.1	138	150
806	29	Pins	12.8	1.6	30	800
808	29	Pins	12.8	1.6	32	700

*Footnote on page 217.

LED: Light Emitting Diode

T-1 size fits ⅛ inch hole

T-1¾ size fits ¹³⁄₆₄ inch hole

Colors: Red, amber, yellow, green.

Maximum forward current 20 to 35 mA

Maximum reverse voltage 3 to 4 V

Polarity: cathode, minus, marked by flat, see sketches.

To operate on 12 to 14 V DC, use series resistor of 470 to 560 Olm, ½ W.

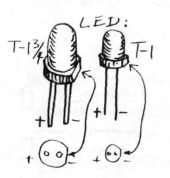

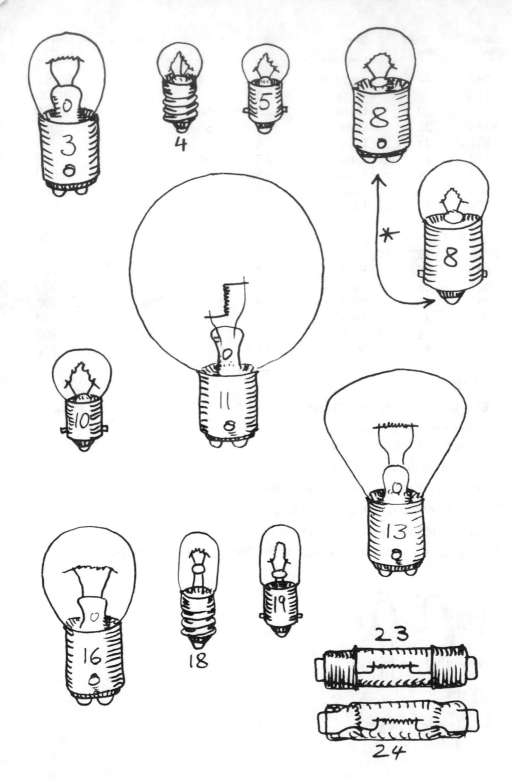

25

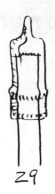

26

27

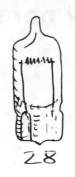

28

29

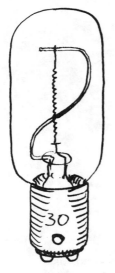

30

For your notes:

Printed Circuit Boards

To make any of the small circuits in the book which involve small diodes, transistors, or the regulator integrated circuits, a printed circuit board is highly desirable because it saves time, space, and wiring headaches. Printed circuit (PC) boards are much easier to make than you might think, and the effort is worthwhile even for one simple project. For example, **Sketch 1** shows a voltage regulator circuit with input, output, and ground terminal and two components: the integrated circuit "7805" and a diode. To make a PC board for it, label all terminals of all components with a letter, as in **Sketch 2**.

Then use a "resist" pen or a waterproof black felt pen with reasonably fine point and mark the terminals and interconnections on a small piece of blank circuit board. For the example, a piece less than ¾ inch long and wide will do. Then use ferric chloride solution, a brown, mildly corrosive and acidic "etchant" available from electronics stores. Pour some into a small plastic dish and drop the board in so that it floats at the surface, copper foil side down. The solution will dissolve all unmarked copper. Do not leave in longer than necessary, wash, dry, sand, and drill holes for the component leads, **Sketch 3**. Mount components on the side opposite the copper foil, solder, and cut off excess wires. Solder the plus and minus wires directly to the copper foil, no holes necessary. After testing, you can coat the foil side and components with varnish or oil paint, to make the circuit completely waterproof.

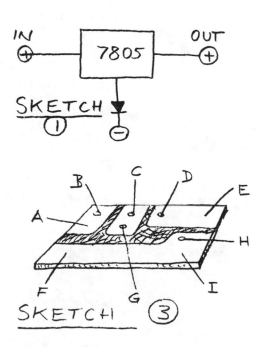

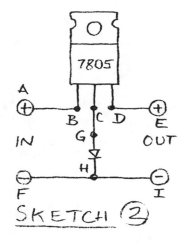

For your notes:

Wind Electricity

Sometimes your boat may be out of commission, out of reach of shore electricity, but with the batteries on board. Power to keep the batteries charged could come from a wind driver generator. Some very small units have been on the market for permanent installation, for example on the mizzen mast. Output of these smaller generators with propellers under 2 feet in diameter is barely able to maintain batteries but too low to recharge or generate power for other purposes.

Larger generators are available with propellers of four to six feet diameter which can be rigged below a stay and a point on deck. The generator will start to charge current when its output voltage exceeds that of the battery, at about 5 knots. At wind speeds of 10 knots, about 5 A can be expected so that an occasional breeze could keep the batteries charged, and steady winds would generate substantial power.

While small diameter propellers can reach relatively high speeds, greater power from the propeller demands greater diameters which lead to low RPM ranges, though at high torque. Both direct driven and geared wind generators are offered, and most use permanent magnet direct current motors as the generator. An isolating diode is needed in the generator wiring to block reverse current which would cause the battery to power the motor and drive the propeller in a calm. Voltage regulators are offered for the larger wind generators.

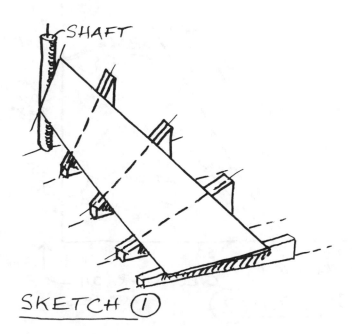

SKETCH ①

If you want to experiment with wind generators and make a propeller, start by selecting the pitch, the distance in inches which the propeller would cut with one turn through gelatine pudding. In, for example, 5 knots of wind, air travels about 6000 inches per minute, and a propeller with a pitch of 6000 inches would theoretically make one turn per minute. To get 100 RPM we reduce the pitch to 60 inches. And because there is slip, the propeller moving through very fluid air instead of threading through gelatine, we should pick a pitch of 30 inches. To make a blade, **Sketch 1**, use blocks with the angles from a graph as **Sketch 2**, to scale, with the circumferences (2 × π × Radius) for a few places along its length. On the other axis is the pitch in inches, to scale. As you interconnect, you get the angle for the propeller at that distance from the center. Since the tip travels

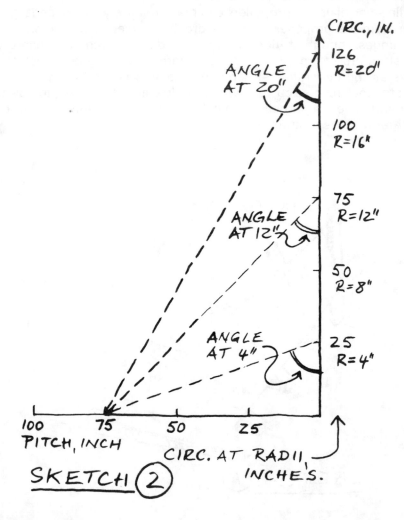

CIRC., IN.

126
R=20"

100
R=16"

75
R=12"

50
R=8"

25
R=4"

ANGLE AT 20"

ANGLE AT 12"

ANGLE AT 4"

100   75   50   25
PITCH, INCH

CIRC. AT RADII, INCHE'S.

SKETCH ②

at greater speed, at its greater circle, it sails more "close hauled" in its apparent wind, compared to places nearer the axis where the sections of the propeller sail more on a "reach," as shown in **Sketch 1**. You could twist a piece of thin plastic and then apply a few layers of glass cloth and resin.

As a generator, use a permanent magnet (PM) motor designed to operate on greater than 24 V, and with a horsepower rating of $\frac{1}{10}$ HP or more. Greater voltage will have it reach 12 V at lower speed, and higher power rating means greater current output. A diode must be used in the wire between plus output and plus of the battery, with cathode toward the battery. Use a type 1N5400, good for up to 3 A.

Or make a generator from a permanent magnet AC synchronous motor, used in many business machines and built like a permanent magnet alternator, only with many more rotor poles. Such motors are designed for 110 V AC and 72 RPM. They have no brushes, output will be AC and must be rectified with diodes. Output currents will be modest but 12 V can be reached with very low propeller speeds. Such motors have eight stator coils in two groups. Use the two groups, or separate into four groups and rectify each separately.

Index

229